Portrait of a Homesteader

*An Ancestral Journey Through
Poland, Volhynia, and Canada*

VICTOR GESS

Portrait of a Homesteader: *An Ancestral Journey Through Poland, Volhynia, and Canada*

Copyright © 2017 by Victor Gess. All rights reserved.

ISBN: 978-0-692-88860-5

Cover photo: Julius Gess seeding wheat, spring 1927.

Published by Missouri River Press
PO Box 1225, Lafayette CA 94549

Editor: David Colin Carr

Cover and interior page design: Jeff Brandenburg

First printing, 2017

Printed in the United States of America

Dedication

Dedicated to the memory of my homesteading father Julius and my mother Alma, the love of his life. To my siblings Helen, Lorraine, and Robert who grew up living the self-sufficent life on the homestead. To my children Catherine and James who left us too soon. To my daughter Cynthia and granddaughter Kelsey knowing that they are there is always an inspiration.

Contents

Preface

For many years I've felt there was a story to be told about my Dad, Julius Gess—the Homesteader. There were thousands of German immigrants who left the province of Volhynia headed for North America. They homesteaded in the prairie provinces of Canada and in the center of the United States. Their great homesteading experiment was fraught with obstacles, yet many succeeded at it. Beside prices for their product, draught, and grasshoppers, the greatest challenge was surviving the "Dirty Thirties" depression.

My Dad was responsible, innovative and, most of all, he was a man made of abundant grit. One evening many years ago, while searching Canadian records online, I went to the homesteading section. I maneuvered to Success, Saskatchewan, the area where my grandfather homesteaded in 1907. Searching for his name, I came up with a record of him filing and receiving a homestead in 1908—at age fifteen. This may have been done to help his Father obtain more land so he could make greater utilization of machinery and ten children that were still living at home. It also may have been done with the thought that it would be his home.

Finally I decided to tell the story of a man called Julius. He demonstrated that grit when getting on his bicycle loaded for the trip to Wolf Point, Montana the morning of July 19, 1915—a trip wholly unlike moving from Volhynia to Canada. It was only 220 miles, and to a country next door, to file for a homestead on the Fort Peck Indian Reservation. Because of the short distance his folks in Success knew they would see him through the decades to follow. The big step on that early July morning took a lot of grit—and it was only the start of a journey that would go on for more than sixty years.

My real interest in the family history began after his death in 1978. We were going through the safe in his home several months later. At the very bottom was a nondescript card-size envelope. I opened the flap and saw an onion skin paper with writing on it. My heart started to pound as I pulled it out. I had a strong feeling that it contained some very valuable information. Written in German were words that I knew would tell a story that I was becoming eager to learn.

I immediately made copies and spread them around, so this precious document would never be lost. The task before me was to have it translated. Little did I know that it would be a year and a half before I would be satisfied it was my Dad's christening record. Because of the old style of German it was written in, I had to ask many people to translate it. Finally I was satisfied with what several of us considered the proper translation. Over the years the document became more and more precious.

Many years later my brother Robert found a box of postal cards and a fold-up pocket map from Julius's Army years. Again, I carefully opened it, anticipating another exciting moment. It was a map of Europe from the World War I era. My eyes moved to Volhynia and I found a small pencil mark indicating my Dad's birth village of Shinufka. It was not uncommon that several villages had the same name, so we were now certain exactly where he was born. It was a highlight of my life to visit that village in 1996. As of this writing in 2016, the Church record of his birth has not been found. I have records of his parents, an uncle, an aunt and his grandfather that place them either in Shinufka where he was born or in nearby villages.

Records in Volhynia are difficult to find and the work goes on to find and index records in various archives. The Society for German Genealogy in Eastern Europe (SGGEE) is busy furthering this effort. In Poland they have extracted and translated several hundred thousand records which are available to members on their website. The extracted records and those submitted by members total over a half million in the Society's database. Their efforts have produced most of the records I found in Poland and Volhynia.

Perestroika during the 1980s resulted in the Berlin Wall coming down in 1989. It was an exciting time for all of us wanting to search records behind the iron curtain. About that same time the home computer was becoming popular—my desk saw its first computer in 1994. One of the first things I did was to install a genealogy program, because it was becoming difficult to manage the two hundred family names I had collected. The computer allowed us to organize what we were finding, and was of great use to search for records that were becoming available online. Instant communication would give access to fellow researchers anywhere in the world.

With all these circumstances, plus my being able to find family records going back to the marriage of my great-grandfather, I felt more and more compelled to write the story of the homesteader and his ancestors' trek through Poland and Volhynia. On January 25, 2015, I sat down at the computer and started to write the story about my father, the homesteader.

Acknowledgments

It is a pleasure to memorialize cousin Emily Arnt, nee Rode, (at six months in 1902 arrived with the family from Volhynia) who provided many hours of oral history that aided my quest. She provided a birth record (in Russian) of her mother, Pauline Rode nee Jess which became a precious document as her birth record has not been found as of this writing.

As the younger brother of Sisters Helen and Lorraine they gladly answered questions whenever I called. Younger brother Robert provided answers when I was stuck with a land, farming issue. Cousin Glenn Sethre said that as a young child he told his mother "Julius was his favorite uncle because he would stop and talk to me." After hearing that I could not have stopped writing this story if I had wanted. Sadly Glenn died as this book was being prepared for the final edit. A big thank you to Lydia's daughter, cousin Wendy Armstrong. Her bursting enthusiasm for even the slightest bit of family history kept me focused.

David Colin Carr provided much needed services, carefully going through the manuscript moving words and fixing what needed.

Thanks to Jeff Brandenburg for the caring touch he used to design the cover and interior pages.

Thanks to Richard Otto Schienke PhD for his digital mail describing the centuries of upheaval, political change and discontent that led our families to emigrate. He urged me on saying, "you have to tell the story."

Thank you to Michaela Brasesco for helping with the photographs and urging me to stay with it.

Thanks to the many volunteers at The Society of Germans Genealogy in Eastern Europe, SGGEE who extracted and translated hundreds of thousands of German records in Poland. German records written in Polish and after 1868 written in Russian—difficult task. Their effort made possible records in this book. Special thanks to Sigrid Pohl Perry, PhD., Karl Krueger, PhD., and their team who extracted and translated thousands of records found in the Lublin Lutheran church. Access to those records were available at the SGGEE website. Records from that effort revealed the Jess family lived in that part of Poland at least two generations.

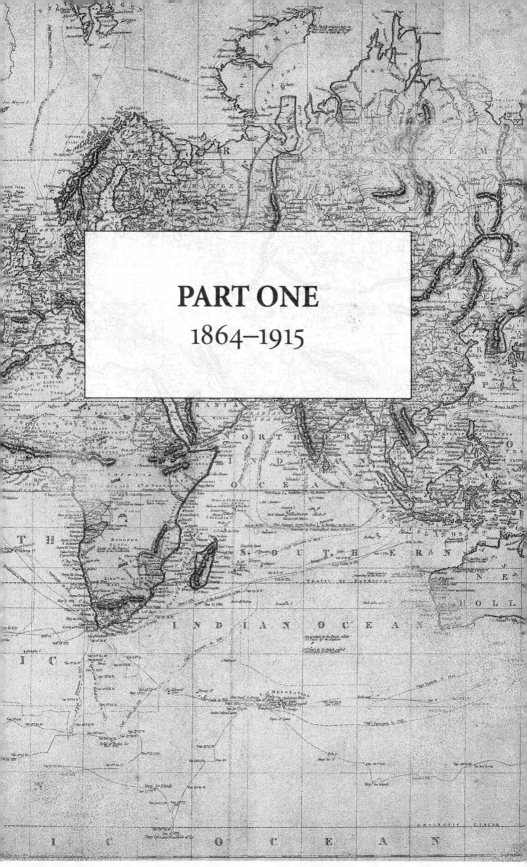

PART ONE

1864–1915

CHAPTER 1

— 1915 —

Viewing His New Homestead

One of the few conversations Victor had with his Father about homesteading concerned finding his property. Julius told him that there were men called Locators whose job it was to help homesteaders find land they were thinking of filing on, as well as land they had already claimed. Locators who were not on an assignment would meet the trains as they pulled into the station with anxious homesteaders aboard. The next step was for the locator to persuade the new arrival that he was the man to show them any potential homestead they may have in mind. Most locators were well qualified, as many of them had worked on the surveying crews that laid out the land in sections and half sections. The sections were marked with a 3 foot steel post driven into the intersecting corner of each half mile. The brass top of the post was marked with the Township, Range, Section Number, and position within that section. With a map, one could know where they were by reading what was on the stake. Before the land was divided by barbed wire fences, the country was freely grazed by sheep and cattle. Victor was told by an old timer that cowboys and sheepherders would tie their horses to those section stakes. This saved them from having to drive a stake only to pull it up when they moved on.

Julius had filed for his homestead of 320 acres on October 19, 1915. He was concerned that the parcels of 240 and 80 acres were separated by a half mile. He needed to make arrangements immediately to view the claim. With all of the homesteading activity, it was easy to find a locator. Arrangements were made with a locator to travel to the land Thursday October 21st.

The fee of $25.00 was paid and 22 year old Julius, full of enthusiasm, climbed onto the one-horse buggy with the locator. Before daylight they left the livery stable at the west end of Main Street in Wolf Point, the site where the new High School was built in 1952. They crossed the railroad tracks, slowly climbing the hill and then dipping into the first of many coulees. On the right was a Swedish homesteader who was building a frame house. The locator commented, "Bet we won't see another frame house like that for awhile," and Julius agreed. Little did Julius know that in about a dozen years that Swedish man would become his father-in-law.

The terrain was not entirely new to him, for he had spent eleven days cycling here from Canada a few weeks earlier. The buggy negotiated some steep hills by going around them. Even with a couple of boggy coulees, that was the quickest way to get to the other side. They passed a few tar paper shacks and a couple in construction. The typical 10 x 12 shacks could be built quickly if all the necessary items and the skills were there. Part of a quick build meant finding a new willing neighbor to volunteer to help. Most homesteaders built their shacks first and then dug the well. These items were the priority.

The trip went well and the abundance of deer and small wild animals was a welcome sight. They traveled a mile east of an area later known as Rosie's Flat, a valley with gentle slopes. The name was referenced only when some event called attention to the area, because there never were farmyards on Rosie's Flat. Climbing the slope out of Rosie's Flat on their right was the homestead of Stone Carlson. Julius would learn later that Mr. Carlson had come out from Minnesota on the Great

Northern Railroad with Julius's future father-in-law, Gustaf Appelgren. The Forseness homestead was a short distance north of Carlson's.

The trail they followed north out of Wolf Point was known as "The Powder River Trail/Road," though no one knew why. It was a cattle drive trail that started in Texas, the final destination being a very wide valley where the grass was known for its high nutritional value. Over the years this was the alternate way to get to the homestead. That valley is located southwest of Scobey and southeast of Peerless.

The locator kept them moving as they were leaving flat land and started traveling down into a wide valley with a view of the valley for several miles to the northwest. From their vantage point they saw a large herd of wild horses about a mile west. They quickly realized that the creek ran only in heavy rains and the spring thaw. They saw pools to the west which they noted as good grazing. When the locator estimated they were now about eight miles southeast of the homestead, he turned the horse and buggy to the northwest to find the section line. Riding a very broad crest of hills, the terrain was easier to navigate, and traveling gave them a better view of the land.

After a few miles the locator started reading the half mile section markers. He had moved west about a mile, and the next section marker was the one that would lead them straight to the southwest corner of Julius's homestead. They simply followed the markers, anticipation growing as they got closer to the homestead. Finally they approached the southwest corner of the east half of section 24, the 80 acre piece.

Despite grass thick and tall, searching on foot they found that precious steel post. The locator suggested they follow the section line a half mile north to the end of the claim. The locator did not quickly volunteer which direction and how far it would be to the next section marker because he wanted the new homesteader to rely on his own skills, knowing he would soon figure out the surveying system himself.

The land ran a quarter mile to the east. The piece would be a quarter mile by a half mile. When they got a half mile north they located the half mile section stake. They looked to the north and saw the hilly 240 acre piece. Though it included a steep hill, the big issue was being separated from the prime land of the smaller parcel.

Imagine the feeling he must have had walking for the first time on his claim. Of course the feeling of his claim being divided—what's over that hill? Is this really mine?—must have been some of the thoughts racing through his head. Julius's brother Emil once told Victor that "your dad is not as serious as he used to be." That is easy to understand. In those first years he was very serious, and kept his mind on building and protecting his homestead.

Julius walked and had the locator follow him with the buggy as he took the first steps on his land. Not a tree in sight, but some wonderful rolling land that he immediately felt would be ideal for growing small grain crops. He looked northeast, and about a mile up a long gentle slope was a homestead. He would soon meet John McClaughlin. Just east of his homestead and across the Powder River Road was Melvin Thompson. South of the McClaughlin homestead was another that belonged to August Nelson from Mankato, Minnesota who would return to his home town every winter before the snow started to fly. Southeast of the homestead and a quarter mile from August Nelson was Red Sutter's homestead. These homesteaders would eventually become lifetime friends. He wondered about those neighbors—who were they, where did they come from, how far along were they in establishing their homesteads?

He stood there gazing at the horizon, appreciating the tall grass. He was a proud man and now he felt his proudest. He knew he could spend hours looking, so he allowed himself time to indulge in what he saw. He knew a smaller part of the land should be fenced off for the horses. Maybe a couple acres at first, which would hold the team while the well was being dug and the shack was being built. They rode only a portion of the acreage that day and then looked for a place to camp for the night.

Imagine the dreams that night under the stars. It was his. By following the rules he would be able to prove up, and then the land would really be his. He needed to build a homestead shack. Fortunately he had carpentry skills, having worked on the construction of the capital building in Regina, Saskatchewan. He had also worked on a framing crew for a housing development in Regina. There were labor issues—

and the whole crew went on strike to get better working conditions and a salary increase. It is hard to imagine this independent homesteader agreeing to go on strike. A well would need to be dug, not an easy task when there was great depth and the dirt would need to be lifted up by bucket. Fencing for the horses was also a priority. It all seemed to be a priority, so careful planning was needed. The highest priority on the list needed to be finished by the time the snow fell, when work would slow down and eventually stop till next spring.

The next morning as the sun was rising, he walked around the area where they had camped. It was a very slight crest with a slope on three sides. He knew then that this would be the location of his farmstead. It was right by the section line which was where land would be given to make a road someday. He now felt comfortable leaving, having looked at the north quarter and established the corners of his homestead. The urgency of starting the return trip was facing them and they began the long buggy ride back. This was the first of what would turn out to be thousands of trips from the homestead to Wolf Point. They turned slightly to the southwest to enjoy a different view as they headed for the bustling town full of men in all the stages of becoming homesteaders.

About a mile from the homestead they passed the homestead shack of Abe Weins. He had homesteaded on land that was quite sandy, however, in later years it proved to be very productive. They passed over the wide valley about a mile from where they traveled the previous day going the other direction. They emerged from the valley and about a mile to the west was where the Hanson brothers each settled their homesteads. The brothers came from Sibley County, Minnesota along with their farm machinery, which included a steam engine.

They moved up a slow incline and arrived at a flat area that was homesteaded by Peter Fast and George Funk. Mr. Fast eventually contributed land at the southeast corner of his homestead to a Mennonite group so they could build a Church. The trip back was not by a road, not even a trail. They headed in the general direction of the town and had to go around some homesteaders' fences, though otherwise their trip had no obstacles. They rode by land that would soon be homesteaded by the Bartels. To the left Nicholas Toaves had homesteaded, eventually becoming a successful farmer with a family of 18 children. On the right side of the trail they came to the homestead of Earl Maltby. On the same side of the trail, later named the Volt road, was Nicholas's brother A.F. Toave's homestead. Several of the brothers' sons would remain in the area and become farmers.

As they traveled on, the terrain was more hilly and they could see some stones through the waving grass on the hilltops. Julius would eventually have to deal with stones on his land. The evidence of home-steading declined as they arrived at the western side of Rosie's flat. The noise of the buggy wheels caused several deer to jump up and run. They headed west in the direction of Wolf Creek, seeking the protection of the trees and brush that followed the water. On the far side of Wolf Creek, they saw a sheep herder's wagon and the sheep herder slowly maneuvering his flock. Sheep herds were in the area well into the '40s. Rosie's Flat was a dry valley with less wild life than in the surrounding area. Julius commented that he was happy seeing as many deer as they had during the two day trip, no doubt thinking they may occasionally be a food source. They climbed a steep hill to climb to get out of Rosie's Flat. On the right side was Bill Minderman's homestead. He was a large man, with a gentle manner and a speaking quality that said he probably had a higher education. I visited his home in the early fifties with my father. My recollection is that his original homestead shack was part of the home he and his wife lived in.

As they made it to the top of the hill they saw a huge steam cloud rise above Wolf Point. This was the late afternoon Number 2 train that was releasing excess steam and an extended whistle blow, spinning its wheels to get the shine off for traction needed to start pulling the load. Julius was looking at what he could now call his hometown from a distance of about eight miles. The buggy was moving slower now, with a very tired horse pulling it, though both of the men seemed to be gaining energy as the horse was losing his, which distracted them from the condition of the horse. Off to the left was a homestead shack fully framed with some shiplap already nailed up. Julius glanced at it, not paying much mind to the claim that belonged to John Applegren.

These two men would become very well acquainted in the middle of the next decade when John became Julius's brother-in-law.

About a half mile further down the section line they were following, on the right side was the bachelor homesteader Shakey Johnson. Victor had met this man, saw him several times, the last being in his later teenage years. His right hand constantly shook. Victor did not recall seeing him any other way. He remembered him as a kind man who always wore a quirky kind of felt hat. Victor never thought about his given first name, and it seemed as though no one knew him by any other.

A quarter mile south of place was the August Hoch homestead. August was a devout, gentle man and the eventual father of nine children. All of his children's names began with the letter E. If someone got mixed up and called a child by the wrong name, at least they had gotten the first letter right. The Hoch family attended the Mennonite Church at the site mentioned earlier.

Getting back to town that night was not to be. The horse was now efforting hard to even walk slow. Both men got off to lighten the load. They walked about two hundred yards with the horse to the base of the hill where there was welcome water for the horse. It had been a good year with rainfall slightly above normal, and in homestead country any rain was a topic for a conversation. They were about four miles out of town and they decided to set up camp and spend the night. Another night under the stars. Exhausted—but still able to continue planning in his head—he struggled with what his priorities were. It was late October and he suddenly realized that he now needed to think about the carpentry job he had waiting for him in Glasgow. It turned out to be a fleeting thought, as the excitement of seeing his homestead had no room for thoughts about a carpenter's job.

It was a night of little sleep and frustration, not being able to finish the trip into Wolf Point. They left before dawn anxious, concerned, and wondering if the horse would make the few miles to Wolf Point. The horse was refreshed and able to maintain a fast walk returning his happy load. The locator dropped Julius off at the Terry Hotel and left for the livery stable. No doubt the horse was happy as he was led to his stall. The hotel had recently been built to accommodate the influx of homesteaders and the people looking for jobs and business opportunities to support them. Julius enjoyed a good night's sleep and after finishing errands he was ready to board the afternoon train for Glasgow.

Julius Gess Claim

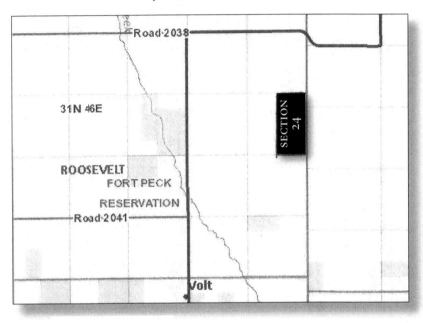

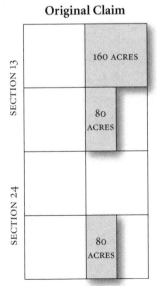

Original Claim

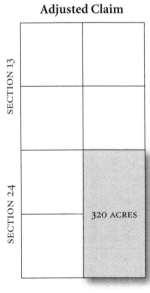

Adjusted Claim

CHAPTER 2

— 1864 —
Bielsk, Poland:
Michael Jess Is Married

About 1844 Michael Jess was born in Klementynow in the Lutheran Parish of Radom to Andreas Jess and Dorothy Heft. Anna Krystyna Riske was born about 1846 in the Kolonia Szczuki, the Lutheran Warsaw Parish, daughter of Krzysztof Riske and Rozalia Weidtman.

Julius's grandfather Michael Jess married Anna January 7, 1864 in the Lutheran Church at Lublin, Poland. The couple settled in Bielsko, a village 27 miles west of Lublin and 85 miles south of Warsaw. The village is at the south end of Lubelski Powiat (county) and at the very eastern end of a large area of arable, rolling meadowland with a forest about one mile north, and some small, damp woods to the south.

The wedding party traveled to Lublin in two wagons, each drawn by a team of horses. Completing the wedding party was Krystyna's uncle Ludwig Riske and a neighbor, Jan Holtz. The wedding couple were well chaperoned by two couples, friends of the wedding party, in the second wagon. They left on the early afternoon of January 6th, a Wednesday by the Julian calendar, so they could return in adequate time for the Sunday Church service. To make the trip as comfortable as possible in the middle of winter, a small stove was put in each wagon, and all available blankets were taken along. The route, which Michael had traveled many times, passed through many small villages and he knew that help would be close by if needed.

It was a bittersweet time for Krystyna, for her parents had both died during her early teen years. She felt it stronger with her wedding fast approaching. Four years earlier her father Christoph, while putting him in a stall, was kicked by a horse. The kick threw him against the wall and his head snapped back against an upright beam, causing a severe concussion. He suffered with headaches so severe that any medical man they consulted advised them to merely keep him as comfortable as they could. He died three weeks later. Krystyna and her mother Rosalie, grieving heavily, started planning for the less than a hectare of cropland and the small goat herd they had to care for. Six months later, after getting out of bed, Krystyna looked out at the rising sun and the grass hanging heavy with morning dew. Her mother usually rose first, so Krystyna checked on her and realized she would not be rising.

As they approached the Church tears were running down Krystyna's cheeks, though she tried to not think about her parents' passing. As an only child, she bore the burden alone and she forced herself to dream of her marriage and her coming family. She realized this could be a very happy time. Being 18 she looked forward to many happy family events.

Michael was a very serious man, who had also lost both his parents. He kept his feelings to himself, appearing reconciled with their passing which he discussed with no one. He had arrived in Bielsko only a few years earlier, and had a small farm. He was respected in the community for having established himself at such an early age. The community felt the couple would have a wonderful life.

They arrived at the Lublin Lutheran Church at 9:00, an hour ahead of the scheduled service. The Church was large and rarely attended by people who lived so far away. The couple and their guests timidly approached the clergy. Realizing their apprehension, the pastors did what they could to make them feel comfortable. The service lasted an hour and the newlyweds were very happy. The minister preached about the importance of working out disagreements right away, and how their love and commitment would help them through the rough bumps for the good of the family and community. As they began their return to Bielsko to begin their married life, a cold breeze coming out of the northwest and snow only on hilltops and in coulees, made them feel lucky that the January weather had allowed them to travel to Lublin and marry when they wanted.

The new couple quickly settled into married life. Krystyna insisted on involvement in Church, though it was of little interest to Michael. With her urging, Michael was soon helping with some minor renovation of the choir section—and seemed to enjoy it. He also helped obtain firewood stored on the other side of Bielsko with his team and his extra large stone boat (a flat, sturdy platform with steel runners held no more than 12 inches off the ground that can carry heavy loads over rocks, dirt or snow). It was the middle of March, and the cord of wood they brought to the Church would help get them through until spring. Michael enjoyed his work at the Church and along with Krystyna began forming relationships he knew would be lasting. He had to admit that he was glad that Krystyna had encouraged his participation.

Michael began planning what he would plant in spring. His farm was in the Głusko Duże borough, 1.5 miles east of their house in Bielsko. Beside his day of farming, he also had to plan time to get there and return after a day's work with his two horses. He owned two hectares of land and he was negotiating a lease of five more hectares. Having grown up on his father's two hectares, leased at a hefty fee that left little to meet the family needs, seven hectares (17.3 acres) was a big undertaking and serious commitment. But Michael had a strong team that could work that much land. He was young, strong and confident.

While Michael guided the plow as it turned a single furrow, he controlled the horses with the reins hanging around his shoulders. When the plowing was done the stone boat was dragged over it to even the ground. After tearing up clods of dirt held together by roots, he seeded it by hand. One hectare was planted with alfalfa type grass as a permanent source of hay. Two hectare were planted to oats, two to barley, and 1.5 to wheat. The last half hectare would supply potatoes for their own use and to barter for other foods.

Michael knew the importance of having a lot of potatoes. When he was a nine years old, soldiers skirmished for six days a few hundred yards from his home. Knowing the neighborhood, he easily slipped into the potato cellar which was hidden by a large tree and an ivy vine that partially covered the entrance. He lived among and ate raw potatoes that whole time. This was not a huge issue for Michael, just an unpleasant experience that he recalled when he thought of planting potatoes.

Michael had adequate time to plan the year's crops, and he was fully prepared when it was time to start farming in the middle of April. The cool weather was welcome as he trudged behind the plow, covering many miles each day. The work went on early morning to early evening, and his pride swelled as he started to near the end of the first phase of planting. His dreams were growing as the sense of accomplishment welled in his mind. Each evening he would share his thoughts and accomplishments of the day. Krystyna's proud feeling was apparent, and she did what she could to encourage him. Michael returned home late one evening the first part of May, completely exhausted. One of his horses had stumbled on a large rock turned up on the previous round of plowing. Though the stumble had ripped a part of the harness, after a couple hours of temporary repair he was able to spend the last few hours plowing.

A very happy wife and a hot supper greeted him. Michael asked Krystyna why she was not eating. She was bubbling with excitement as she blurted out, "Michael, you'll make a wonderful father." Being so tired from his day working, along with exciting news, he tossed and turned most of the night.

He left early the next morning to go to the harness maker who quickly handled the repair. Michael continued on to the farm with a new sense of purpose and a huge feeling of responsibility that kept turning over in his head all day. After the grains were planted. Michael prepared potatoes from last year's crop, carefully cut each potato into several pieces each containing an "eye." While Michael steered the team down a row to create a furrow of freshly turned soil, Krystyna planted the seed potatoes two feet apart with the eye on the top. When the next furrow was created it covered the seed with about four inches of soil. With the warm weather, the eye of the potato would sprout a potato plant above ground and potatoes in the soil.

The newlywed couple happily watched a bountiful crop develop. A lot of planning was needed to prepare for the harvest, which needed to be done quickly when the crop ripened. Michael traded some of his potato crop to a man in the village for two scythes, promising to deliver the ten sacks of potatoes as soon as they were harvested. He knew that if the crop developed the way it looked, he would need help harvesting.

The second scythe was needed because harvesting potatoes was slow and help was needed to get them out of the ground and stored before the first frost. He delivered potatoes to pay for his scythes and had plenty to provide for home use and for bartering. They were well prepared for the long winter.

The birth was January 17, 1865 at 9:00 in the evening. Krystyna and the midwife were quickly aware of the labored birth of Rosalia. They boiled water for steam to direct toward Rosalia's nostrils. Minor relief gave them hope that this would not become a permanent problem. Though as time went on her breathing did not improve, Rosalia appeared healthy and strong.

Rosalia, her parents and two witnesses—August Frolich and Jan Holtz—went to the Bielsk Lutheran Chapel at noon January 22, 1865 for the christening. The Chapel was part of the school, and the School Master was Chapel Cantor and provided most of the Church services. The Lutheran Minister from Lublin, who visited twice a year, recorded all performed events in the Church record book. He also performed marriages which the Cantor was not able to do.

The birth record states:

> *This occurred in Lublin on 22nd January, year 1865 at noon when Micha Jess, a farmer, 22-years-old, residing in Bielsk personally came forward in presence of witnesses August*

Frolich, 31 years old and Jan Holtz, 58 years old, both farmers
residing in Bielsk and presented us a female baby and declared
it was born in Bielsk on 17th day current month and year at
9 p.m. from his lawful wife Krystyna nee Riske, 20 years old.
That baby was baptized today and was given a name Rosa-
lia. The godparents were the above mentioned witnesses and
Krystyna Riske from Bielsk. That certificate was read by us
to the witnesses and subscribed by us only, because they can-
not write. Priest Karol Jonscher, pastor. (Translation of record
written in Polish.)

Rosalia's condition concerned her parents and they were anxious to get her settled into her familiar surroundings. Krystyna continued having melancholy feelings and she wanted to share them with Michael. She worried about how he would take it, and finally she felt so strongly about it that one Sunday after Church services she blurted out what was on her mind. To her surprise he was very receptive and encouraged her to tell him more about how she felt. Michael's mood had been very positive since last spring, after the crops were sown and the outlook for a good harvest was possible.

After Rosalia's birth and christening Michael was again helping at the Church. The committee welcomed his strong body and fine team of horses that were needed for some heavy jobs. Michael assured Krystyna that his love for her was very strong and that he was there for her no matter what. She realized that this was part of what she had been sad about. Now that she knew Michael was there beside her, she began to feel much better. She needed to concentrate on her health and build up her body. She knew Rosalia would need the steam day and night to keep her lungs open. Their relationship was more relaxed and even seemed much more enjoyable. Krystyna knew that Michael would soon be making plans for the new year's crops. She wanted to help him get ready and, if possible, help more than with planting the potatoes. With Michael helping at the Church and being available in the winter months, the committee was contemplating building a new parsonage. Michael also did some handy work for several of the elderly villagers who appreciated his efforts, and he enjoyed the food and lumber that were given him in appreciation.

Winter was passing rapidly and Michael was preparing for planting, following the same plan as last year, hoping and praying for another successful year.

With the crops planted and the potato seedlings pushing up through the sandy soil, Michael and Krystyna planted a large garden near their house. The garden was full of vegetables that would keep in their root cellar. The sufficient rains meant that Krystyna did not have to worry about creating ditches to water their garden. It would have been very difficult to water the garden with Rosalia requiring constant attention. Please Lord, help her get better.

Krystyna was very happy, for Michael had fulfilled his promise to be there and discuss any issue she wanted to raise. If only their daughter would begin to show improvement, she would feel so fulfilled. A doctor traveling from Radom told them to keep the steam near the baby day and night. If only that dear little baby would get better, even show a slight improvement, Krystyna would be so encouraged.

With crops sprouting, Michael got down on his knees to look down the rows of green coming up through the earth. He was such a proud man, if only he could have a few minutes to show his father, Andreas. The rains were coming in adequate amounts and it looked like it would be another high yielding crop like last year. He rode back anxious to tell Krystyna the wonderful crop was developing. Michael still went to Glusko Duze each morning, as it was the time to repair a jointly owned fence on the west and north side of the property. There was always maintenance and upkeep that needed his attention, and he just liked to be on his land and watch over his crops. Late one afternoon he was asked by a neighbor if he would help him move some dirt to fill in a coulee that a fence was stretched over where the neighbor's cattle were coming into his field and trampling his crops. Michael was eager to help and the work continued into the dark evening. The job was done, thanks given, and Michael began the short ride home.

Krystyna usually came running out to meet him, and because of it being so late he was eagerly looking forward to her greeting. As he approached, the meadow just beyond the house he could see a shadow of Krystyna emerging from the front door. She started running, and as he got closer he sensed something was wrong. He dismounted in time for Krystyna to collapse into his arms. He asked if it was Rosalia, and through sobs she told him she had died. Michael held her as he tied up the horse to be tended to later. It was many minutes before she could tell him that Rosalia stopped breathing about an hour earlier. Michael wished he had worked faster so that he could have been with them. Krystyna was expecting him any moment so she did not think of going to the field to get him. Their hearts were heavy, and they had much to do right away as well as being with their heavy grief. A neighbor went to contact the Cantor whose job was to help them wash the body and lay her out. That meant to dress her and then get someone in the village to help them build a small casket for burial the next day. The Cantor officiated at the funeral service the next day. The traveling pastor recorded the event in the Lutheran Church records of Lublin:

> *Number 87. Bielsk. This occurred in Lublin on 5th, year 1865 at noon when Micha Jess, 22 years old and August Frolich, 32 years old, both peasants residing in Bielsk personally came forward and declared that yesterday at 6 p.m. Rozalia Jess died in Bielsk, a daughter of the first above mentioned person and Krystyna nee Riske, Jess spouses, at the age of 4 months and 17 days. We convinced ourselves about Rozalia Jess death. That certificate was read by us to the witnesses (second informant is not related to the deceased person) and subscribed by us only, because they cannot write. Priest Karol Jonscher, pastor. [translated and recorded here exactly as written in Polish] The death date was Thursday June 3, 1865 by the Julian calendar.*

Michael arrived home from the fields the next day to find three neighbor ladies with Krystyna, as she continued calling for Michael soon after Rosalia was laid to rest. Her demeanor changed after Michael arrived, and she cried out again to the well-meaning ladies to leave her alone. They understood and could leave, now that Michael had arrived. Most residents of the village came by to bring food and express their condolences. It was appreciated, and Michael was able to politely handle the many visitors. Michael and Krystyna ate little of the food that was on the table and in the ice chest.

It was a week later that Michael rose, still with a heavy heart and the urge to step out in the yard and do some little jobs that really did not need attention. He went through the motions and soon retreated to the comfort of the home and Krystyna's arms.

Two weeks later they talked about going to Church on Sunday, but that morning there was no discussion of it, as they both knew people greeting them would be too difficult to handle. Sunday afternoon they were able to take a walk, and actually stopped to visit with neighbors who were working in their garden. The visit was cordial and Krystyna later remarked that the visit was very positive and a first step in the long healing process. She knew and told Michael that they would never get over Rosalia's passing, even though they both knew there would be more children. They discussed the passing of each of their parents, and both agreed there was no comparison. To them the villagers were generous gifts, and they appreciated the many meaningful expressions of care and concern. Many had suffered the loss of a child or had a close friend or relative who had. Because of that many of the villagers were feeling some of what Rosalia's parents were going through.

Michael had not gone to see his crops in a couple of weeks, so he decided that Monday May 24th he would go. That morning at breakfast Michael watched Krystyna carefully to determine if he felt he could leave for a few hours. They discussed it and Michael promised he would be back in late morning. He rode to his cropland with a lot of grief and feelings of guilt. His thoughts went back to the 7th of May, that long day that he was at the fields and riding home feeling proud and happy that his crops looked good, and pleased that he could help his neighbor repair his fence.

But he also felt it was good for Krystyna to have him be away for a few hours. She was a very strong lady, but even for a strong lady the good Lord had asked her to shoulder a lot. Michael checked his crops and was surprised at how much they had grown in two weeks. He also checked the coulee, satisfied with the way things looked. He was anxious to get back, though the bright sun told him that it was still a couple hours before noon.

As he walked in the house Krystyna was visiting with a neighbor who had just dropped by. Michael greeted them both and went to put the horse in the barn. He pulled some weeds in the garden which looked like it had not had any attention recently. When the visitor left Michael went in to greet Krystyna. She was very happy to see him, to sit down with him and discuss her day. She asked about the farm and Michael reported that it looked very good. He said that the potatoes were growing exceptionally well, that even the weeds in the potato patch were growing rapidly. They needed attention and that he would have to go back very soon and start hoeing them. Krystyna surprised Michael by asking if she could go along and help with the weeding. Michael stuttered an answer: yes, of course it would be wonderful to have her along. The patch was large, and hoeing around each potato plant meant being careful to not cut the vines. It would take one person two days, from sunrise to sunset. Michael would appreciate the help, but he knew it was even more important for Krystyna to be out of the house and with him.

Two days later Krystyna packed a lunch and Michael prepared one horse and the wagon. They left by mid-morning, Krystyna talking about how she was enjoying being out in the sun. She mentioned Rosalia's name and for the first time broke out in tears. Michael was overjoyed that she had decided to come along and help. They arrived at the potato patch and Michael cared for the horse while Krystyna picked out the row closest to the wheat field and started to hoe.

Michael noticed some cattle near the east side of the field so he went over to check the fence. He felt the cattle were no threat so he came back to begin hoeing weeds. They worked for a couple hours enjoying the warm sun and the fresh air. Michael had started far behind Krystyna and when he finally caught up to her their first words were "Time to break for lunch." They ate their lunch leaning against the wagon wheel. They did not talk much, but finally Krystyna said that she wanted to return home after a little bit more work. Michael agreed and was feeling so good about Krystyna being able to leave the house and go to the field with him, though he knew he would have to return the next few days to finish the long hard work in the potato patch. But he knew it had to be done immediately to produce a large potato crop like last year provided they got a few more rains.

Krystyna's life became a routine of preparing food and doing the normal housework. She began to visit her neighbors, which she had not done since she became pregnant. She found it comforting, even though most of the neighbor ladies were twice her age. She enjoyed their sharing of household hints acquired over the years. Krystyna was amazed at their ability to make tasteful meals when it appeared they did not have much to work with. One morning while visiting at the house of her neighbor, another lady dropped by. The discussion turned to the lady's granddaughter and how she was allowed to finish the fifth grade, and now was employed by a villager on his farm . She worked long hard hours but was very happy with her employer. Her parents felt she was paid well and the farmer did not overwork her. She was 12 years old and the oldest child in her family, so when she was home, most of her time was spent helping her mother take care of her seven siblings. There was much work to do and she felt happy that she could help her mother. Her salary in cash and food was paid directly to her parents. After listening to this discussion, without thinking Krystyna blurted out that she was pregnant. The women all shouted out with joy and congratulations. Krystyna wondered why she told them when she hadn't even mentioned it to Michael.

Krystyna was so happy and could not wait for Michael to come home from the field to tell him the happy news. For the first time since Rosalia died she was singing as she prepared dinner. She smiled and laughed, even though no one was around. Michael arrived tired and happy, having put in extra time to finish hoeing the potato crop. Rains were plenty and the weeds had grown. He thought this would be the last time he would have to hoe the potato patch.

Krystyna ran to him before he dismounted and gave him the news. "Michael we will have a family again," and she grabbed him as he was dismounting. He held her tight and told her how happy he was. He knew this was what she wanted more than anything else in the world.

The mood that evening was joyful, which had not been present in their house in many months. The news was all they could talk about as they were eating their supper. A dream had come true to have another baby, and they would constantly pray that the baby would be healthy. Surely God would not challenge them with another baby who was not healthy.

Sunday morning they arrived at Church early. They did not share the news with anyone. People remarked about how good Krystyna looked and that she was such a strong lady. She and Michael smiled to themselves as they greeted people and heard similar comments from many of the parishioners. They settled into their seats and after the hymns were sung and the liturgy finished, the Cantor began his sermon on the Beatitudes from the fifth chapter of Matthew.

As the Cantor slowly moved through the Beatitudes, Michael became more interested. "Blessed are those who mourn, for they shall be comforted." Michael sat straight up in the pew, squeezed Krystyna's hand and listened intently as the Cantor discussed that Beatitude. Michael felt as if the hand of God had reached out and touched him. An almost unbeliever, Michael now realized the Church truly was there in time of need. All he had to do was to present himself and Krystyna with an open mind. Michael enjoyed the rest of the service as he had never appreciated a sermon before. As they made their way out, Michael felt relieved and happy, greeting everyone like a long lost friend. He couldn't wait to thank the Cantor at the door for his clear explanation of the Beatitudes.

All the way home Michael expressed his happiness at finding comfort in the sermon and the arrival of a baby early next spring. Krystyna was uplifted by Michael's enthusiasm for the sermon. She had never seen him excited about a spiritual matter. The rest of that Sunday was spent in a relaxed mood. They talked all afternoon like they had never talked before, and both of them felt very happy and in a way burden free. Of course there was sadness and always would be about the death of Rosalia. They felt they had reached an acceptance of what had been taken away from them. They worried that the joy they were feeling would leave them. They both vowed they would do everything to lead lives that would ensure the joy they felt.

The field crops were not quite as good as last years, however the potato yield was much better. That was important, for this year Michael would use much of his potato crop to barter. The fall weather arrived early and Krystyna was able to help Michael with much of the harvest. Michael got two village school boys to help pick the potatoes and load them in the wagon and store them in the root cellar near their home. The crops were all in before the early frost arrived. Because of the rush to get the crops in, some of the vegetables froze before they could be picked. This did not worry them as they knew that many villagers had large gardens and would be glad to trade for Michael's potatoes.

Christmas came and went as Michael and Krystyna's faith continued strong regarding their acceptance of Rosalia's death. They were more involved in the Church and regularly attended services. More work was being done to upgrade the cry room in the Church. Michael was happy to work on that project, for he could see his wife and the new baby using the room. The use of his team and a wagon were again requested as chopped wood needed to be delivered to some of the elderly folks in the village. He was always glad to help, and his pay was usually a hearty thanks and a satisfied look on the receiver's face. He was glad to help because he had learned that he never knew when he might have to ask for help. The winter dragged on with unusually cold weather, but the preparations Michael and Krystyna had made put them in a good position. They had enough wood and food to last months longer than the cold weather would.

A male and a female name had been settled on weeks before the baby arrived March 7, 1866 at 4:00 pm. With the help of a midwife Krystyna easily delivered a healthy baby girl, Anna Julia Jess. Rejoicing, thanks and laughter with some bittersweet moments greeted the new baby. Anna Julia years later would become known only as Julianna. All her legal papers up to her grave stone would carry that name. It was only after her birth record was discovered that her real name was revealed:

> *"This occurred in Lublin on March 10th, year 1866 at 1:00 in the afternoon when Micha Jess, a farmer, 23 years old, residing in Bielsk personally came forward in presence of witnesses*

Krzysztof Henkel, 27 years old and Ludwig Neumann, 38 years old, both farmers residing in Bielsk and presented us a female baby and declared it was born in Bielsk on 7th day current month and year at 4 p.m. from his lawful wife Krystyna nee Riske, 21 years old. That baby was baptized today and was given the names Anna Julia. The godparents were the above mentioned witnesses and Elizabeth Neumann from Bielsk. Certificate was read by us to the newly married and witnesses and scribed by us only, because they cannot write. Priest Karol Jonscher, pastor."

She was a healthy baby and would remain so. She was also very strong and sat up and walked much sooner than other children. Her smile and laughter delighted her parents. Anna Julia eventually became the mother of eight children and lived 80 years.

It was a happy day when Anna Julia first attended Church with her parents. Michael was very proud as he saw his wife and daughter in the cry room that he helped renovate. He was thankful that Krystyna had encouraged him—maybe more like insisted—that he get involved helping out at the Church.

The winter weather did not last as long as it had the previous year. Michael was happy—this meant he could prepare early and would be ready to plant his crops when he felt the weather was right. He would sow a half hectare less of wheat and use that land to plant more oats. There had been requests for more oats and Michael had bartered it all and still could not supply the need. He felt needed in the community, and realized that he was becoming a respected members. He worried that he would not be able to live up to the responsibility he felt.

Krystyna was always busy watching Anna Julia and preparing meals. Michael was proudly feeling the responsibility of providing for his family.

He was starting to take an interest in what was happening in his country. Poland had ceased to exist in 1795, and his area was under Russian rule. He listened intently when the elders in his village discussed political and economic issues. How could he learn more? He listened and eventually started asking questions.

He was illiterate, and aware of the handicap. Maybe someday he would be able to ask someone if they could teach him to read. He hoped and prayed that his children would have an opportunity to attend school and not have to drop out like he did after only a few months. Michael had overheard rumblings of unrest in the country and he wondered what it would mean in the future. The villagers did not appear to have any concerns about their future, other than jobs and having successful crops.

The village was led by men who knew how to manage, and that resulted in happy residents. Michael had felt the contentment when he moved to Bielsko several years earlier. It was the first place he had lived where he felt settled and had the feeling of home. Any hint that this might not always remain that way was of great concern to him, especially after the birth of Anna Julia. What kind of future was there for them? He would ponder this as he rode to his cropland and back. For sure he would raise them up in the Lutheran Church. He would do all he could to help them find the joy that he found as he became closer to the Church teachings.

Krystyna was also concerned, as Michael found out, when he voiced his private thoughts to her. Her concern was much less than Michael's, for she lived round the clock with her child. In a few weeks Michael relaxed, after overhearing conversations as often as he could. He was getting back to putting his full attention to his family and the crops.

Krystyna would soon be giving birth: two children and a wife. Since his late teens he had dreamed of a day like this. Now his dream was being played out every day. Krystyna looked forward more than Michael. She had developed close friendships in the village and had a comfortable relationship with the Cantor and his wife. She could call on her friends who were mothers to many children, even one woman who had 11. Large families were normal, though a couple mothers in the village had only two children. They had more children, but lost several when a severe flu swept through the village. There was much sadness and much joy as Krystyna related to them, and the older mothers were happy to tell her of their experiences with illness and death.

Krystyna was approaching this birth with a feeling of excitement and confidence. She had experienced two births and had the knowledge of many hours talking to the mothers in the village. She was ready, but did not discuss her positive feelings with Michael. She felt strong, almost independent—and wanted to keep this to herself. Michael was so supportive, and it was a proud moment when the conversation with her friends would turn to her for comments on fathers.

Krystyna had never been close to her aunt Krystyna Riske, whose namesake she was. Finally after living in the same village for years Krystyna decided to try to build a relationship with her, though she had felt it was up to her aunt to do it. Now her feelings were different and she would take the first step in trying to bridge any reason her aunt had for being distant. She planned her visit for weeks. Finally in October 1868 she borrowed a little wagon from a neighbor, and on a bright sunny day she pulled Anna Julia over to visit her aunt who lived at the far end of Bielsko. Her aunt Krystyna was so excited and happy to see her that she cried out loud as she invited them in.

Anna ran all over the comfortable home, and Krystyna tried to calm her down. Her aunt insisted that she let Anna do what she wanted. Aunt Krystyna was overwhelmed, and she kept repeating how good it was to see her and meet her daughter. She could not stop talking, but after an hour or so she was able to settle down and offer her niece some coffee and cookies. As she was able to get over the excitement, Anna approached her and wanted to sit in her lap. Aunt Krystyna gladly picked her up and she winked to her mother that she had a new friend. Krystyna was careful to leave at an appropriate time and not overstay her welcome. She was able to leave only after her aunt made her promise that they would see each other soon.

As she pulled the wagon home she was overjoyed that she had decided to visit her aunt. When she arrived home Michael had the house nice and warm. She was bubbling with excitement as she described the visit. It was puzzling to Michael, as he knew there had been an issue between his wife's parents and her aunt. He listened intently as Krystyna told him all about the afternoon and how glad she was that she had made the visit. Michael was happy and proud that Krystyna had taken the first step to build the relationship. Their world was expanding, and with it came some responsibility. They were glad to accept it, as they knew this was how they would build more friendships.

Ludwig was born without incident, and the happy parents took their baby to the Chapel the next day to be christened. The birth and christening were recorded in the record book at the Lutheran Church in Lublin:

First Son Ludwig was born Wednesday December 30, 1868 at 10:00 pm.

> *"This occurred in Lublin on 19th/31st December,[1] year 1868 at 2 in the afternoon when Micha Jess, 26 years old, a colonist residing in Bielsko personally came forward in presence of witnesses Augustyn Freising, 35 years old and Andreas Neuman, 22 years old, both colonists residing in Bielsko and showed us a male baby and declared it was born yesterday in Bielsko at 10 in the afternoon from his lawful wife Krystyna nee Riske, 24 years old. That baby was baptized today and was given a name Ludwig. The godparents were both witnesses mentioned above and Godmother Krystyna Riske nee Kwast residing in Bielsko. That certificate was read to the father and the witnesses and subscribed by us only. Karl Jonscher, Pastor"*

Krystyna realized that the new boy in the family might cause some jealousy for Anna. Not as much time would be available now for her. Krystyna gave little jobs to Anna so she would feel needed in taking care of Ludwig. Baby Ludwig was as strong and healthy as Anna at the same age. Michael was happy to have a son and he gladly helped with his care. He went through the village telling people about his son. He went to the east end of the village to thank Krystyna's aunt for being Ludwig's godmother. She appreciated the visit and promised to visit in a couple days.

---

1. There is a 12 day difference between the Gregorian and Julian calendars, so both dates are often presented on German baptismal records.

Michael returned home and they enjoyed supper while he told the family about his walk through the village. He told how the people he met asked about the family and complimented him on his daughter Anna's manners. He had been invited to go hunting the next day with one of the men about his age. He declined, preferring to stay close to home. He was happy, and he told Anna that a lot of people had asked about her. She kept asking what he told them. She repeated her question several times that night, and as he put her bed. He hoped a good night's rest would end the questions.

Krystyna was very tired, restless and needed help taking care of the children, but she felt uncomfortable telling Michael. She struggled with her problem and went to visit a neighbor lady. She was happy that she felt comfortable about going to talk to her acquaintance. She was greeted with excitement and was welcomed with open arms. Her neighbor was especially warm with the children. This being the first visit that had been made since returning home after the christening, they talked about their families over coffee, and eventually Krystyna brought up her feeling exhausted all the time. Her neighbor Lydia listened intently and asked many questions to the point that she thought she may have crossed a line. Krystyna gladly answered them and realized she had missed such conversations since the death of her mother eight years back. The concern shown by Lydia was affecting Krystyna in a positive way. She told Lydia that Michael was selfless and she could not expect more from him. She said she really did not know what she was looking for, with things being positive at home. Lydia mentioned several times that she was welcome to come over with the children any time. Kystyna finally suggested that Lydia visit her sometime. She was feeling better, and as noon was approaching she knew it was time to return home. She thanked Lydia several times as she prepared the children for the walk home.

Arriving home she greeted Michael and went about preparing a light meal for her family. She told Michael about her visit with Lydia and how she was invited back, without mentioning what they discussed, for she had decided to work on the issue herself. He was inquisitive about her visit, as this was an unusual thing for her to do. She had been a homebody ever since they were married, so the question was a normal one.

He was happy with her response and started to talk about raising his son to help him in the fields. Little did Michael even think that Ludwig would have a son named Julius who would be a Homesteader in Montana USA. He thought a lot about showing Ludwig how to use tools, and especially how to be a confident man. He had great hopes that he would be able to learn to read and write. He desperately wanted to be there for him and not die at an early age like his own father. Tears ran down his cheeks as he thought of his father's passing. Krystyna knew something was touching him, she put her arms around him, told him she loved him and everything would be all right. She was well aware that Michael had some soft spots, and she was proud of that. He presented as a serious, deep thinking man, accentuated in a German standing six foot one. He was such a proud man, and since the birth of his son he was changing rapidly. Krystyna told him that she loved the way he was absorbing his responsibility.

The fall of 1874 Ludwig started school in the building attached to the village Chapel. The Cantor served as the school teacher, helped by a Church member who had been kicked by a horse and was not able to do manual labor. Though uneducated, he kept fires burning and helped the Cantor manage the children. Ludwig enjoyed school, though he received no help at home for his parents were illiterate. But they provided much encouragement. Anna Julia, like many girls of that era was not able to attend.

They marveled as he learned, and there was great excitement the day he came home and showed them how he could write his name. Any documents needing their signature was always signed with an X.

There was much to live for and now their attention was turning to threatening weather. They were prepared for normal winters. However, in times of heavy snow it was difficult even living in a village. It was easier to stay in the house where it was warm and go out only to take care of the horses. Michael's concern about the weather drove him to walk across the village and talk to an elder resident, 86 years old Heinrich, who had lived in this part of Poland all his life.

The door opened as he approached the house and he was warmly greeted. Michael sat down, politely turned down an offer of Polish liquor and immediately voiced his concern about the weather and asked Heinrich what he thought. Heinrich told him about a storm when he had been 11 years old in 1794. He and his father were traveling home to their village, Kazimierz Dolny, from the village of Wilkow. About a mile after they started the clouds became thicker and the wind, which began as a gentle breeze, picked up speed and the temperature dropped. Their trip was slow as the wagon was pulled by their oxen.

They had only done about half of the five mile trip when it became apparent that they would not reach home before the snow began, pushed by a strong wind. The temperature fell quickly and going forward was not possible. They unhitched the oxen and led them to the side of the wagon. His father told Heinrich to dig out some snow beside one ox after it lay down for protection and his father lay between the oxen. Although not as protected as Heinrich, he thought their bodies would keep him warm enough to survive. The storm continued, and at night with a full moon they could tell it was a very heavy snow fall. Toward morning the wind and snowfall had stopped, but the temperature stayed extremely low. Heinrich pushed out of the snow and called to his father. When he heard no response, he started to dig. With his gloved hand he felt his frozen father. He said, "Michael I'm telling you that story because the clouds and the cold wind look and feel today the same as they did that day 75 years ago."

Michael knew that he had been the person who helped Heinrich tell the story and possibly relieve a burden that had been with him all those years. They exchanged some pleasantries and an emotional Michael thanked him and walked home. He related the story to Krystyna and as he neared the end of it, tears started to run down her cheeks. She felt very sad because she knew who Michael had gone to visit. But they felt confident that they were well prepared for the worst kind of weather.

As the storm subsided they found out that the village had survived well, with the exception of some horses that had broken out of an inadequate barnyard fence and drifted away with the storm. Immediately the two owners of the horses and two other men packed supplies and left to find the horses. The snow had covered any tracks and all they could do was to use their best sense as to where they had gone.

Four hours away from Bielsko they came to the intersection of three valleys. They decided to ride down the two outside valleys in pairs. If the horses were not found they would camp and resume the search in early morning. Twenty miles beyond where they separated the three valleys would rejoin. They rode hard the second day, but because of deep snow they were still several miles from the place where the three valleys rejoined. The forest provided comfortable places to camp for the night.

By mid-morning they had reached the joining spot and the two men on the east side waited for the other men to join them. By noon they were all together and the men traveled faster as the weather had warmed up and there was less snow in this valley. There was no sight of the drifting horses and the men were becoming anxious about where they may be. Had they gone further than the ground they had covered? The discussion concluded that it was not likely. They rode on and thought that with good conditions they might be able to get back to the village by evening. The discussion while riding was a repetition of all the possible places the horses could be. With no sight of the horses, they pressed on, determined to get home. The last mile it was obvious their horses could not go much further. With no sign of the strays they slowed the pace and toward midnight they could see some lights of the village. As they rode down the street at once they all saw the lost horses tied up at one of the owner's barnyards. Though they knew that horses had a sense for returning home, they also knew that they could just keep going on. An elated group of tired men cared for their horses and put them in the stable. Each man quietly went to his home with no further discussion of the trip. The storm and drifting horses no doubt would be the topic at family gatherings for many generations to come. But the lost horses and the men who bravely went out to find them were not discussed in the village. Everyone knew that had it been them, they would've done exactly what the four men did.

The weather settled down and the good part was that the snow lay deep across the fields, in some places as much as four feet with still a couple months before the spring thaw. Michael had some typical winter work to do that he had been putting off and decided to get it done before other people decided the same thing. He had harnesses that needed to be repaired and strengthened. He used one horse to take the harnesses over and ask the harness maker to do the repair work. Michael offered to pay him with three sacks of potatoes. The harness maker said he would take one sack of potatoes and five bushels of oats for the considerable amount of work he wanted done. Michael did not feel comfortable bargaining anymore and agreed to provide the barter. Within a day after the harnesses were repaired.

He was always worrying about how the crop would turn out. It was a part of him, from recalling the very small farm his father had and how hail had once completely destroyed their one hectare of oats. Though his dad also did farm work for those that needed extra help, it was not regular work and could never be counted on. The struggle was endless, between raising a garden, having a milk cow, and doing some outside work. They managed to get by. Michael realized that, as bleak as his upbringing had been, it was in those young years that he learned the skills that he put to use on his own farm. He knew those tough years could come again, and that always concerned him. That reminder caused him to carefully plan the crops that he would seed each year.

He found that the more experienced farmers would give him advice, though they gave it sparingly. Maybe they wanted him to learn it on his own. Maybe they wanted to hoard some of what they had learned over 30–40 years of experience. He learned to respect that. Only years later did they loosen up a bit and divulge a little more.

Everyone in the village knew Michael's land, as most villagers knew everyone else's land. The great benefit was that he could ask most any-one what would happen to the lower southeast corner of his crop in an extremely heavy rain. He acted on many answers that he received from such subtle questions. He could tell that the experienced farmers felt complimented when he sought their advice. A few years went by and Michael began to feel he too was an experienced farmer. He was having good crops—and in a way this bothered him because he knew that things could turn out the other way. But for the time being the whole community was doing well.

Being remote from the bigger towns and cities, the residents of Bielsko were vaguely aware of political happenings. Michael very well remembered the January 1863 uprising that began as a spontaneous protest by young Poles against conscription into the Russian Army. They were soon joined by high-ranking Polish-Lithuanian officers and various politicians. The uprising covered present day Poland, Lithuania, Belarus, Latvia, parts of Ukraine and western Russia against the Russian Empire.

It began January 22, 1863 and lasted until the last insurgents were captured in 1865. The insurrectionists, severely outnumbered and lacking serious outside support, were forced to resort to guerrilla warfare tactics. They failed to win any major military victories or capture any major cities or fortresses, but they did blunt the effect of the Tsar's abolition of serfdom in the Russian partition, which had been designed to draw the support of peasants away from their national feelings. Severe reprisals against insurgents, such as public executions and deportations to Siberia, led many people to abandon armed struggle and turn instead to the idea of regular work and economic and cultural self-improvement.

Although the insurrection was widespread, it involved mostly young people who felt very strongly about their cause. Michael did not get involved. He concentrated on marriage, farming, and his children. The insurrection was felt for many years. Many young people had been killed or wounded, and the concern right after it ended was severe reprisal from Russia.

There were rumors of ethnic Germans moving eastward toward the Ukrainian border. If they heard that things were better in another area or country, Germans would gather up and move, several related families moving together, sometimes whole villages trying to improve their living conditions. Again Michael was concerned, and any questions he asked were responded to with vague opinions. This bothered him enough to wonder if he should consider moving to another area where maybe he could have more land.

By the end of August 1878 Anna was 12 years old and Ludwig was going on 10. His family was doing well, with both children helping him in the fields. Ludwig was not quite big enough to handle the scythe, but Michael was happy that he kept trying. Maybe next harvest he would be big enough to swing it like his dad.

Michael and his children were in the field shocking the oats—standing each bundle on end with the head at the top surrounded by several more bundles. This allowed rain water to drain to the ground and the heads would dry out quickly when the rain stopped. Soon they would be going home to a warm meal and much needed rest. As they were putting their harvesting tools away in the shed, the widowed owner of the land they leased arrived in a wagon. She quickly stepped off the wagon and advised Michael that she would not be able to lease him her land anymore—she had just married and her husband would be farming what Michael had leased. Michael politely thanked her for the many years that he had the lease. She responded saying she appreciated that he had always done a good job farming.

There was nothing to do but go home, tell Krystyna the news, and start talking about the future. Everyone was tired and the news of the day hung heavy over the supper table. Krystyna did her best to cheer up her family and Michael realized he needed to help her.

There was very little of the harvest left and the fall would give them a chance to discuss options. Two families had left Bielsko and moved eastward. Michael decided he would try to find out where they went and what they were doing. He was not well acquainted with either family, however he knew some of their relatives who had stayed and he would ask them at Church or as he happened to meet them in the village. He was aware that if he was obvious with his questions people would wonder if he was thinking of moving. He did not want that impression in the village for now. It was enough to be known as a confident man with strong feelings for his family. Michael had learned how to gather information without appearing to probe.

Michael learned that with the abolition of serfdom, opportunities were more available. The Russian leadership felt the void would be filled in by the children of the freed serfs. More incentive for production would be one benefit. More families would be needed to till the land for large land owners.

Losing the five hectare lease was a major blow to the family. Michael was growing more restless and his anxiety bothered Krystyna. They talked for hours at a time about the possibility of moving where there might be better opportunity. He was having trouble deciding which option would be the best for his family. He would let the villagers know when he was ready. If he decided not to move they might think he was weak for not trying. And he realized that by not talking he might miss some wise counsel. He and Krystyna were troubled by having to face the biggest decision of their 13 year marriage.

Within a week Michael Krystyna's uncle Ludwig Riske, Michael's son's namesake, visited when he knew Krystyna would not be home, as he wanted to have a private visit with Michael. Though they had not visited much over the years. He said that he had been thinking about moving and wondered if Michael would like to hear of his plans. The two farmers talked for several hours and agreed to take a trip to Karolinow, a village five miles northeast of Chelm. There was farmland available to lease and communal grazing for cattle. Michael expected Krystyna to be opposed to the idea, but she was very supportive. He felt the closeness to Chelm was what interested her.

Michael and Ludwig met several times in the next days, deciding to leave as soon as possible, as it was already turning cold. They left Monday September 16, 1878. Karolinow was about 65 miles from Bielsko and the trip would take over a week. They prepared the wagon with a rounded roof covered with canvas to keep their provisions dry. The difficult good-byes stayed with them as Bielsko was faded out of sight. Ludwig was in his early fifties. He hoped to find a place to settle in and live the rest of his life. Michael listened intently, as he had great respect for Krystyna's uncle. He was only looking for the best for his family. If that meant moving again, he would. Learning is what he wanted to do. He was illiterate, but that did not keep him from wanting to discover what he could do. He certainly knew how to talk to people. He was realizing that even if they did not move to Karolinow he would be more respected in the village for having made this trip.

Ludwig was optimistic about what they would find. They decided to stay as long as needed to learn everything they could about the area. They questioned each other to figure out every issue they would need to know. Once they realized that they were a resource for each other, they continued raising issues no matter how small. The further they traveled the better they felt. When they left they had no idea the trip would produce mutual respect, so even if they never moved they would feel the trip was worthwhile. Passing through Lublin reminded them about Michael's wedding. With a lump in his throat, Michael told Ludwig how lucky he felt to be married to Krystyna. With the death of Rosalia and some other tough times, he felt they were better for it.

Very late on the third night they made camp on the edge of Chelm. The next morning they made their way to Karolinow and met with an agent who knew all the land around the village. The questions began to pour out of both of them. They discussed rainfall, lease rates, snowfall, the Catholic Church and the Lutheran Church. They looked at some land that was available. Most of the leased land had a house on it. The agent left them and let them take another look at what he had shown them. They looked over everything a second time, and some parcels a third time. The idea that a home would be on the land they would be farming was especially attractive to Michael, after traveling so far to his fields. By the end of the second full day they were convinced that this was the area for them.

Early the next morning they spent time with the agent and committed to side by side pieces of property. Because it was late in the year, they told the agent they did not know if they could take care of their affairs and return and to take ownership this fall. But the properties were secured and two happy men prepared for the trip home. They camped again on the western edge of Chelm and started early Saturday morning for Bielsko. The cool weather was good for traveling, just right for the horses, which they worried about. They camped beside a creek below a gentle sloping hill where the horses had plenty of grass and water. They woke up during the night to a heavy downpour. The horses had been securely tied and were safe, and the goods in the wagon were dry. The only concern was the rapidly rising creek. Ludwig moved the horses a short distance to higher ground, and they both got under the cover of the wagon. The rain pounded so hard that sleeping was impossible.

Early morning the rain stopped and they moved further away from the creek to a flat spot where they could start a fire and dry their clothes. They were happy they had done such a thorough job of making the wagon cover secure and waterproof. In this part of Poland heavy rains come along with very little warning.

It was early afternoon before they got fully under way, but they were not concerned about the time. The important thing was that the horses were healthy, and for that an extra day would be a small price to pay, for Michael had heard many stories about horses and oxen going lame, getting sick, and even dying in harness. Ludwig said he had been involved in such himself. It made them more cautious and less anxious to push their horses.

They picked a campsite and prepared to settle in for the night in an area known for an abundance of wildlife. As the sun was going down they saw many deer coming out of the forest and heading to creeks. Michael was intrigued because of the farming activity. In the Bielsko area they did not come out much during the day, except on the cold winter days looking for hay or grain. Ludwig said the wildlife used to be much more abundant with many more kinds of animals—so many that it had been hard to protect growing crops.

They broke camp early morning Wednesday to make it home that day, but they would watch the horses closely. Shortly after leaving camp they met a caravan of about a dozen wagons and many cattle being led by people walking. They were Germans from an area east of Radom on the way to Volhynia, a Province in Ukraine with the Bug River on its western border. Their entire village was moving because they had heard that with serfdom ended, large land owners needed competent farmers to till the soil, and Germans had a reputation for being skilled craftsmen and good farmers.

Late afternoon Ludwig suggested that they camp on the edge of the village of Poniatowa, four and a half miles from Bielsko. They arrived home next noon, happy to discuss what they had done the last ten days.

After many hours of conversation Michael's only interest was rest. Krystyna was especially excited that they had committed to property side by side. While Michael slept she wanted to go tell the neighbors, but then she realized they would soon find out. It did not take long for the news to spread in their village.

The next afternoon the family was talking about the move when Ludwig came over. The first decision to be made was to move now or wait till spring. If they moved now, they could start to settle in before the heavy snow fell and could plan for next year. So many things to discuss. Their house would be wanted by newly marrieds in the village, but they may not be able to sell their land. The land records for Lubelskie Powiat were in Karczmiska, a three day trip. With the loss of his lease things were simplified for Michael and he was feeling like things were falling into place for he and his family. Ludwig and his family could leave this fall, having several family members who could handle the details.

Ludwig mentioned another family that might want to move with them. They had five young children, four horses and two milk cows, and had thought of moving eastward for several years. Ludwig said their animals would be an asset to everyone. The day was spent discussing all aspects of the upcoming move. Krystyna fixed supper and the discussion went on through the meal until late at night. Without anyone mentioning it, their discussion brought the decision to go as soon as possible. Michael left early the next morning for Karczmiska to find out if he could sell his property. He would be back late on Saturday night.

Planning was going on and the mood of everyone was very serious. Even the children began asking more questions than usual. Ludwig was there much of the time evaluating which possessions duplicated his and could be left behind, though they would not know until the actual packing started. Ludwig would take two wagons, so he began bargaining for another team. Michael returned to report that their home and two hectares of land could be sold, though for less than they hoped for. He would need to go to Karczmiska again next week to complete the transaction.

The Sunday service was an emotional experience for Michael's family. The village knew they were leaving, and many good-byes were said. It was difficult for Michael who remembered how his involvement in that Church had helped him create a loving home for Krystyna and their children, though they would be involved in the Lutheran Church in Karolinow.

By Tuesday the sale was completed. Michael decided to buy another team so he could take his farm implements. Michael assured Krystyna there would be enough funds for the trip and to help them get started in Karolinow. The next few days were extremely busy.

Michael was not happy with the disposition of the dapple gray horse in his new team, but he had to take both because of the pressure of time. Ludwig was a more experienced horseman, so they felt they could handle the horse. Michael spent time with the harness maker because the spirited horse was smaller by at least 200 pounds. The heavy girth belt had to fit both horses properly, which required altering a girth belt that the harness maker had on hand. And each horse required a different size collar. After the special fittings both men were happy with the equipment and the wagons. Having just traveled with a team and wagon, Michael was particular with the wagon covers. Each family had a high cover on at least one wagon for weather protection. The other wagons were covered but not arched over the top. He was satisfied that their property would be safe regardless of the weather.

Though only ten, Ludwig was large for his age and had a natural ability to work with animals. He would drive the wagon and their faithful, experienced team. Krystyna and Anna would ride in the wagon. Michael would lead the caravan driving the new team, keeping the dapple gray in tight control. The trip would last four or five days if the weather held and there were no mishaps. They would be trailing six head of cattle, a colt, and on one wagon a cage with 30 chickens. The plan was to leave Wednesday October 2, 1878.

CHAPTER 3

— 1878 —

First Move: To Karolinow, Poland

Final packing was not finished until midnight October 2nd, and everyone was restless except the children, who fell asleep from exhaustion. Michael and Krystyna happened to meet at the side of the wagon. They hugged and leaned against the wagon wheel. Michael said he was "sad and happy leaving our village to join another. Many of these people we will not see again."

Krystyna answered, "We'll make another home, have a good life for our children. Maybe we'll have a bigger family." Tears were running down her cheeks as she took a long last look at their home.

When it was time to move the caravan, Michael took the lead and the six wagons started to roll out of Bielsko as the sun began to show itself. Ludwig felt very grown up controlling his team and wagon. Michael was weary and he knew it would be a long journey. Packing for the trip had been hastily done and not organized well. Hope that the weather would hold for them occupied his mind.

Michael still felt uneasy about his high-spirited dapple gray gelding, though he harnessed up well and was pulling like the horse beside him. Maybe it was having a new team that gave him concern, but he knew that the team his son was driving was the best. It was a cool crisp morning, the bright sun promising a warm day.

Though the caravan moved slowly eastward, the village of Bielsko seemed to quickly disappear. The reality of the move was being felt by everyone in the wagon train, though most of the travelers kept their thoughts to themselves. Some chatted, seeming not to care who heard their conversations. Most seemed to realize the trip would be over in a few days, and a new world would be theirs. They would soon prepare to settle in for the long winter.

Michael was leading in the first wagon with the plow and farm tools and whatever household goods could fill up to the canvas covered arches. The second wagon was doing well, his son proudly in control of the reins beside his mother and Anna. There was a small space on top of household items where a couple of people could sleep, but the hope was that the weather would hold so they could all spend the night under the wagons, which had plenty of canvas to wrap around three sides.

The third wagon was driven by Krystyna's uncle Ludwig, and two of his young sons rode with him. A young man of 19 from the Church had agreed to make the trip for ten dollars and was driving Uncle Ludwig's second wagon, the fourth in the caravan. His saddle horse was trailing behind his wagon.

The fifth wagon belonged to the Heinrichs family—Gene, his wife Emily and five children aged 3 to 7. The twins were the oldest. His wagon was full and his nephew Howard drove a second filled with their goods. The saddle horse, a colt, and four milk cows followed.

As the sun reached its peak the caravan stopped for a meal. The men started a campfire and saw that the animals could graze, drink small amounts of water, and stay securely tied. The women prepared the food. The men were very busy during the food preparation, in a rush atmosphere, for at least two hours were needed for the stop. With the sun going down early this time of the year and despite a half moon, they needed to settle by dusk.

The heavy draft horses seemed to be only half working, with the exception of Michael's gelding. But even he seemed to settle down except for a few nervous head throws. Michael, Ludwig and Gene had decided to try to make it to the village of Belzyce, keeping as straight a line as possible to Chelm. This route would take them south of Lublin a few miles, though they would have liked to stop at the Lutheran Church they had attended a few times. The trip moved slowly toward the goal of the day. At one brief stop late afternoon Krystyna joined Michael, talking about how proud their son was to be driving a team pulling the wagon. She said his whole conversation seemed like he was years older than he had been yesterday. They were both pleased, and Anna seemed content sitting beside Ludwig, carrying on a conversation which Krystyna could see as the road curved. They had not realized that her visit with Michael would be a good time for their children to talk.

The caravan stopped by a creek within walking distance of Belzyce the wagons pulled in a circle. The cattle, being very tame, were turned loose inside the campground. The horses were tied to various anchors; some to wagons, some to trees, one to a wagon wheel. The fire was burning and the evening meal was being prepared. Cows were milked, chickens fed and the canvas protection wrapped around three sides of each wagon to provide windbreaks. Most of the people had at least a few good hours of sleep, though the first night out brought some apprehension. They worried about wild animals and their weird sounds, though they knew that they were safe.

The caravan got an early start. All the animals were calm, some even anxious to get under way. The colt, halter broke months earlier, led well and often pranced, kicking up his heels to burn off youthful energy. Krystyna was enjoying riding with Michael as they left camp and in a mile or two would go back to their second wagon. The other children were comfortable did not show the restlessness of yesterday. They had planned the trip with help from elders in the village who had told them about water sources along the way. There were many creeks and several farm wells they could use if needed. There was adequate food even if the trip should take some extra days. Just like yesterday the morning was cold, but soon the sun warmed them. Michael and Krystyna talked together about the house and land in Karolinow. She was anxious and worried that it might not be what Michael had described, though she had no reason to feel that way. But it is late in the year and hard weather could arrive anytime. Even if it arrived soon, she told Michael that she was glad they left now rather than waiting till spring—a long wait like that would have been difficult, a time for second guessing themselves.

After Krystyna joined Ludwig and Anna, the caravan went up a long slope. The trail was straight and not difficult. Just slow, steady and long. When they reached the crest they stopped for a few minutes to let the horses rest, and they enjoyed the beautiful view. The road ahead was flat for a short distance before dropping down into a big valley, the decline was a little greater than the incline.

As they moved Michael kept looking back to see that the other wagons were moving as they should. As he was turning to sit back down, a deer jumped in front of his team and the dapple gray reared up on his hind legs then bolted. Michael lost his balance but grabbed the brake handle. He was able to pull himself up to his seat, but the gelding was running while the other horse was pulling back. The gelding pulled off the trail and was running hard despite Michael pulling on the reins. He stepped in a hole about the size of a wash tub, stumbled, fell, and lunged forward. Then the wagon hit the hole. The horse did not get up. Stunned, Michael surveyed the damage. The front wheel was broken and the gelding was crying in pain. Michael saw that his leg was broken. The rest of the caravan had stopped and was gathering. The mothers kept the children back from the scene. The men huddled and without speaking knew what had to be done. Since there were no guns in the caravan, Gene volunteered to use a heavy steel hammer. They butchered the hind quarters to use in the next few days.

It was decided to make camp for the night and start repairing the broken wheel. Michael would need another horse to pull the load, and most of what was on the wagon had to be repacked. Krystyna was pale, worried that Michael might have been hurt. That she had just left the seat a short time before the accident may have contributed to her feeling faint. Michael was lucky the harness had suffered only minor damage.

Each wagon carried an extra wheel, but it took most of the afternoon to replace the broken one. Then they had to get the wagon moving, which required shoveling dirt into the hole. Each man took a position to push while Ludwig drove the one horse team. After a couple of tries the wagon was freed. Michael took the reins and positioned the wagon in the circle for the evening.

The men discussed using the saddle horse to replace the dapple gray. The young man who owned it said that it had been used to pull a light wagon several times, but never a heavy load. What appealed to them was the horse's easy disposition, which was important when harnessing a horse next to a seasoned work horse. They discussed other options, like limping into the next village, storing part of the wagon load, and coming back for it later. None of them liked that idea. Someone suggested spreading part of the load among the rest of the wagons. They had to admit that the same thing could happen to another wagon. The owner of the saddle horse suggested that they give it a try in the morning. The men agreed it was worth the time they had taken to discuss the other options.

Michael and Krystyna spent hours repacking the wagon. They talked about how lucky they were that the accident wasn't worse. The only cost was losing their horse, and they both felt that it was an accident that was bound to happen eventually. Now it was over. Though there had been something that bothered Michael about that horse, sort of an untrustworthy nature, he was sad that he had lost it. But now he had to look ahead.

They traveled about four miles that day of ups and downs. The evening was quiet and everyone was looking forward to a steady peaceful day of travel. The daily duties were becoming routine, and all did their part and things ran smoothly. Michael was feeling uneasy, but he knew that it would soon pass. Young Ludwig did not say much, thinking about his father being in the accident and his mother having just left that wagon. He realized that if his team had been spooked, they would've run into the first wagon, causing further damage.

Michael was nervous watching the saddle horse in harness. The first mile was going well. The horse was doing a good job and pulling his share of the load. Michael felt good about it and conveyed the message back to the other wagons. Maybe he was overreacting after having been so concerned about the dapple gray. He told himself to relax and pay more attention to the caravan and his son driving the wagon behind him.

The group agreed to keep a steady push and go as far as they could, pulling off the trail for water about mid-afternoon in case they could not camp by a water source. If they could reach Metow before dark, setting up camp would not be difficult. There were no problems and they reached Metow as the sun was setting. Camp was set up quickly, a cooking fire was started, and everyone helped, so a meal was soon enjoyed. Tending to the animals took a couple of hours and most of the people were anxious to get a few hours of sound sleep.

At breakfast they talked about their progress and realized that the trip would take much longer than they had planned—on the fourth morning they still had a long way to go. As long as the weather held out they would be okay for they were well provisioned for the trip. The quarters of horse meat would help save their preserved meat. By noon break they had covered a lot of ground and not stopped for water. They were alongside a stream which they would be following for many more miles. It looked like today they would cover the most miles of any day so far. That lifted their spirits. Family members wanted to stay close to their wagons, not visiting much with other families. They were concerned about their wagons and especially their animals.

The weather was much colder next morning and the sun not as bright. It felt better to keep moving and no one wanted to stop. Well past noon the animals were watered and everyone rushed their jobs so the caravan would get moving. The land was flat and lightly populated. The trail they were on was a popular one and they noticed that most of the traffic seemed local.

Michael thought he would see more Germans moving eastward. Even if they were all traveling in the same direction, they might pass a group resting or camped early for the night. They would feel better knowing there were more people on the road than just their caravan. Maybe others had not started the trip because of the time of the year.

He still felt they had made the right decision—and they would be six months to a year ahead of others who decided to move east in the spring. He was happy despite weather risks. They made it to the west side of Bystrzejowice Pierwsze and set up camp for the night. Ludwig had been there years before, having heard of a relative who might be living there. After spending a full day looking and inquiring about his cousin he was satisfied that he was not there.

That fifth night away from Bielsko the evening was much colder, which changed preparations for sleeping. The canvas covers were pulled in to create a smaller space to contain body heat better. The small children all slept in their respective wagons, which were very comfortable. In the morning the adults getting up very early were greeted by about four inches of snow on the ground. This was not a disastrous event, however it did slow their movement. They were late getting started and they knew they would not match their previous days. The sun came out and by noon the snow had melted. The wet earth created some mud sticking problems which slowed them some. But they were moving better in the afternoon and covered the same distance they had the day before.

On the sixth night out they camped east of the village of Biskupice. A very happy bunch of travelers had their evening meal and most went to sleep early. They used their tighter sleeping arrangements again, as the temperature had dropped even lower than the night before. Michael was anxious, but at the same time trying to not let it show. He had led the caravan out of town thinking he would trade the lead with the other men. No one suggested it, and from the start they assumed Michael was the leader. They all just knew. He tried his best to fulfill that responsibility. He was admired and acted more and more the leader. A big man, he had a commanding presence. They all looked up to him, even Uncle Ludwig, who occasionally sought his wisdom.

It did not snow and it looked like it would be another sunny fall day, though it was cold. Son Ludwig was having a little problem with his left horse who was not responding to Ludwig's direction. The horse was starting to drag a bit while the other horse led the way. This held up the caravan's start, so they decided to swap horses with Michael who was happy with the saddle horse and confident of putting it under Ludwig's control. With the trade, Michael would be able to figure out what the problem was. They got underway late, but the caravan moved steadily closer to Chelm. Michael had no problem with the horse, and finally concluded that the horse had been playing Ludwig. When Michael commanded him, he responded as he always had. When they finally made the noon stop Michael talked with Ludwig about driving a team. Horses knew who was driving them and would respond better when they knew the driver was strong and knew the commands.

The afternoon was sunny and Michael stopped the caravan south of the village of Anusin. He felt that they would arrive in Karolinow in three more days, so he decided to slow the pace a little to take good care of their animals. The cattle had traveled well, the chickens in their cage had survived the wreck. By stopping early they had more time to prepare meals and prepare their sleeping areas. The horse meat would run out tonight and they would go back to salted meat the next two nights. The women enjoyed the time together preparing meals. Krystyna became much better acquainted with her aunt and uncle. The Heinrich family mixed and seemed to enjoy it. Though they seemed to want to become closer with the group, for some reason they held back a bit, seeming to want to go back to the comfort of their wagon.

The next morning, Wednesday October 9th, they left a little later since Michael said they had the time to. The horse that Michael had swapped with Ludwig was no problem. He pulled well and was easily directed. Krystyna enjoyed sitting all these miles beside her son. They talked a lot and she felt she knew him a lot better. The day went well and they arrived mid-afternoon and set up camp on the edge of Janko-wice. The early arrival was welcome and they put the wagons in a circle as best they could. Some of the animals were loose in the enclosure, the rest were tied to their respective wagons. Michael, Ludwig, Gene, and Uncle Ludwig walked up the trail about a half mile to watch a man training workhorses.

In the morning camp came to life earlier. Everyone had slept well, and the thought of being very close to their new home was exciting. No one had to be encouraged to get ready for their last long day on the road—they would be able to get within a mile of Chelm by late afternoon. The following day they would camp there and the next day they would reach Karolinow by early afternoon.

They were meeting more people on the road as they approached Chelm, locals as well as a caravan of about 30 wagons that had stopped for the day. By their wagons Michael could tell they were Germans. They told him they were going to Volhynia and planned to make their home in the Rovno area, about 110 miles east of the Bug River. Some of them were craftsman, most were farmers who had come from the Pultusk area, thirty miles north of Warsaw. About half of them were from that village. They were moving to Volhynia because the large land owners were still looking for people to farm their land. Land owners purchased forested land because the soil was good. Several of the men in the group were land clearers who could saw down trees and pull out the stumps, work that they could get throughout the winter. After a long visit the inquisitive Michael hastened back to the caravan and they started toward the west end of Chelm.

Michael's interest had been piqued by the resting caravan. He thought about it the rest of the afternoon. Is that where he should be going? Are there really good opportunities there? It's still Poland, so he would not have had to cross into another country. Michael's Volhynia thoughts stopped when he realized they were about a half mile west of Chelm and they needed to find a campsite. The mood was very cheerful. Everyone gathered around the cooking fire early. They were so anxious to see what their homes would be like.

Most of the camp stayed around the fire talking about the trip and the new life they were about to start. Michael was anxious, and took his son to walk around the camp with him. He asked him how he liked driving a team. Ludwig had grown up quickly with the responsibility for the wagon and his mother and sister beside him. He told his dad that he might become a drive master hauling wagons of freight with teams of six or eight horses. Michael was proud that he was dreaming and had ambition. He recalled having worked in his neighbor's fields a full day when he himself was only nine. He wanted better for his children and he was working hard to that end. When they returned to their wagons Krystyna told Michael she was glad to see the two of them wander off together.

Krystyna noticed her son's confidence, even that he now walked with a bit of an arrogant swagger. She smiled, wondering what he would be like in ten years. He was big for his age, but would he keep growing? There would be plenty for him to do when they got to Karolinow. The whole family would work hard to get settled before deep winter set in.

People felt so comfortable around the fire that Michael had to put it out to get the group to rest. It would be a big day tomorrow. Soon the last lantern went out and an exhausted group of travelers were sound asleep.

Many slept late and had to be urged out of bed. They left even later than Michael had planned, though he saw no reason to push them. As long as they left by mid-morning, they would get home by mid-afternoon if there were no unforeseen events.

The excitement continued as they went around the northern side of Chelm. They only had four miles to go, and then they would be home. Everyone in the caravan was chatting and laughing. Michael had never seen such expression—neither here nor at home in Bielsko.

The adults were all curious, watching the open terrain. They liked what they saw. It was similar to what they had left, and forest land was much further away. The road followed a creek most of the way. It was difficult to judge the soil as they were riding by, though Michael and Ludwig had liked what they saw when they had visited earlier. With the village of Karolinow in sight, a loud cheer went up. They wanted to stop, but Michael kept going as he knew the house was within a thousand feet. Michael pulled up to his house and Uncle Ludwig continued past Michael's wagons to his own home.

Gene's wagon followed Uncle Ludwig to his home, just a hundred yards further. As in many German villages, one road went through it and people lived on both sides. Their outbuildings were close to the road and the homes set further back.

The colony of Karolinow was about five kilometers long. It was founded in 1870, largely by settlers from the parishes of Wengrow (east of Warsaw) and Pultusk. Karolinow had 64 farms, 89% of which were German.

The surrounding area had been very swampy and at times hard to travel through. Many drainage channels had been dug and countless loads of dirt hauled into the low places. It had taken a lot of work by former farmers to bring it up to the productive land it now was. This was the reason that the Germans were always sought after. They knew how to make land productive—and most importantly they were willing to do the hard work necessary. Catherine the Great, a German princess, who became the Tsarina of Russia, issued a proclamation in 1763 inviting Germans to migrate to Russia via the North Sea and St. Petersburg. After a rest in St. Petersburg they could sail down the Volga to occupy and develop the south of Russia.

Karolinow was situated on the Serebryszcze Estate owned by Josef Zawadzki. The relationship with Zawadzki was very good, but after he died the relationship with the new owner, Lechnicki, was rather stormy. He wanted to raise the rent substantially or even chase out some of the colonists. The day after arriving Michael, Ludwig and Gene had to deal with Lechnicki's representative. They felt their rent was high, but after a conversation with the representative they considered it fair. Given good crops, they felt that they could provide for their families.

By early evening the wagons were unloaded and a fire was going in the stove. Krystyna had carefully planned the unloading of the household goods, to place them where she knew she would eventually want them. Her magic touch had created a homey atmosphere, even though the house disappointed her, though Michael would be the last to know that. Michael and his son got help from Uncle Ludwig unloading the plow. They returned the favor and went to help Ludwig as soon as he was ready to unload.

Michael had taken the harnesses off the two teams, since Ludwig was too short and not strong enough to do this job. He watched with an interest he had not had before the trip. They rubbed the horses down with extra care and carefully brushed them. Michael was impressing on his son the need to take care of their horses, which were key to their movement as well as to what would be put on the table. Ludwig understood what his dad was saying to him. To have the dapple gray destroyed before him had shocked Ludwig. That vision stuck with him. The dapple was always a misfit, and Ludwig asked if maybe he had been raised wrong. Michael said he thought the dapple had some thoroughbred blood in him, being highly spirited. Michael was so proud of the questions Ludwig kept asking. He was elated beyond words and couldn't wait to discuss it with Krystyna before they fell asleep.

Krystyna was exhausted but happy. She told Michael it had been a wonderful experience because of his careful preparations. She was proud of him. Now they were concerned about their children blending into the village, since it was much bigger than the one where they were born.

Michael, Uncle Ludwig and Gene had an immediate issue—they each only had a couple armfuls of firewood. They met the next morning, Saturday October 12, and decided to go to the Mayor's house to ask where they could get wood.

The Mayor, Otto Duerr, warmly welcomed them. Before he would hear about their concern he wanted to know where they had come from and all about the journey. He and his family came from the Gostynin Parish, northwest of Warsaw, about a dozen miles south, across the Vistula River from Plock.

He had arrived in Karolinow shortly after the settlement was formed in 1870 and had been mayor since 1874. He told the three men to relax and not to worry—they could come back with their wagons and fill them from his wood pile. This would give them time to find some dead trees to cut down. After many thanks, he made them promise to come to him for help or advice no matter what it concerned.

They left happy and excited. It did not take long for three wagons to be loaded with fire wood and unloaded at their homes, sheltered from the snow that was sure to come soon.

The next day Ludwig and Gene went into the forest looking for trees they could cut down. There were many dead trees and they took back two that they had cut and sawed into six foot lengths. They had brought only one wagon, for the trip was exploratory. That evening the three men met, and included the young man who had helped on the trip. They talked about going out early the next morning to start building the wood pile needed to get through the winter. They would pay the young man five dollars if he would help them chop down trees for the next week. He wanted to stay a few days anyway to give his horse a much needed rest. Michael again heaped thanks upon him for the use of his horse when the dapple had to be put down.

The morrow being the Lord's day, Gene opined that biblically they were doing the correct right thing. He quoted something that he'd heard in a sermon years ago that "if on the Lord's day, the ox is in the mire, you should get him out." After all agreed that being right with the Lord, they would meet at sunup in front of Michael's house. When Michael told the family, Ludwig said he was going too—there was no way he was going to stay home. Michael resisted an appropriate amount, then told him he could, knowing what he would have Ludwig do. It would be the same as having a grown man work for him.

The day was very cloudy, the coldest so far. All the more reason to rush. Soon they started swinging axes and the trees started to fall. Ludwig was put to work using their team to drag the fallen trees back to the wagons. They felled 20 to 30 foot trees and they cut them into six to eight foot lengths, depending on the diameter, so they could lift onto the wagons. Their wagons were full by noon. They were very happy.

The next day they left under darkness so they could bring in two loads, being nervous about the weather. Michael knew he could barter his carpenter skills for wood if necessary, but he kept this to himself. It was a fallback plan. He encouraged the guys to chop, saw, tow and load until each family had seven loads of wood stacked at their homes. With the cold weather creeping up, Michael suggested that the next day they aim to bring three loads in. Ten loads per family might last through most of the winter. They all agreed to include Ludwig and set out in the middle of the night.

Gene rode with Michael on his wagon. The young man who owned the saddle horse drove Gene's team. Gene thought the wood would not last through the winter, if it lasted longer than normal. He said even if it snowed today or tonight they should go back out for more wood. If there was extra wood in a big village, there would be people needing to barter for some of it later in the winter. As they approached the village with the third load it started to snow. They unloaded it into a barn where they could saw and split it. The snow was heavy that night and they stayed home chopping firewood in their respective barns.

Happy, thankful, and appreciative to the mayor for their warm homes, they took several days to get their wood piles ready for a long winter. Michael and Krystyna talked about going to Church on Sunday October 27th. They would attend the Lutheran Evangelical Augsburg Parish Church in Chelm. They had seen a Church in the village, but their neighbors said it was a small Lutheran Church without a Pastor. A local school teacher who also served as a Cantor held services the first and third Sunday of the month, a typical arrangement in small villages. On the Pastor's visit to the local Church he would perform marriages, sanction baptisms and make necessary Pastoral visits.

But Michael and his family wanted to go into Chelm to attend. They would attend in the village after that. There was a lot of snow on the ground Sunday and the air was crisp. They left early to have enough time if something caused a delay. The trip was uneventful and they arrived with extra time before the service. This was the first time they had been in a large Church since Ludwig was baptized. Michael and Krystyna were holding hands as they walked up the steps. The children were close behind them entering through the huge door. They walked through the narthex, walked through an open door and entered the sanctuary. They stood, awed and overwhelmed by the size and beauty of the sanctuary.

They were ushered to a seat and sat in silence listening to an organ prelude. Krystyna whispered to Michael, "Isn't it beautiful?" He whispered back, "I've never seen anything like it." He leaned forward and winked at the children.

His thoughts went back to Bielsko and his helping at the Church, some of his finest days. Tears filled his eyes. Was it possible he could do some work here and get acquainted, maybe even get to visit with the Reverend? The liturgy was finished and Pastor Schmidt began the sermon, but Michael did not understand much because his mind was wandering. He let his eyes gaze from side to side as he thought about all the beautiful stained glass windows and the wood carving on the altar. He was sad when the sermon came to an end. Part of him wanted to stay and enjoy the Church interior. But Anna nudged her mother.

On the way out a member said hello to Michael, who returned a stuttered hello. No one else attempted a conversation and they were soon in front of Reverend Schmidt. The Reverend greeted them warmly, recognizing they were first time visitors, and invited them back. Mixed emotions filled Michael on the trip home. When he entered the large Church his thoughts had gone back to the trip to the Lutheran Church in Lublin for their marriage. Maybe he was thinking about his parents. Whatever it was, Krystyna did not bother him with questions. Instead she talked about the beautiful Church and the fine choir. The last mile nothing was said, with everyone deep in thought. Krystyna later commented about it to Michael. "We have been to Church and the Lord works in mysterious ways. Maybe he was telling us that it was good we had made the long trip to go listen to His Word." She had been proud of the silence of the last mile—that lapse was unusual with children.

They decided that Michael would spend this week sawing the logs and splitting them. The pressure was off, so they went through the village to see what craftsmen were there. Michael was interested in what services they could get if the need arose, now that he had an adequate wood supply to barter. He did discover that there was a widow who might need some wood soon. Her husband had died last spring and some wood had been given to her. She would need much more to get through the winter.

Michael decided to go out and get some more wood. He would have Ludwig take the other wagon with one horse, since the saddle horse had gone back with the owner. The single horse could pull only a third of the load that two could. The snow was not too deep to prevent them from going. They were able to make four trips before the snow stopped them, but Michael was happy.

The winter had heavy snowfall and was a little longer than normal. When it finally warmed enough to plant the garden, Krystyna was in a hurry to get it done. The garden they planned was huge—two morgen (about 1.2 acres). One quarter was for vegetables, the rest was for the potato patch. Michael had found out that, as back home in Bielsko, potatoes were good for bartering. People always ran out and Michael let the word out that he was going to have extra. He had traded some of his wood toward the end of the winter. He wanted to be known as a man who would trade and a man who would drop what he was doing to help a neighbor. He knew the importance of getting along and especially showing his willingness to help.

The garden had been planted and the crops had been sown. Michael's crop land allotment was four morgen. He had divided it so he had 1½ morgen of hay, 1 morgen of oats, ½ morgen of barley, 1 morgen of wheat. The hay should be enough for the winter. He had sold his horse so he only had the team and his few cattle to feed. He felt good about the way the farm looked—it had rained at the right time and his crops sprouted the way they should.

After the crop was sown Michael was approached about putting up a barn on a man's property for cash. He would actually lead the job with Michael as his helper. Michael gladly accepted. He and Krystyna lived at the southern end of the village and the barn was to be built at the northern end. Michael rode one of the work horses to the site. They started working shortly after sunup and stopped by late afternoon, since the owner was in his late 60s. The job lasted only ten days, but the man had him help clean up and move several piles of wood and junk. A passing neighbor commented that his farmyard looked very good and told them to keep at it—the property had been a mess. Michael stayed to help clean up for a few more days.

When he was paid and getting his horse ready for the ride home, the man called to him to say that of all the men who had worked for him over the years, Michael did the best job. "You were here when you were supposed to be, and I really appreciated it." He thanked him again and an elated Michael rode home.

As Michael was finishing the story to his family, there was a knock at the door. A Mr. Krushel introduced himself. He was also new in the village and he had spoken to the man Michael had worked for. He was living in a tent with his family and was about to start building a house. He was a carpenter himself and would like to hire Michael to work for

him till the house was built. Michael invited him in and introduced him
to his family. They discussed the project and what would be expected
of Michael. It was well after dark before Mr. Krushel got up to leave.
Michael said he would work for him, but would need a day or two off
as his farm needed his attention. They agreed to the terms.

Michael and the family were thrilled that things were going so well.
With the added income Krystyna would be able to buy some household items that she had wanted. Michael said one of the first things he
needed was to get the harness properly repaired that had been damaged
in the wreck.

The building of the house moved forward slowly. The man was very
particular, which slowed construction. It was a little bigger than the
typical house in Karolinow, but was needed for his seven children. It
was a typical German village house, with a stove in the central part for
heating the home and cooking. A barn was to be built onto the house,
though so far Mr. Krushel had not asked Michael to help with it. A
month later the family moved in. Everyone was very happy, and the
man made the final payment to Michael for his wages. As they were
preparing to say goodbye, Mr. Krushel asked if he would like to help
him as he built the barn. Michael said yes, if he could have the rest
of the week to tend to his farm. He was certain the potatoes needed
weeding and he wanted to get the harness maker started on his repair.

The following Monday Michael was on the job and anxious to learn.
He asked a lot of questions, for the man was an accomplished carpenter.
Michael had done a lot of that kind of work, but most of it on rough
projects—outbuildings and such that did not require finish carpentry
skills. The man was very generous in answering questions and would
sometimes take extra time to explain an answer. They were forming a
bond, enjoying each other's company. They discussed the village and
the Church. Mr. Krushel, and his family had been to services there.
They were conducted by the Cantor who conveyed a strong message.
They had moved from a village about ten miles west of Chelm. His
wife's parents lived here and she wanted to be near them. They had
only been married ten years and her parents were about the age of her
husband. The oldest of the seven children was eight and there was one

set of twins. Michael thought a lot about their family, and mentioned them to Krystyna. Maybe they should have another child before their two got much older. They did not spend much time on the topic, but both of them probably kept thinking about it.

The barn building went well, and Michael told Krystyna that it was one of the better jobs that he had ever had. He'd learned a lot, was treated well, and he had been paid. He thanked Mr. Krushel for the work.

He was glad to get back to his farm for much needed work on his house, using a lot of what he had learned to complete an extra bedroom that had been framed in years earlier. He fixed some slumping doors and built Krystyna new shelves in the kitchen. She was elated—she had not expected these things so soon. Michael's skills had improved dramatically.

There was field work to do and the potato patch needed attention. The rains promised one of their largest potato crops. Two morgens of potatoes meant a lot of hoeing to kill the weeds. Michael worked from daybreak till noon in the potato patch. In the afternoon he did errands in the village. He got his repaired harnesses back and made arrangements to trade some wood for some cured meat.

The summer went by quickly and they were feeling that their village was the best possible choice. They felt accepted and even appreciated. Michael was doing a little bit of work at the Church when he could squeeze in the time.

Michael had overheard some talk about land being available in Volhynia not too many miles east of the Bug River. He wondered why this kept coming up. There must be something real happening there.

They celebrated October 11, 1879, the one year since their arrival in the village. Sunday they would go to Church in Chelm. They all remembered the beautiful building, an easy sermon to comprehend and a wonderful choir.

When Sunday came they left extra early and arrived with time to spare. This time they felt more comfortable walking into the sanctuary. It was just as beautiful. They relaxed and took in all that was offered that special morning. They were not out of place, even if they felt so. The Church was attended by many colonists from the surrounding

area. Their Lutheran roots were deep, and Michael was well aware of
that and wanted to instill that into his children. The service began, and
after the sermon a lady sang a solo that brought tears to Krystyna's
eyes. She commented that it reminded her of a friend of her mother's
who was a soloist in her Church, whom she had heard many times.
They were near the end of the line to accept the Pastor's greeting. Pastor Schmidt greeted them and asked where they lived, seeming very
interested in knowing more about them. Krystyna asked him if he ever
called on their village. He did not, but if they were ever in Chelm they
would be welcomed if they would like to stop by and receive a blessing.
They thanked the Pastor and soon were traveling back to Karolinow.

The noonday ride home was much warmer. The sun on their faces
felt good. There wasn't a lot of conversation on the way home. Maybe
everyone was reflecting on the service. Maybe they were just tired,
anxious to get home and rest. Sundays were observed at Krystyna's
house, except for the necessary work to take care of the animals, bring
in wood, fix meals and keep the house warm.

There was only a small job in the village for Michael and he proudly
did it and was promised more work before spring. The last winter he
had traded wood to some of the villagers and the word was out that if
you needed wood, Michael was the man to see. He had hauled in many
more cords than they would need. He had stacked the best wood so it
would be easy to get to if someone came to get it. His barn was close to
the road, so a buyer could see his full supply with the best in front and
available. He dreamed of people in the village buying or trading for all
of his extra wood. Krystyna felt well prepared for the long winter. Her
garden had produced abundant vegetables and she had preserved a lot.
It was only a few weeks before the Christmas season started. This year,
as last, would be spent with her uncle and aunt. Even with the children's
difference in ages, they still enjoyed the holidays together.

Uncle Ludwig and Aunt Krystyna arrived late afternoon for a Christmas eve meal. Much of the discussion was about their leaving Bielsko
and the journey to Karolinow. It was a warm evening and all of the
children were outside, even the team driver Ludwig. They were glad
they had made the move. In a brief lull in the conversation, Krystyna

said that she was especially happy they were here because she wanted them all to know she was pregnant. Just before the announcement Krystyna had put the wine bottle back on the table. Michael gave her a hug and a kiss, he grabbed the wine bottle and made sure that everyone had a glass of wine. He toasted the event and said his only wish was for a healthy baby. When the children came in they were told about the news, and it was greeted with great excitement.

It was near midnight when Krystyna's uncle and aunt left amid many wishes for a Merry Christmas. Michael's family finally got to sleep. They were up early to enjoy the traditional Christmas morning with presents that were under the tree. They attended the services in the village conducted by the Cantor with assistance from two lay men. Krystyna enjoyed hearing the Christmas carols being sung, which brought back many memories of the time before her parents died. Even though it was difficult, she enjoyed the service.

There was much for the family to look forward to in 1880—a new baby and discussions about Volhynia. There had been some warm weather in the middle of January, leaving spots of ground showing. Mayor Schmidt was out touring the village and meeting with people who would take the time to visit. Michael invited him into the house. The conversation started about issues in the village, and Michael told him he and his wife were very happy the way the village was being run. He said the community meetings that the Mayor held every month were a good place for people to voice concerns. There were usually not many complaints, so most of the meetings turned out to be informative.

Michael asked the Mayor if he knew any reason why people were moving to Volhynia. He had only heard some of the same things Michael had, however he knew a family in the village he should meet. Daniel Holtz had several siblings, who with his parents, had gone there two years ago in a caravan. He felt that he would be glad to tell him everything that he knew about Volhynia. Michael thanked him for stopping by and thanked him again for the wood when he first moved to the village. After the Mayor left, Michael kept thinking about Volhynia and wondered what the attraction was. Daniel Holtz might have answers to his many questions. Of course if there were all kinds of opportunities, he wondered why Mr. Holtz stayed here.

Because things were good, Michael began to think about replacing one of his draft horses, aged eight and fourteen. His team worked well together. If he found the right horse he would team him up and keep the horse being replaced. It would be ideal if he found the right horse and the owner would take wood and money in trade. He would seek a horse from four to eight years of age. A team like that, if compatible, would be with him a long time.

He spent a lot of time looking for that one special horse. He traveled to other villages, always looking. He got lost one day returning from a village and ran into a German settler who had about a dozen horses in his pasture. A man near the haystack saw him and started toward Michael. They introduced themselves and chatted mostly about where they came from. The man had come from the Gabin area in Poland about ten years ago. Michael asked if he had his particular kind of horse for sale or knew anyone who did. He only owned four of the horses that Michael had seen. He took horses in to break, mostly for use as draft horses. The man acted as if he might know but wasn't going to let loose the information. Michael asked him for the best road back to Karolinow, thanked him, said goodbye and was on his way.

When he returned home Krystyna was visiting with a neighbor lady. Michael joined in and told them about his day and how his spirits had gone up when he saw the dozen horses, for he was becoming disappointed about not finding one. The lady said that her husband had two draft horses for sale, horses that Michael had often admired. Michael went right over to talk to his neighbor who wanted to sell his five year old gelding. Michael said he noticed his wood supply was low and asked if he would take some of the payment in wood. He jumped at the chance. Michael had seen the gelding as a team pulling a wagon several times and did not have to check him out. They bargained and reached an agreement. Michael would give him four cords of wood, his 14 year old horse and a small amount of money. Michael took the horse the quarter of a mile home.

Michael went into the house where Krystyna was alone. He was shaking. He didn't know why—maybe because the hunt for a horse was done. It took him several hours to settle down. This reaction had never happened to him. He was so happy with his new horse, and now he had one of the better teams in the village. He thought about the many people he had met while he was looking for a horse. He had such a good experience during his search—he had learned a lot and someday he would certainly cross paths with many of the people he had met.

One day when Krystyna was helping Michael plant potatoes, she said she was getting sick and had to quit, though they were only half finished. Michael helped her to the house and returned to the potato patch. It was difficult planting alone. He plowed a furrow then went back with a bucket of prepared potatoes pieces. Then with the horse he carefully plowed another furrow which covered the first row and provided the proper spacing between the rows. The next furrow that he plowed was ready for seeding. It was very slow working alone, but Michael realized they were planting early, so if it took longer it would be all right.

The summer was going well. Ludwig and Anna spent time with friends in the village. Ludwig helped a lot in the fields and he especially enjoyed using the team, which he handled like a man who had done it for years. Cautioned that things can happen like with the dapple gray, he was cautious for his young age, but seemed a natural around animals.

Anna wanted nothing to do with animals. She had a strong interest in harvesting the garden and working the few fruit trees on the property. She learned the proper way to prune them, which was her source of pride.

Both children were very excited about the prospect of a new brother or sister. They kept asking when the child would arrive. Krystyna took the opportunity to explain how humans reproduce and the fact that it did not always work out as planned. Children might be born with illnesses, perhaps crippled, though the prayer is always for a healthy child. Ludwig did not ask a single question, however Anna was full of them. She also asked a lot of questions about the family. She wondered where everyone was born and she wanted to know how they were related. Were they all farmers or were there any craftsman in the family? Her questioning at times was relentless, which frustrated Krystyna, but she did not let that get to her as she was so proud that Anna was interested and would be able to pass the information on to her own children.

Krystyna's pregnancy was difficult and many days she stayed in bed. Anna was there for any help that was needed and wanted. Michael was very sympathetic and did what he could to comfort Krystyna. Her time was close and she knew that she should restrict any unnecessary movement. The midwife had been visiting regularly, and Krystyna tried to follow her suggestions carefully. She thought that twins might be delivered. Anna told her mother that she would do whatever was needed, so she should not worry. In the middle of July the hot weather seemed unbearable to Krystyna. But she was comforted knowing Anna, now 14, was there for her all the time. She suffered continuously and only found relief the few hours she slept during the night and early morning.

Very early in the morning of July 30th she called for Anna. Michael woke her up and while she cared for her mother, Michael went for the midwife. Immediately after they arrived the midwife began making preparations for the birth.

Mid-morning Krystyna gave birth to twin girls. Anna noticed the midwife's expression of concern. The names they had ready were Pauline and Andreas after Michael's father. The healthy first born was named Pauline. After a quick family discussion the other girl was named Eva, after the midwife. Their lives dramatically changed that morning.

There was excitement and concern that Friday in the Jess house. Eva's breathing was very difficult and the midwife quietly told Michael and Anna that she did not expect her to live but a few hours. They all watched her and realized she would not get better. She breathed rapidly a few times and then she was gone. Happiness and devastation all within a few hours. Krystyna was aware as it happened, and she was devastated. This was the second infant death the family had suffered, but Pauline needed to be cared for, and Krystyna told Anna again how she appreciated her help.

The word quickly spread. That afternoon Krystyna and Ludwig heard the news and came to visit. Michael was busy that afternoon, asking neighbors to come back the next day or Sunday. He went to the local undertaker and asked him to prepare a small casket for Eva. Michael, Krystyna, Ludwig, Uncle Ludwig and Aunt Krystyna, with the minister, laid her to rest. They requested a private service and burial, with the Cantor serving in place of the Pastor. Many condolences were offered as the neighbors promised they would come back. Unlike the other children, Pauline's baptism would not be immediate, it would be on Sunday August 9th. Eva did not live long enough to be baptized. Krystyna was very weak, realizing that she was old to be giving birth. She needed all the help Anna gladly provided, and her appreciation for her family grew daily.

This year's crop did not look promising. At best it would be below average, so Michael started making plans to offset a poor crop. He was adding to his already large wood supply. The wood he and Ludwig were cutting now was green. When they brought it home after it was cut and chopped, they placed it in the sunlight so over the next two months it would dry sufficiently. They would lay two chopped logs a foot apart and stack two chopped logs the opposite way on top, bringing the stack up to five feet. This allowed air to flow through as the sun was beating down. Though this took much more time, it was a necessary step so to assure any buyer that the wood had been thoroughly dried. Michael had been in the village long enough to establish his reputation as a man who had good wood cut to the right length. He knew that he would have more calls for wood this winter, and that made him feel better as he and Ludwig continued to bring in more wood.

The christening—part of the Sunday service at the Church in Chelm—was beautiful and Anna was there to help and assure that her father felt proud in his role. They had not been there since they celebrated one year after their arrival in Karolinow. Michael and Krystyna both felt very comfortable in the Church. Krystyna was very sad and could not hold back tears during the baptismal ceremony. But she now had three healthy children and they were her source of strength.

Weeks after the births visitors still arrived to offer congratulations and condolences. Most brought food, which was the custom in the village. They realized that most people in the village knew them—and many came whom they had not officially met. They felt honored, and Michael commented that he felt more at home here than he had in Bielsko. He had much love and respect for the people in Bielsko and many times he longed to go back and visit. Since that was not possible, his appreciation for the people in Karolinow was even stronger.

The harvest was indeed poor. However, the potato crop was much better than the small grain yields. That was welcome, as they had planted more than they needed for their own use. For the first time Ludwig could help cut the grain crop. Michael had purchased a scythe for him, though realized he might not be tall enough to wield it. At the very least he would give it a good try. If he had to wait till next year to do the job, at least he had a scythe. The harvest dragged on because of rains—which they had needed two months earlier. They managed to harvest enough oats and barley for their animals, though there would be none left over. They would have some wheat that they could barter, but even that crop was skimpy. He might need to buy another milk cow, as one of theirs would soon be dry and it would be sometime before that cow would calve again. They certainly needed to be aware of their food production, now that the family had increased. They decided to get by with their two cows and try to keep one of them milking at all times.

The winter was not as cold as other winters, however there was more snow. That was welcome, for there was not much runoff with their level land. There was more social interaction during the winter time in the village. The long evenings gave them a chance to visit with some of their friends. Michael had talked several times with Dan Holtz. One evening Michael and Krystyna took the team and went to see the Holtz family and visit about Volhynia. Dan surprised them by saying they were thinking about joining Dan's siblings and parents who lived in the area of Torczyn village in the Rozyszce Parish—15 miles west of

Luck/Lutsk and 15 southwest of the town of Rozyszce. Dan said that his family were farmers and that the land owners were still looking for more farmers who wanted to lease land. The Styr/Sirna River ran through the area and the top soil was deep, which was of great interest to Michael. He knew good soil was necessary to raise good crops. The soil on both of the places he had was good, but not loamy and deep like that soil. Dan said the yields were very high for small grains, and gardens produced abundant vegetables. Michael asked many questions and told Dan that if all this was correct, he would consider moving there. Krystyna did not want to hear about moving again when she only recently felt that they were settled down. However, her ear did perk up again as she heard the men discuss the topsoil and the many Germans who had migrated to Volhynia. Dan said that Torczyn was about 70 miles from Karolinow, which Michael compared to the trip from Bielsko. He recalled his suspicion about the dapple gray, its death, and how the rest of the trip was uneventful. A caravan leader could not wish for anything better. It was a pleasant memory. The conversation went on longer than a normal visit. Finally Michael and Krystyna thanked Dan and his wife Emily and said good bye, hoping to meet again soon. Their conversation continued on the short ride home. This was the first time that Krystyna had been away from the baby Pauline for more than a few minutes, and she was anxious to get home. All was well when she arrived, and the baby was happy to see her mother.

Michael and Krystyna continued talking about Volhynia. It was heavy on their mind and soon they got together with her uncle and aunt. To their surprise they were both eager to learn more about Volhynia and even meet Daniel and Emily, whom had they met casually at Church services.

Daniel had heard a lot of good things about Volhynia including that many Germans had been moving there for 50 years. There were hundreds of villages and the people seemed to be content. There was some rocky soil, some swampy areas, and a lot of forest, and there was work available clearing land to ready it for farming. That work was very hard. Uncle Ludwig said he would leave that to the younger men. They agreed to continue their discussion and visit Daniel soon.

Michael was fortunate that many people in the village needed wood that winter. He and Ludwig gladly sold or traded wood. The pile for sale was getting low by the middle of March. Having sold or bartered that much meant that the income made a big contribution to providing for Michael's growing family. They had brought in so much wood that Michael really felt he would be lucky to sell half of it. He now knew that all of that wood would be sold. This summer he would go out earlier and cut more wood. He was happy that he now had a very good side business and felt they could live comfortably even if the crops were not good. Carefully preparing the wood and cutting it the exact right size made his wood preferred over any other in the village. He explained to his son how he had carefully built up the business and that it developed much faster than he expected. Ludwig was not interested in the business end of the piles of wood. His father knew that it would come with time and a lot of what he was saying now he would remember later on. At age 13 Ludwig had done a lot of man's work and had done it well.

Anna was a big help to her mother who was very appreciative. She had just turned 15, an age where she could take on more responsibility. Pauline was healthy and Anna spent a lot of time playing with her. Anna's mother told her all about their discussions regarding Volhynia. To her surprise Anna seemed interested. Perhaps the adventure of it appealed to her.

Michael and Krystyna invited Krystyna and Ludwig, as well as Dan and Emily over one Saturday evening for a meal and a Volhynia discussion. Ludwig asked if Gene Heinrichs and Emily could join them.

They sat down to eat and after a few pleasantries the Volhynia discussion began. Dan surprised them saying they were going to move to Volhynia next June. They were all surprised, and happy. Maybe it was that they realized Dan and Emily knew enough to make the decision. Of course Dan's family was there. Their motivation was different than the other families sitting around the table.

Dan's announcement changed the discussion and now the others were talking more about when being a good time to move, rather than the economic opportunities. Dan said that if those in the room wanted to move, they were welcome to join up with him and Emily next June.

Both Krystynas started talking at once, wondering where they would go when they got there. Daniel said he understood that there was still a lot of land to be leased, even some to be bought. It was his impression that the opportunity was as good there was anywhere in Volhynia. The Church headquarters for the Rozyzcze Parish was 15 miles away in the town of Rozyzcze. Torczyn had a large chapel unlike in Karolinow where the school master was also the Cantor. Everyone in the room was trying to get a feel for what the others were thinking.

Michael spoke up and said he would leave with Dan next June. There was a year to plan, but this was not a contractual obligation. If they decided they did not want to go, it would be okay. Before the evening was over all four couples said they wanted to move. It was a long way off, which gave them plenty of time to think about it and get ready for the move. Underlying people's willingness to move was having to deal with the representative of Mr. Lechnicki who owned the estate. He had not caused Michael any angst, however there was an uneasy feeling that most of the villagers felt. The evening ended with everyone feeling very happy. The guests thanked Krystyna and Michael for getting the group together. They all felt this was the beginning of a great relationship.

Michael and Krystyna talked about how it was hard to get settled into everyday life after the group meeting. They thought of nothing else the next day, but finally they settled into taking care of the seasonal work. Michael had to make plans for the wood cutting he and Ludwig would do in a couple months. His attitude toward his farm and what he had to do had changed. The decision had indeed been made to move next June.

He and Krystyna knew from experience what they would do differently. They had not accumulated much more than what they had arrived with from Bielsko. Michael had traded wood for a silage grinder, which he used all the time. It had a platform where the corn stalks or corn ears were laid down. There was a wheel about four feet in diameter attached to one end that someone would turn as another person was pushing the corn stalks toward the end where the wheel was. As the wheel was turned it would grind the corn into short pieces that could be put into a small silo or fed, as it was prepared. Michael had to take it with him. They would move again with two wagons, like before. Now Ludwig would be a seasoned team driver at age 14.

Michael's manual silage grinder

The summer went well. Pauline was a healthy active child, and Anna enjoyed taking care of her whenever she was asked. The family got along well and enjoyed being all together. Michael and Ludwig started cutting wood in July. Ludwig was much better at swinging the ax than he had been the last year, growing into a stout young man. He was a big help to his father, able to do any of the jobs. He harnessed the horses that first day without being asked, anticipating jobs that needed to be done. This made Michael a very proud father. They would haul several loads, not so big of a pile that it would look like an impossible task, then stop to saw the logs and split the stumps into firewood.

Throughout the winter the four families met to prepare for June. Several other families asked about joining the caravan. One of them had siblings who had recently moved to Volhynia. The four families decided that if they wanted to join they would be welcome. There was a relationship with all the people in the village through at least one of the four families. Most people had moved at least once, and anyone who had done that would be an asset on the trip.

The destination for the four families would be the Torczyn area, and anyone going further than that could leave from there. There was a buzz in the village for months about the caravan starting out in June. Michael was asked a lot of questions about the upcoming trip. His answers were respected because of his recent move from Bielsko and his good standing in the village.

The departure date was set for Monday morning, June 14, 1881. Four families were deciding whether or not to make the move. Michael knew that they would decide in time, and he would not say anything to influence them either way. Each of them eventually decided to go. Each of the eight families would be pulling two wagons. Thomas and Anna Gerlach, Rudolph and Elisabeth Schulz, Wilhelm and Emma Scheier, and Simon and Bertha Baumgart were joining the original four families.

The Gerlachs had four children ranging from four to ten. Rudolph and Elisabeth had five, three to nine. Wilhelm and Emma had two, seven and eight. Simon and Bertha, seven children between five and twelve that included two sets of twins. All families were going to Torczyn except the Baumgarts who were going to Klewan, northwest of Rovno, to join cousins who had lived there for five years.

When the Schulzes told Michael of their decision, Elisabeth said she was wishing that they would go later. She was concerned, given the health of her husband. The last few months he had lost some weight, his complexion was pallid, and she said he did not seem to have as much energy as a few months back. But they both wanted very much to go. However, she thought they should have decided to wait for another opportunity. Michael listened carefully and all he said was, "I think he'll be all right." The planning meetings had been held and everyone was comfortable that they had considered all possibilities that might confront them.

Michael and Uncle Ludwig decided on the position of each family in the caravan. Michael and his son would be the first two wagons. They decided to put the two Schulz wagons next because of Rudolph's health. Uncle Ludwig followed. They both decided they could not have chosen a better position, should the Schulz need help. Next was Gene Heinrichs followed by Dan and Emily Holtz. Dan was not interested in leadership and he gladly took the position assigned. Next were the Gerlachs followed by the Scheirs family, and last the Baumgarts.

Michael and Uncle Ludwig talked many hours about the route. They decided to go straight east to a crossing in the Bug River, which was 115 miles of the border between Poland and Volhynia. They could cut many miles off by going southeast from Karolinow, but first they would have to cross the Udal River and then the Bug River. By going straight east they would have only one crossing where the Bug River was wide and slow—and they were familiar with it. It was not deep, which had been considered by the men who built the bridge. There was a large clearing on both sides where rocks had been hauled in and dumped in the river, but would not act as a dam. Even if there was high water from spring runoff, there would only be two feet of water above the rocks.

CHAPTER 4

— 1881 —

Second Move:
To Sablotche, Volhynia

Tuesday June 14, 1881 was a perfect morning. Everyone assembled at daybreak in their assigned position to start the journey to Torczyn, Volhynia. An hour after the sun appeared Michael let out a shout and they started to move, forming a caravan that stretched out for a quarter mile. Michael realized now they would have new issues with a wagon train this long. He wished he had a saddle horse so that he could ride back to see how everyone was doing. He was worried about Rudolph, even though he was the second one to arrive that morning. Maybe there was nothing to worry about, but a sick man with five children was something that would not leave his mind.

They were moving well toward the rising sun on a warm morning. Everyone was excited. The first day out they would get within a few miles of the crossing. The caravan moved steadily and the decision was made to stop a short time at noon to eat and take care of the animals.

Everyone was happy, doing the jobs that needed to be done. By late afternoon they were a little more than two miles from the crossing. Michael's son Ludwig was a veteran wagon driver, so Michael put his concerns elsewhere.

Michael decided that a short distance before the crossing he would go back and talk to the men about the crossing and how rough it would be. He would walk and lead his team across, thinking the horses would be less likely to spook if he was beside them. When they got to the bridge there was water over it in a couple of spots, though the rocks were mostly dry so it looked like it would be an easy crossing. The bridge of rocks was 22 to 25 feet wide, so wagons could pass if they met, though most team drivers would wait for any traffic to cross before they started. Elisabeth decided to ride in their second wagon to comfort one of the younger children who had been fussing. She was concerned the crossing would frustrate him more. Rudolph was alone and looked as though he had put in a full day's work already, giving Michael second thoughts about having let the Schulz family travel with them.

Finally the caravan of sixteen wagons, several milk cows, and a few colts were ready to cross. The crossing was 300 feet long. Michael led the way, holding one of the long reins that went back to the wagon seat. Slowly they moved toward the other side. Michael kept turning to watch the wagons approach the bridge and start to cross. All was going well.

He was about fifty feet from land when he turned again to check on the caravan. As he turned, Rudolph slumped forward. Michael quickly jerked the brake handle back and tied a single rein to it and ran to Rudolph just as he was falling out of the seat. Michael was able to grab him and soften his fall. He laid him down and tried to straighten him. By then Uncle Ludwig was there and Elisabeth came as quickly as she could move on the rocks. Others from several wagons back came to find out what happened. Michael's son and Krystyna kept the young children back. Gene Heinrichs arrived, the only one in the caravan who had an interest in medical issues and had studied some on his own. Gene kneeled over Rudolph briefly, got up and put his arm around Elisabeth. "He is gone." Screams filtered through the caravan with news.

Someone covered his body. Gene stayed with Elisabeth as Michael and Ludwig went to Michael's wagon to discuss what to do.

They decided to put Rudolph's body on one of the Schulz wagons and bring everyone across the river to a clearing big enough for all the wagons near a small creek that drained into the river. There they would decide the next stop. Michael, Ludwig, Gene and some of the other men met to discuss the next step. Ludwig saw two options. The first was for the two Schulz wagons to return to Karolinow. The other was to proceed to the next village, go to the Church or Chapel, and talk to the Pastor about having a funeral and a burial there. They decided that Gene, Michael and Ludwig would talk to Elisabeth. She would be in shock, but they needed to make a quick decision.

As they started to tell Elisabeth about their discussion, she blurted out that she wanted to go home. Her response startled them, but soon the whole mood of the camp was to do everything they could to help Elisabeth get back to Karolinow. William Scheir volunteered to go with her. He said he could get a friend from the village to take him back to the caravan. Each would ride a horse and his friend would trail the horse William rode back to Karolinow. William would take the lead wagon, and Elisabeth's cousin who was helping them move would take the reins of the wagon he had been driving for them. The group prepared an early noon meal and fixed some food for them so they would travel all night to arrive back home by daylight. There were many hugs and tears, others realizing it could happen to them. Several men followed them to the crossing to be sure they safely got over. Two hours earlier they had been going in the other direction.

Now the caravan must reassemble and continue their journey. The sadness and frustration was too much for some of the travelers. Michael decided to stop early, thinking it may help to get the cooking fires going and let people relax. It also would save William many miles on his return to the caravan. It would be an all night trip to Karolinow and a hard ride back to the caravan, even on a fresh saddle horse.

It was late Friday afternoon when William caught up with them. That evening before the meal was served Michael would have him tell the group about helping Elisabeth and her family get back to Karolinow. This would give them a chance to ask questions and relieve some anxiety. William's return was a big relief to Michael—knowing the trip was successfully done, he could concentrate on the rest of the trip.

They were at a crossroads as to which route to take. Michael called in the men for a meeting to help decide. The road they were on, going straight east, would take them to Kowel. They would then have a choice of roads to take to get to Torczyn. Either one of them would require a wide swing out and then turn back in to reach Torczyn, adding many miles to the trip. The plus was that those roads were well traveled.

The other route would have them continuing east on the same road for several miles to an intersection. A short distance north was the village of Luboml. Southward was the route that would take them eventually to the village of Werbe, where they would turn to the right toward Wladimir Wolynski, then east to Torczyn. That would be much shorter. For the first 20 miles or so there would only be a few villages, but after that there would be many German villages all the way into Torczyn. Though they had extra time, the majority felt they should make the most of it and get to their destination as soon as possible. The decision was made, to take the shorter route.

They did not have to be concerned about water as there were many creeks and springs. There were adequate trees for shelter near their camps. They felt that starting early in the morning they could cover most of the less populated area by late afternoon. On June 16th the days were very long and it was good to have that extra daylight if needed. The decision was made and everyone seemed pleased.

The caravan came to life early and everyone jumped into the chores. Though the caravan was shorter now by two wagons, with the many milk cows and several colts, it took time to get it going. It proved very helpful that every driver knew his place in the line and pulled in when it was his turn. It was about 30 miles to Wladimir Wolynski, and if all went well they would pass it by Saturday afternoon.

Michael had to stop second-guessing his decision regarding the Schulz family, though as the caravan moved along he thought about Elisabeth and her five children. He wondered how they would find a place to live. Maybe she could claim back the house they moved out of two days earlier. Krystyna knew how bothered he was, but she knew he had to work it out and that he would. His responsibility as wagon master required his full attention and everyone appreciated this fact. He would often stand up to check back at the wagons. Each time he got a huge smile and a big wave from Krystyna, which made him feel good after he sat down to watch his faithful team pull his wagon.

Michael and Uncle Ludwig had hoped to find land to lease side by side. They could work together on their land and share tools and teams when needed. They worked well together. Maybe this evening when the work was done, they could huddle and talk about that dream. They had heard that there was still land available in some of the outlying villages. Michael was thinking about how their life would change again in a few days as they began to search for a lease.

Daniel had told them that northern Volhynia was known for its forest and marshes, and there had been clearing and draining of swamps for many generations, so they expected to find an adequate land supply. What they had to do was not new to them—but they would be doing it in a new place. Michael and Ludwig did meet that evening. They talked for a couple hours, and some of the discussion was about how the trip was going so far. They envisioned the trouble Elisabeth would have raising the family. The only positive thing about it was that Rudolph and Elisabeth were very well regarded in Karolinow. They had been as active as they could be in the Church, having five children. They prayed the best for them. The hour was late and the caravan had to leave at that certain time, so it was off to get some rest for both of them.

There were no problems as everyone in the caravan was very responsible and quickly got their chores done. They arrived at Werbe and turned to the right on a more traveled road. By late afternoon they were traveling around the side of Wladimir Wolynski and heading east for Torczyn. A mile out of the village they found a camp area and began setting up for the evening.

Michael went to Dan and asked him to arrange for someone to drive his team so he could sit with him on his wagon. Dan had parents and siblings in the area and knew more than anyone else in the caravan about Torczyn and the surrounding area. He had visited his family and the area several years ago, so he was familiar with it. They needed to decide where they would set up and have a meeting place while they were looking for leases and homes. Dan said his brother August had a large two hectare meadow used for grazing. He thought they might be able to camp there for as long as it took them to get settled. He was sure that the family had a lease and a home ready for him and his family.

They covered several miles as their discussion carried on. Finally Michael suggested Dan go back to his wagon and they would talk more the following evenings. Michael estimated they would be in Torczyn by afternoon June 24th. They would not push it. The weather was very warm, so there was concern for the horses and all the animals being trailed. More than half way there, he decided to continue at a slower pace. They would arrive at a good time of the year. If they could get settled soon, they would be very thankful. Daniel thought that most of the men would be able to find some work helping on farms. In a couple months harvest would be starting and there would probably be demand for help. They were all optimistic about the possibilities, though there was probably a little too much reliance on Dan's family for guidance in their new area.

Michael noticed that as they got further past Wladimir Wolynski, their people were more talkative, there was even some laughter which had not been heard for days. He had Krystyna join him as much as she could. Son Ludwig was doing well, a proud young man sitting on the wagon seat driving the team. Pauline would celebrate her first birthday in a couple of months. Krystyna was very proud, but tears welled up in her eyes whenever she thought about Rosalia and Eva. So sad and yet so thankful for the family she had with her. She had hoped for more children and maybe someday it would happen.

Most of the children traveled well and were not a noticeable bother. They all knew the seriousness of what was going on, especially after the death of Mr. Schulz. Everyone knew they had to move on and look to the near future.

They passed several villages which were of great interest to all of the adults. A couple times Michael halted the caravan, as they wanted a longer look at the construction of the houses. Hay was being cut, men sweating as they swung their scythes. It took work, but farming was all that Michael and most of the people in the caravan knew.

Michael pictured his land having good loam soil, easy to work and very productive. From the wagon seat he had seen a variety of crops. Most of them looked very good, though some crops were not so thick and healthy looking. He felt it was because of the soil, not necessarily how much rain they had. He also pictured a home adequate for his family. He did not care how it looked inside or out, for he could fix whatever was needed. He just wanted it to be big enough.

A day out of Wladimir Wolynski, Michael began to feel some anxiety and noticed that he was hoping they would get there much quicker than he had planned. Krystyna noticed this sudden change in Michael and she made it a point to talk to him several times a day and listening to what he said. He knew that he had to concentrate, but realized that he had not talked to Simon and Bertha about their destination. That evening he met with them and asked about the journey to Klewan after they reached Torczyn, another 45–50 miles. Simon said that he felt comfortable traveling with just his two wagons. He was very experienced, and after a day or two of rest they would be ready to go. His seven children had quickly adapted to life in the caravan and he said it was a very enjoyable experience for them. Simon and his wife did ask that if they could help them replenish some supplies. They voiced appreciation. Michael said he would see what he could do when they got to Torczyn and got settled. Simon told him he thought he had done a fine job leading the caravan. He would be thanking him again at the end of the journey. As Simon and Bertha left Michael assured them that he would do whatever he could to help them get to Klewan. Michael also said that all of the families would be concerned about their own situation and might not be able to help as they would have liked.

The caravan moved well the next couple of days. Late afternoon as they set up camp, Simon came to Michael and asked him to look at his second wagon, especially the two right wheels. After their immediate chores were complete Michael walked over to meet Simon. After the wagons created a circle for the evening there were extra wagons which were usually parked beside the circled wagons. This double circle meant that no one was very far away from anyone in the group. Simon showed Michael the two wheels and they both looked them over. Michael was concerned about them. He mentioned that they would probably be in Torczyn by tomorrow late afternoon. It would not be a big job to repair them or to replace the wheels, but both men agreed that they could make it to Torczyn. Some rough ruts a few miles back had caused the damage. The road was much better now and it seemed it would be better as they approached Torczyn.

They left early in the morning under rain clouds. They were all glad they had followed Michael's suggestion of preparing their wagon covers before they left. Everyone was talking and very excited that they would reach Torczyn late afternoon. Michael could even hear some chatter and laughter in his front wagon. With a slight breeze and the wagon noise he usually couldn't. He knew his group was happy. A couple of hours after they left camp a slow rain started—the type a farmer would enjoy: slow enough to soak in, with no water running off. The road was good, the terrain slow and rolling. Nothing that should slow their travel. They would arrive today.

After an hour of slow rain, it started to thunder and there were a few sharp bolts of lightning. Before long it was a downpour. They kept going, everyone inside under canvas. The soil was a type of gumbo that stuck to the wheels, though it would fall off so he did not pay much attention to it. With the rain much heavier the caravan was barely moving.

Michael heard shouting and immediately stopped his team. In the heavy rain rather than walk outside he made his way to the back of the wagon and opened a small port. He shouted to his son Ludwig and asked what was the problem. He said he thought he heard something about Simon's wagon being lost. He told Ludwig that as soon as the rain allowed they would pull off as soon as he could find a spot. At about noon Michael saw some clearing skies in the west. When the rain let up in a couple of hours, Michael asked his son and Uncle Ludwig to find a clearing to camp and to guide the wagons in. Michael turned his team around and headed back to find out what happened.

The caravan had just come over a small hill and Simon could not see his second wagon. He was in a tight spot with little room to turn to head back over the ground they just covered. Michael helped him with his anxious team that did not want to cooperate in the slippery mud. They got turned around and soon were on the way and anxious to reach a point where they could see the wagon. They soon saw it sitting at an angle pointing to the left side of the road. The right rear wheel was broken and the axle was resting on the ground. The front wheel appeared to be okay. When they looked closer they wondered why it hadn't collapsed. The driver was shaken to say the least. He said all had been fine, but when it started to rain very heavily he noticed that they were going slower than the wagons ahead of them, riding in the ruts created by the first thirteen wagons. He felt the best thing to do was to drive the team slightly to the left, to get them on better ground. As they were moving forward, the team moved a bit to the left, but the wagon had stayed in the ruts. He moved the team left a little more, shouted and made some quick movement with the reins as they lay on the team's back. The wagon lunged but it did turn, as the back wheel was still in the rut—crumbled under the wagon and twisted. The driver shouted to Simon, but in the heavy rainfall he could not be heard. It was another half mile up and over the incline that Simon realized the last wagon was not there anymore. The men checked the axle and found that it held up well, but they needed two complete wheels. Michael and Simon rode their wagons back, leaving the driver to watch his wagon.

There were a lot of anxious faces as they pulled into camp. The men figured out who had the wheels and tools to repair the damage. They got what was needed onto Michael's wagon, and two men volunteered to go along and help. The weather was cooperating, but as soon as they arrived at the wagon they noticed they had overlooked bringing a lifting device. Two men with axes went off toward a creek with a lot of trees. They picked one about five inches in diameter for eighteen to twenty feet. They felled the tree, which was green and very heavy. They trimmed the branches off and at eighteen feet chopped off the top. Two men carried the long tree, and the third man carried a six foot section from the top. Meanwhile the other men had dug mud out from under the axle. Three men got on the pole and shoved it under the axel. The six foot section was chopped into three short pieces which were placed at right angles to the pole. When all was in place the men on the pole pulled down and at the same time moved back toward the end. Though the wagon was heavily loaded, it was lifted high enough for one man to easily slip the good wheel back on the heavily greased axle. After the nut was tightened, the men slowly let the pole down. The same was repeated on the front wheel, much easier because it was still whole. As evening darkened the three wagons joined the camp to clapping and cheering. Everyone was glad to see them all back and all anxious to hear what had happened. They had to find place for the two wagons. Michael would not have chosen this campground, which sloped toward the creek . But now with rain coming down he realized how lucky they were. Shelters were put up and tied securely against the wind. At midnight the rain came down much heavier. Most of the adults slept very little that night.

Saturday June 25th it was not raining as daylight broke, though threatening clouds hung above them. The men felt uneasy, and by mid-morning it started to pour. They were glad they had not tried to move the caravan. Everyone was huddled in their wagons. Finally at noon it let up and the sky cleared a little. Michael, Uncle Ludwig and Gene Heinrichs discussed what to do. It did not take them long to decide they would stay put. If it continued to clear off they would be ready to travel in the morning. There was no disagreement with the decision—people were relieved that the caravan would not move.

Late afternoon brought rain showers and more threatening clouds. Several hours after dark it started to rain heavily, but after several hours it suddenly stopped. Not too long after sun up the sky started to clear. It looked like they might be able to travel today, maybe even get to Torczyn by the next evening. They left later than usual. One of the wagons had some leaking because a corner of the canvas was not tied as tightly as it should have been. The heavy rains had impacted everyone. Some had damp clothes. Some of the flour had been soaked and had to be thrown out. Everyone had muddy shoes and boots. Being only a day drive out of Torczyn is what kept everyone in a happy mood.

The wagons were moving slowly and Michael was happy to keep it that way in the beginning. The weather was still a question and all they could do was to keep moving as their destination was getting closer. Michael was thinking about how each family should be positioned if Dan's brother August would let them park in his meadow. One of the wagons of each family would be used to look at land, their other parked for several days and possibly for weeks. The meadow would be like a village, leaving the grass tramped down and certainly cutting its yield. He needed a way to overcome that objection.

When they stopped for the noon meal Michael was disappointed that they had only covered a few miles, what with the late start and muddy roads.

Michael asked Dan to sit with him. He suggested that the way to ask his brother August to park on his meadow was to offer him rent for a month. Dan agreed that it would make that much easier for August to consider. Michael asked the rest of the men to join them. He proposed the same thing to the group and they all agreed, as it took away some of their uncertainty. Michael asked them to give some thought about what to offer. Maybe one or two of several calves in the caravan would be adequate rent. They would all give it some thought and have an offer ready when they arrived.

Michael and Uncle Ludwig decided they would travel only a few hours and then look for a camp site. That would leave them with a four or five mile trip to Torczyn for the final leg. The men who drove the teams were happy to have a short day. Beyond controlling their teams, it was being alert every minute that took so much energy. The mud slowed the wagons, making it harder for the teams to pull. The horses could always use a rest, and they would have a longer one by stopping early.

That evening after the meal Michael and Uncle Ludwig asked the men to meet again. With the weather looking promising and the road being a little drier, it looked like they would be at Dan's brother's place by noon. Michael told Dan to have both of his wagons go past the others and get to the front as they got closer to his brother's place. He would lead the caravan to August's place.

The night went by quickly and everyone was up early. The excitement was shared by everyone. Mid-morning Michael's two wagons pulled onto the road and each one fell into its designated space. Son Ludwig was by now a seasoned team driver with past 100 miles to his credit. Krystyna was so proud and of course Michael was also, although he did not show it. He felt he demonstrated it by giving him the job of wagon master.

Outside of Torczyn Dan and his two wagons passed forward to take the lead. Imagine Dan's brother August seeing a fourteen wagon caravan coming up the road with Dan leading them. Another hour and they were pulling into August's farmyard. He and his wife met them with salt and bread, which was the custom. Each person tore a piece of bread from the loaf, dipped it in the salt, and ate it. August was so happy to see his brother. He warmly greeted each of the families and told them that his helper would direct them where to park the wagons. He said they had made preparations for a big meal that night. It would take a few hours to prepare because they did not know when they would arrive, thinking it would take a couple extra days because of the rain.

Michael and Uncle Ludwig approached August about giving him two calves as rent for the large group staying there. August's eyes dashed between them, and finally he spoke. He thanked them for the offer and said that he was happy to provide whatever he could for them. He would not take anything for it, even if some of them stayed several weeks. He said he felt that the group had helped his brother get there safely and he was happy to see him. Michael and Ludwig thanked him again and walked to the meadow for a short rest before the meal.

It was early evening when the bell rang for all to gather for the evening meal. Since Gene Heinrichs sometimes served as a Lay Assistant to the Cantor in Karolinow, Michael asked August if he would mind if Gene gave thanks before the meal for their safe arrival and the meal. In fact he encouraged it. Michael asked the people to form a circle with the children in the middle. Gene stepped forward and the people fell into a prayerful mood. He thanked God for the safe arrival in Torczyn, the good health of the travelers, and for His servant August who welcomed them to his home. He closed his prayer asking God's blessing on Elisabeth and her family.

The group was more than anxious to fill their plates and enjoy what August's family had prepared for them. A feeling of relief ran through the crowd, and also awareness that some very intense days might be ahead. After the meal there was still daylight. Michael gathered the men together and August said he would be glad to meet with them.

Surprisingly, Thomas asked the first question, wondering how the climate compared with Karolinow. The questioning quickly moved to farm leases and availability. They were pleased to learn that the representative of the owner was an understanding man to deal with and no heavy demands. It seemed that the owner knew how difficult it was to provide for a family on a few hectares. August had talked to the representative and Mr. Whist said he would gladly meet with them when they arrived. They agreed to meet him late the next morning and start talking about leasing land.

The families felt good about staying put for at least a few days. The wagons were their homes for now and they all gladly made the most of it. It was already late June, but they still had time to find their homes and get settled, though they would not have a crop this year. However, all felt there would be work for the men and they would have time this fall to prepare for seeding their crops next spring.

Most of the group slept soundly and they woke with a view of an area that would be their new home. Simon Baumgart and his family would be leaving in a day or two for their destination of Klewan. He decided to go along with the men and maybe get some information about the road ahead for him. He asked about two wagons traveling alone to Klewan and was assured there were many villages along the way. It was suggested that at mid to late afternoon they approach a village to stay, or at least camp very nearby. Simon felt comfortable with the trip he was about to start. His teams were healthy and his wagons were in good repair. He did ask about getting a wheel from someone just in case he had trouble with his.

The men felt good about their time with Mr. Whist. Both Ludwigs enjoyed the visit and young Ludwig especially appreciated being asked by his father to go with them. The men had an available lease to look at on the way back to August's place. It was on the north side of Torczyn and about a half mile from August's home. They all looked at it as a possible location for Daniel. It was close to his brother and the Church was nearby, though the improvements needed a lot of work. The pluses about the property made up for its condition. He would talk to his brother and give it a lot of thought.

The only topic during the evening meal was about the outing the men had. There were many questions from the women, though most of them could not be answered from their few hours of riding over the area. They would go out again tomorrow and circle Torczyn to find out more about the terrain. They would see where the river was and look at land that was near it. It would give them a better feel for the area.

Simon and his family were getting anxious to get back on the road to Klewan. This would be their second night in Torczyn and they were appreciative of the August's providing for them. They kept thinking of getting to Klewan to see Simon's cousins. They were part of the Germans who had moved on about ten years ago, after living twelve years in eastern Poland. They decided that they would prepare tomorrow and leave the following day. They would be able to move faster not being in a caravan, and they looked forward to being in their new home no later than a week hence.

The next day the Baumgarts were busy preparing for their departure. Everyone was generously giving them travel food and helping wherever needed. They would be missed, as Simon was right there whenever help was needed on the trip. His large family of children were helpful and fit in very well with the group. Krystyna in her goodbye complimented them on the good manners of their children. When they left the following morning, everyone was there to wish them well as they pulled out of the meadow.

The only prospect for side-by-side farm leases was in a small village about four miles northeast of Torczyn. The village of Sablotsche was on the west side of the Sirna River and appeared to have very good soil. The terrain was similar to their farm in Bielsko. The two families looked at other land and discussed the property at Sablotsche. The

other three families—Gerlachs, Heinrichs and Scheirs—were also looking at property. They had various opportunities, and before long made
decisions about what to do. Gene Heinrichs had a chance to work with
an established farmer and rent an adequate home for this family which
met their needs.

Michael and Uncle Ludwig decided to take the property in Sablotsche
and would be moving out of August's meadow and into their new village in three or four days after all the necessary paperwork had been
completed. August's meadow was getting back to normal and within a
week all the wagons would be gone.

When Michael rolled out of the meadow he stopped to visit with
August. He expressed his appreciation for kindly helping them
while they looked for their new homes. As Michael was on the road
to Sablotsche, he knew he would never forget the help that August
gave them all. He only hoped that someday, some way he could help
someone and pass on the good deed. His concentration was now
on the short trip to Sablotsche. Ludwig was following in the second
wagon and Uncle Ludwig followed with his two wagons. They arrived
in Sablotsche, their permanent home, June 30th.

There was much work to do and they were glad for the time of the
long summer days. There was an adequate barn attached to the house,
and a pasture for the horses and cows. They would buy or barter for
some chickens. It did not take long for Michael to be satisfied that the
livestock were secure and he would not have to worry about them. After
that the house took all of their attention for the next couple weeks until
it was up to their expectations. Michael was able to work outside and to
start thinking about crops to be seeded in the spring.

There was a very small chapel in the village. Michael's family and
Uncle Ludwig's decided to attend Church in Torczyn before they started
attending the chapel. The families enjoyed the service and were glad
they had chosen to go. They met many German families, particularly
the Ferdinand Wunnik family. On Sunday was April 4, 1881 the Wunnik
family had moved to the village of Bujany, on the edge of Torczyn. After
the Church service they had a long visit. They talked about moving and
the Wunniks said that their destination originally was rich farmland

near Dubno, southwest of Rovno. But they had friends who had lived in Sablotsche and decided to settle here. They had four children of similar ages to Michael and Krystyna's children, baby Gustaf being the first child born in Volhynia. Andreas had been born in 1864, Ferdinand in 1866, and Johann Julius in 1869. The Wunniks came from the Gostynin area southwest of Plock across the Vistula River, largest and longest river in Poland at 651 miles. It begins in southern Poland and flows north to drain into the Bay at Gdansk. Several generations of Wunniks lived in villages to the east and north of Gostynin. The earliest Wunnik record is of Ferdinand's grandfather Michael, born about 1786. They all lived within a few miles of each other. Records suggest the Ferdinand Wunnik family was the first to move out of the area.

The following was written by Pastor Rosenberg of the Gostynin parish in 1875:

> There is a second factor (besides the conversion to sects) that caused the people to be overcome with the fury of emigration to Volhynia. Here the people made a good living from difficult ground and they were always well off. The value of the land went up every year, and the Pole now finds himself in possession of this abandoned place. I believe that not ten years will pass before there are no more dead to bury. The remaining will, from year to year, decide to take up their walking sticks for the pilgrimage to Volhynia, abandoning the dead and their graves to their destiny. In villages where there used to be 30 Evangelical families, there are now only two. As they move out into the wide world, it is inevitable that the Pole will apply his ploughshare to the consecrated places and Church yards (cemeteries) and they will just be a memory.

Michael and Uncle Ludwig and families had enjoyed the outing to Church. They would pass through the village of Bujany on their return to Sablotsche. They were happy. In a month they had moved, gotten settled into their home, and were pleased with the way things were going. Pauline had reached one on July 28th. Anna was 15, Ludwig 13, Michael was 38 and Krystyna was 35.

It was decided that Ludwig would look for work, going from farm to farm asking if they needed help. He was big for his age and looked older than he was. He was an experienced young man and he would not have trouble finding work. Michael would do the same after he was satisfied that he had done all he could to prepare for spring. Anna would stay at home with her mother, help with Pauline and whatever house work was needed to be done.

Their farmyard was down in a small coulee west of the Sirna river. Michael liked that, as it gave protection from the north winds since it did not have a tree windbreak. The leasing rep pointed out the hill behind the house that would give them protection. Their land and Uncle Ludwig's was west of the buildings and it gently sloped west for about a mile. Michael knew that when the winds came from that direction it would be very cold on the hill behind their farm yard. He was glad that they were down from the hill.

He and Uncle Ludwig met quite often to discuss crops and their small herd of cattle. They knew they would have to buy a bull so they could have him to turn out with the cows next May. Between them by next spring they would have ten cows. It was a big saving for both families to be able to share the cost and maintenance of the bull.

Michael was very happy that Uncle Ludwig had traveled with them. The older he got, the more he appreciated Ludwig. He seemed to Michael to have had much more experience at the age that Michael is now. Michael could not imagine how he had learned so much in his years. Michael's father had died long before Michael got married, and he never had the experience of learning more adult things from his father. He would occasionally tell Ludwig that he appreciated his friendship and all that he was able to learn from him. He tried to guide his son Ludwig the way he would have liked to be taught, and he used a lot of what he learned from Uncle Ludwig to do that. Barring any unforeseen events they should have a good year in 1882.

As they were working in the house one day Krystyna commented that she hoped they would be able to get back the feeling of community that they had in Bielsko and to a lesser amount in Karolinow. She acknowledged that the presence of her aunt and uncle were a big help in that regard. Michael felt that would return when they started to raise their own crops. He was meeting many of the villagers who happened by, and most were very friendly. Krystyna kept close to home taking care of Pauline.

The fall of the year was similar to Karolinow and the preparation for the long winter was on schedule. Michael had to tear down the chicken coop that was there when they arrived. It was very small and in bad need of repair. The new one would accommodate 100 chickens. They would have extra eggs to use for barter by next fall. They would have to prepare for having a dozen hens setting on fertilized eggs early in the spring. They prepared a wooden box big enough to put a thick layer of straw in the bottom to form a nest. A dozen eggs would be placed in the nest and then they would put a hen in the box. The hens would have to be trained to stay on the nest. This was done by covering the box with boards and placing something heavy over them so a small space between the boards for adequate ventilation. The hens would be let out briefly to eat and drink. Soon when the hens were used to sitting on the eggs, the boards could be removed and the hens could get up as needed, but never leaving the eggs for very long so they wouldn't cool off. After the chicks started to break through their shells, within a few hours they would all be hatched. Then help was needed to get their chicks out of the box. The hatching had to be planned when the weather was warm enough so the hen could take care of them, for the first couple of weeks chicks were very delicate and at risk for survival.

Late winter Michael did the set up for hatching chicks, and his hens provided over 100 chicks. He was prepared for seeding the crops and was anxious for the seeds to germinate so he could watch their progress.

Ludwig had worked short jobs into late fall and had hopes of being able to get some repeat work as soon as the weather was favorable. Anna was always busy helping her mother with Pauline.

In was the middle of August Michael was talking to his family over the evening meal. He was so proud that he lost very few chicks and they are now full size chickens. The crops were looking good and he was happy with the way things were going. Michael told about meeting a man from the village who had lived in Karolinow and left many years before Michael and his family arrived. Michael related several stories that had been told to him. It was amusing him, though the family did not follow much of what he was saying. Maybe because the stories were being retold too many times. Krystyna interrupted. "Michael I've been wanting to tell you that you are going to be a father again." That stopped Michael and his face changed from very relaxed to surprised and bewildered. This was the last thing Michael was thinking about. Finally he was able to smile. He got up from the table and helped get Krystyna on her feet and gave her a big hug, though there was not much public affection shown by Germans. It was not uncommon to see mothers shake hands with an adult son when arriving or departing. They sat down at the table and all of them talked about having a new Jess family member. Anna and Ludwig were very happy and told their parents that they would be ready to help when the time came. It could not have been a better day and evening.

Krystyna suggested that they go to the Church in Torczyn this Sunday. Early that Sunday morning they were all up and getting ready. They were eager to go as they thought the Wunnik family would be there. They hadn't seen them for awhile and they wanted to visit with them and tell them the news about the new baby. The trip to town was very pleasant as the warm summer sun fell on their faces as they moved toward Torczyn.

The Church was as crowded as it had been on previous visits. The beautiful sanctuary was breathtaking and Michael stopped to admire it. He was quickly moved along by parishioners moving toward their pews. Michael said that he enjoyed the sermon and Krystyna especially appreciated the choir as they sang two special numbers.

The Wunniks invited the Jess family to join them and a neighbor family to enjoy a Sunday meal. Soon after they started eating, Ferdinand announced that they would be moving in another month after the harvest was finished. Michael was stunned. Ferdinand said that a cousin of his had moved there years ago from the Gostynin area southwest of Plock and they were moving to be near them. Their cousin had a lease for them west of the village of Maschulki about 40 miles from Torczyn. Another reason they were moving now was that Julia was pregnant and was expecting the baby around the end of the year. Of course Michael mentioned that they were also going to have a baby. There was a lot of discussion about babies and children.

Michael offered to go to Ferdinand's place Monday or Tuesday and help him with whatever he needed. There was packing to be done and the time was short. Ferdinand accepted his offer and asked if he could come back the next morning. Michael said he would be there and he would bring Ludwig along to help. There were many thanks exchanged between the families. They said goodbye and Michael got the team ready and they were on their way to Sablotche.

The following morning Michael and Ludwig left before sunup to help the Wunniks prepare for their trip to Maschulki. When they arrived Michael got Ferdinand to talk about the trip and tell him what they were taking. He also had Ferdinand show him the wagons they were taking. They both looked them over carefully and Michael pointed out an axle that Ferdinand had not noticed, worn enough that on an extended trip the wheel would flop and possibly break. Ferdinand did not have a replacement but Michael did. He offered to bring it down in the morning. Ferdinand said he thought he had a wheel somewhere on his place, but he was not an organized person and he asked Michael to go with him as he went to look for it. They did find two wheels in some tall weeds and they pulled them out and rolled them over to where the wagon was. One of the wheels was not good enough to replace the worn wheel, but the other one was.

Michael told him about the experience moving to Sablotche from Karolinow. Ferdinand asked him to do whatever he could to prevent a breakdown now before leaving. Ferdinand began to appreciate what Michael had been saying to him. It had been years since he had moved, and it was obvious he had not given the trip much thought. The next morning Michael arrived with an axle, and it did not take long to replace it. Michael and Ferdinand lifted the old axle onto Michael's wagon. He would take it home where he might be able to find a steel sleeve to replace the badly worn one. Michael and Ludwig helped him several days that week, and when they left, the Wunniks were almost ready to travel. All they had to do was to put the last of the household items that they used for cooking on the wagons. They were very grateful for the help that Michael and Ludwig provided. Julia was especially thankful that they took the time and gave them the axle.

Everyone agreed that they were well prepared to undertake the journey. It was not a long one, however it was long enough and on roads they'd not traveled. Michael and Ludwig said goodbye and wished them the very best as they traveled to Maschulki. The Wunniks left two days later, on Sunday. It was a beautiful day to travel and their children were in a good mood as they loaded up. Ferdinand was planning on this being a four day trip and he felt it would put no pressure on him or the team to do that.

Michael and Ludwig left mid-afternoon on Friday, discussing the Wunniks preparation for the trip. Michael asked Ludwig how he thought it had gone. Ludwig talked about the badly worn axle. He had remembered the Baumgart's broken wheel and how it should've been fixed before they left on the trip. Michael was happy to see him thinking about them undertaking the trip and being fully prepared to do it before they left. He wondered if the three cattle trailing would be tied properly. He asked about many things—food, water, dry fire wood. Michael was thrilled that his one question had Ludwig really talking about what to do before traveling. Ludwig asked his dad if they were ever going to move again. Michael said that he was interested in the good soil that Ferdinand had described southwest of Rovno and northeast of Dubno, but he thought they would probably live a long time in Sablotche. He was happy there, and he thought the family was also. He told Ludwig that if an opportunity for better living was open somewhere, that they should consider it. Then he surprised Ludwig— his real dream was to move someday to America or Canada. Ludwig had heard of those places, but this was the first time he had heard his dad talk about them.

At home they enjoyed the evening meal with the family. Ludwig carried a lot of the conversation as he told about the repair work on the wagon. He also told about how he was able to pack the boxes a certain way to leave more space for the children. His proudest moment was when he suggested to Mr. Wunnik that he should be sure the wagon was waterproof. He also said the canvases had to be tied down tight in case of high winds. After they had traveled half a day, he said, they should check the canvas. Michael and Ludwig would have a little catch up work next week, having been gone for a week helping the Wunniks, but they were both very proud that they were able to contribute toward getting them ready to move.

The autumn was spent in final preparation for winter. Food, wood and hay for the livestock all had to be in place for use during the coldest months. The blessing for making their winter life comfortable was that hill behind their house. It would block the winds—and that was a big item.

The winter arrived mild, as related by the long-term residents of the village. Snow was late falling, which soon concerned the villagers. They wanted those banks of snow to provide moisture for the coming year. In January when it started snowing heavily, there was great rejoicing along with some grumbling about the snow and cold. The snow was heavy enough at times during the winter to cut down Sunday attendance even at the Chapel. None of the villagers would go to Torczyn for Church services.

The first of March showed no signs of winter ending soon. There was snow everywhere and the cold weather continued. Krystyna was regularly visited by a midwife. The pregnancy seemed to be progressing normally, but the midwife was bothered by Krystyna's complaints about pain that she had a hard time describing. Anna was doing all of the housework and watching after Pauline. She had acquired many of the skills needed to take care of the family.

The last two weeks of her pregnancy Krystyna spent in bed. She felt sick most of the time and did not have the energy to get out of bed even to walk a little for exercise. Michael was worried about her and felt comfort knowing that Anna was there to take care of her every need.

On the fourth of April 1883 Anna sent her father to get the midwife. She arrived and quickly knew that a baby would be born very soon. After noon the delivery began, very slow and not the way the midwife knew it should go. Krystyna strained and strained. As the baby was born, Krystyna breathed her last.

The joy of a healthy baby's arrival was drowned out by crying sobs of disbelief. Michael, Anna, Ludwig and Pauline, only three months short of three were all in shock. Krystyna lay motionless with sharp strains showing on her face. Without saying anything, Michael left to get the local undertaker. They arrived back shortly and the undertaker solemnly went about his duties. Shock and responsibility were on the mind of the adults. Pauline was confused and Ludwig did his best to comfort her. Anna tended to the new baby boy, whose previously chosen name was Heinrich. Everyone was numb for days. They went through the motions doing the minimum necessary to keep everyone healthy so they could get through the next few weeks. Michael moved slowly and talked very little. It was Anna who tried to get him to talk, asking a lot of questions hoping for more than a yes-or-no answer. It was nineteen years and three months since Michael and Krystyna were married, and Michael was a very sad man.

After the funeral service, all of the villagers were there to be with the family during their time of grief. It was a couple weeks after the service that Michael, Ludwig and Anna would talk in the evenings at Anna's suggestion. Michael started to participate more and it seemed to relax him a bit. It was obvious that there would have to be a division of the household duties, as it was too much to expect Anna to do it all. This was all being decided as the weather was getting much warmer and soon the field work would be starting. At different times for each of them it seemed to be too much, but one would gain some strength about the time one of the others would fall into overwhelm. The pain was heavy for them all—to think only a month ago everyone was happy and waiting for a baby to arrive.

The death brought back memories for Michael of Eva's and Rosalia's birth and death. It was a sadness that he knew would get better—and he hoped it would not be too long. He needed to feel better so he could help more in caring for Heinrich and be a father to the rest of the family. Many families in the village had been bringing them food and offering to help. Anna accepted the offer of Martha, a young lady two years older than she who came several times a week to stay most of the day. Her help was not needed as much at home and she was glad to do this meaningful job. She and Anna got along well and would end up being very good friends. Martha and her family felt very good about being able to help the Jess family during this tragic time. After two months she came over less, as Anna was able to handle most of the work. When she came it was mostly to spend time with Anna and the baby. They both enjoyed taking care of him and being able to at last laugh a little.

It was the middle of July when Uncle Ludwig and Aunt Krystyna came over for a visit one evening. Michael sensed that something was on their mind and it involved them. They sat down around the family table and Ludwig started to talk. He was making small talk and doing a poor job of it. He stuttered some, trying to buy time and not knowing when to get to the reason they were there. Anna soon understood his being uncomfortable, and did her best to engage him. She knew that it was so soon after his niece had passed that he felt uncomfortable saying why he came.

Finally Ludwig took a deep breath and told them that they were going to move. He said he felt guilty about moving and he was really there to explain what they planned to do and get Michael's blessing. Ludwig said that they did not feel comfortable in Sablotche and they wanted to leave, planning to go to the area close to Dubno. He kept hearing that the soil was very good and the landholders were needing people to farm. He said they wanted to go by way of Maschulki and visit with the Wunniks. They had made a connection and even though it would add more days to the trip they wanted to do it.

Michael was stunned and had to pull himself together so he could speak to them rationally, having just lost his wife—their niece—and had a baby to raise. And now this news. Uncle Ludwig and Krystyna had no idea the news would affect Michael that way. Ludwig knew that what he had to do now was to be as pleasant as possible and leave soon. He apologized to Michael, Anna and Ludwig that the news was difficult for them to receive. He and Krystyna said they would be back soon to visit.

After they left Michael, Anna and Ludwig sat at the table in silence. Finally Anna said that they would get by as a wonderful family with everyone working hard. They would have a good family life. Michael told Ludwig and Anna that he needed to think this over and was going to bed.

The next morning Michael arose earlier than usual. He even smiled a little, and as each child woke up he had a cheerful greeting for them, drinking coffee and talking. He said to Anna that he thought maybe her uncle leaving was a good thing. Uncle Ludwig had taught him so many things—items that one would not think much about, like showing him an easier and safer way to climb up on the wagon, and planting corn rows closer for higher yield per hectare. Ludwig had been a big help showing him better food preservation techniques for the root cellar. He felt tremendous sadness over them leaving and realized he would no longer have an uncle to go to. But he began to see that maybe this needed to happen. Now he would be his own man and he would have to work things out by himself. That could be a good thing. He still had a lot he could pass on to Ludwig. They would work together for many years to come and he now realized how much he was looking forward to that.

The Ludwig Riske family did move that summer. Michael and Ludwig helped them, although they did not need as much help as the Wunnik family. Their departure was another sad day for everyone in the Jess family, even though Michael in particular had thought it all through and felt that he would do all right with Uncle Ludwig not around to answer questions.

The summer season moved on as the roles in Michael's house were being redefined. The biggest and easiest adjustment was for Anna. On April 4th she had become a stand-in mother to Pauline and baby Heinrich. She also was the head of the house when it came to preparing food, asking Ludwig to help and making all the decisions needed to keep a home functioning. At 17 she certainly was capable of taking on the added duties. Her mother had prepared her well. Many times she thought of that and realized how lucky she was, given her mother's sudden death. Ludwig quickly learned to respond to any request that Anna had. He knew that if he was to continue working with and learning from his father, he would need to be a big help to his sister. All summer the pall hung over the family—disbelief was still there, although waning. She said to her father one day that the two opposite things happening at once were hard to reconcile—a birth and a death not even a minute apart made it so difficult to accept.

Life did go on and late into December, as Ludwigs 15th birthday was nearing, Anna noticed a lighter feeling in the house. Her father was laughing a little more and Ludwig seemed happier. He had developed friendships with some young men in the village. He was looked up to by some of the boys after they learned he had driven during the family's two moves. He was enjoying the friendships, even though his time was limited because of responsibilities at home. Being able to develop friends had helped Ludwig think beyond what had happened to his mother.

Michael had volunteered to help at the Chapel on an inside renovation project that had started and needed more help. One side wall had never been finished, and the door to the cry room needed to be replaced. The cry room was a very small room in the back, with windows for the mothers to watch and follow the service. Michael worked whenever he felt he could put in a full day. This work gave him a chance to have conversations with his fellow villagers. He enjoyed this exchange and liked that there was time as they worked to have more than a casual exchange. He was able to talk freely about his wife and children for the first time since Krystyna had died. Michael was able to work five days, till the project was done. The work was well received by the parishioners and Michael was happy to have been a part of it. It was another step of healing for him—he realized that his contribution was a benefit to him as well. He knew he had to get out and mix with people. He decided to ask Anna to help him mix more. She was an outgoing young lady who had no difficulty meeting people and spending time with them. Michael could mix, however it was best in a structured setting like working at the Church. He was now a single father with four children. His hope was that Anna would be with him a long time to help take care of her siblings.

At the start of 1884 Michael and his four children were ready for a much better year than the last. The household duties were done well by Anna with help from Ludwig. Being a sister and mother to Heinrich was difficult, but Anna knew she had to be that mother. He would need her loving care for a long time, as would Pauline.

Michael had to force himself to think about farming in spring, especially taking on Ludwig's land for three years till the lease expired the end of August 1888. Ludwig would be a big help, but Michael had to do the planning and make sure that all was ready when the time came. Perhaps he was losing interest in farming his lease. The trauma of losing Krystyna needed much more time for him to recover from, but he kept on preparing and deciding what crop would go in each field.

Sometimes he could not remember what he had planned for a certain field. He did know what was bothering him, so he tried to work slower. Starting early in the season was saving him. He finally realized that with a couple more months to go he would have time to get everything worked out. He had also taken over Uncle Ludwig's cattle, continuing to raise them on shares. If four calves were born Michael would get two. They would settle up at the end of each year and make contact to decide if his share was to increase the herd or go to settle up by a money payment.

When it was time to plant, the weather was cooperating and Michael was ready. He and Ludwig had a lot of work to do and by nightfall they were tired. It happened to be the activity that Michael needed to take his mind off Krystyna's passing. Ludwig would not talk about it, and Anna noticed that and worked very hard trying to get him to discuss his mother's death. He would have none of it until a year had passed. Anna felt so accomplished and fulfilled that her brother was finally opening up and mentioning his mother. She hoped that it meant he was beginning the long-term healing process.

The crops were planted, the cattle and horses well taken care of. By mid summer all was looking good, though certainly not a bumper crop. If this carried through to harvest, the family and the livestock would all be taken care of through the winter.

In the first week of August 1888, the lease was soon terminating, Uncle Ludwig and Aunt Krystyna arrived in Sablotche to visit and go over his crop sharing arrangement with Michael. They intended to stay a week. Michael and his family were very happy to see them. For the first couple days they caught up on Michael's farming and the news in Sablotche. Ludwig told them about the settlements in the Dubno area. They said that they liked the area and planned to stay a long time.

Uncle Ludwig told them that the Wunnik family had settled in a village called Julianowka, north of Dubno by five miles. He talked about the differences from Sablotche.

They spoke of the difficulties the family had after Krystyna died. They could not help but talk about the birth of the energetic five year old Heinrich who was running around the house. Anna was now 22, Ludwig 20, and Pauline 8. Pauline had been going to school regularly since she turned six. Heinrich would start school in a few weeks.

Michael became very interested in learning more about Uncle Ludwig's area. Most of the conversation the rest of the Riskes' stay was about the villages and the land in the area. Michael was especially interested in the topsoil which he had heard was excellent and deep.

Michael began thinking about moving there, and the perfect time to move would be soon with the leases ending and school starting. He brought the family together and with Uncle Ludwig and Aunt Krystyna there they began discussing a possible move, despite the short notice. The children were all excited. Michael did bring up Krystyna's grave but he knew that should not keep them from moving. He wanted to let the children know that he was thinking of their mother. The more they talked about it, the more it seemed like the right thing to do. They would be near the Wunniks and back with their aunt and uncle, who would be leaving the next day—it was already ten days.

The morning of their departure Michael told them that they were going to move as soon as possible. They had many matters to take care of, but with the able help of Anna and Ludwig they would be ready to move in a couple of weeks.

Michael and Uncle Ludwig estimated it was over 40 miles. If the weather held it would be a three or four day trip. Ludwig would begin looking for land to lease in the area and a home for Michael and his family.

Anna and Ludwig knew what had to be done to get ready for the move. It was only a matter of structuring the time and knowing what to do on certain days for it all to fall into place. There were legal matters that Michael and Ludwig would need to handle. Ludwig was needed to interpret and sign papers as his father could neither read nor write. They decided to take two cows, one currently being milked and the other dry. They would sell the rest, and the same with the several hogs they had. Every year they raised a lot of chickens and they would sell them also. With the help of Anna and Ludwig the preparations were easy, compared to previous moves.

All was ready, and at daybreak on the morning of Tuesday August 28, 1888 the two Jess wagons left Sablotche for Julianowka, Volhynia, planning to arrive by the weekend. They would travel east to Lutsk and then go south southeast toward Dubno. About four miles before Dubno they would head east and go a mile to the village of Julianowka. It was an ambitious trip, but they felt the time allotted was reasonable. They were all anxious, but little Heinrich was especially happy to be on his first long wagon trip. Another unknown awaited them—and Anna and Michael felt it the most. It had all happened quickly. Now that they were underway the reality of it all was hitting them. They thought of all the people they knew to whom they were not able to say goodbye, but they would soon be at the homes of relatives and friends. Their anxiety was high, but they seemed to gain energy from it. All they thought about was being with family and friends again.

CHAPTER 5

— 1882 —

Wilhelm Rode Moves to Shinufka, Volhynia

Wilhelm Rode, his wife Justine Gering Rode, and their daughter Julianna arrived in the village of Karlswalde in the spring of 1874. They had come from the village of Chmielewo in Poland, where Julianna was born January 18, 1870. That town is three miles north of Pultusk, which is 35 miles north of Warsaw. Wilhelm was born in the village of Stara Rzeka, Powiat Swiecki Kujawsko-Pomorskie Province, 170 miles northwest of Warsaw. He and Justine had married October 30, 1866 in Pultusk.

Karlswalde was four miles south of Ostrog and 23 miles southeast of Rovno, the largest city in Volhynia. In the 17th century, Ostrog was surrounded by fortifications with a moat, a rampart and five bastions. During the partition in 1793, the town was annexed by the Russian Empire, in which it remained until 1918. A railroad built in the 19th century bypassed Ostrog, leaving the town to stagnate.

Son August joined the family in Karlswalde January 6, 1876. Their second son Charles was born July 6, 1884 in Shinufka. In 1872 word got around that the very religious Mennonites in Russia were selling their farms—being pacifists they did not want to serve in the Russian army. The Russian Government had given them land tax free, and promised them that their sons would never have to serve in the army, but broke that promise in 1865 and the Mennonites left for America.

Karlswalde (name later changed to Prykordonne) village was composed of 42 German families. In the center of the village was a Church, school, and store. The village also had a blacksmith, a tailor, a shoemaker, an oil press, and a grain mill. One main road, lined with trees, went through the center of town. Secondary roads went into the woods and to Jadwonin, a mile southeast. Both villages were in the woods, so their income source was firewood and lumber.

The houses were one-story with an attic. Barns were attached to the houses because of heavy snow. There was a large walk-in chimney area with a cooking kettle. The oven and cooking stove, in the kitchen, were fired separately in closed fire boxes to preserve heat. A large brick warming wall in the center of the house was used for heating the interior. The only entrance to the house was through the large hall or *Hausgang*, that ran between the house and barn, along one side of the building. There was a pantry off the kitchen, a large kitchen and dining room area, a living room or *grosse stube*, and two bedrooms. The floors were wooden, and the outside walls of the house were wood covered with plaster. The roof was thatched.

The newly built schoolhouse, a brick building, replaced the old schoolhouse. The schoolteacher, Albert Benke, lived at the end of the building. There were a total of four grades that encompassed 8 years of education. The schoolmaster earned extra compensation by how many children passed the examination which was administered annually by an official examiner. At first the lessons were taught in the German language, but when Mr. Benke came, Russian became the official language of the school. Children were taught the 3 Rs. They worked on slate tablets and recopied their work in notebooks. The one-room school had a heating wall similar to the village homes. School was held 5 days a week from September to May. Most children finished school at 14. Anyone desiring higher education would then attend school in one of the nearby cities. Children learned domestics, farming and household arts at home. Anyone desiring to learn a trade worked four year apprenticeships as bakers, butchers, builders, tailors, cabinet makers or musicians.

Each farm contained about 30 acres of pastureland, cropland and fruit orchards. The major crops were barley, rye, oats, buckwheat and potatoes. Livestock consisted of cows, pigs, horses, and fowl. Garden vegetables raised were beets, beans, peas, onions, turnips, carrots, lettuce, potatoes, cabbage, and turnips. Every home had a flower bed around it. Gooseberries and currants grew along the picket fences. Herbs included dill, parsley, chamomile, fennel, peppermint and hops. Food was preserved by smoking, drying, and pickling. The barn attached to the house had a horse stall, a cow stall, and a large storage area. A trough carried water from the well to the barn, though the horses were watered from a pail. The pig barn was located in the barnyard. Hog food—beets, potatoes and grain mixed together—was cooked in a large kettle in the house chimney fireplace. Most farms had an upper pasture near the woods, and a lower pasture near the creek.

The Karlswalde congregation were Evangelical Lutheran, with services conducted in German. The older Mennonite Church in the village was beginning to deteriorate, so their parishioners wanted to build a new Church-house. Some people wanted it to be more central, and Jakob Schairer donated land and it was built across from the schoolhouse.

The Church, built by Mr. Peblau and his apprentice, Gottlieb Laibrandt, was similar to the Redeemer Church in Lebanon, Connecticut built at a later date by Mr. Laibrandt. However the Karlswalde Church was much larger—with two balconies, one in back and one on the side. The focal point of the altar was a large painting of Jesus with a lamb. Since there was no organ, members of the Church played on brass instruments on the back balcony to accompany the singing. The side balcony was reserved for the choir. The men sat on the left side of the Church while the women sat on the right side.

Schoolmaster Benke also conducted services, although he was not an ordained minister. A Lutheran Pastor from Rovno traveled 30 miles several times a year to Karlswalde to affirm christenings, confirmations, offer communion, and perform wedding services.

Worship services similar to The Missouri Synod Lutheran service in the U.S. were conducted every Sunday morning. Entire families came to Church, even the Petrofsky family, a Polish family who lived in the Karlswalde woods. Each family also held morning and evening prayers as well as daily Bible readings. The Church played an important role in the life of the community.

Wilhem Herman Rode had bought one of the former 30 acre Mennonite farms. The family enjoyed the life in Karlswalde and would go to Ostrog on special occasions. He heard from Germans in the village about the rich soil in and around the village of Shinufka. He traveled there to check out the area and very much liked what he saw. The availability of land was good, as a few people were selling and moving to the United States, Canada and South America. Before returning to Karlswalde he had made up his mind that he wanted his family to live in Shinufka.

They moved in September 1883. Their new home was in the valley, on the main street with houses on either side. From the top of the hill behind the houses on the main street the sight north was of a slope to a valley and a long slow rise to the trees at the end of the field. This prime land around Shinufka had many takers when it became available twenty years earlier.

One of Wilhelm's neighbors, Heinrich Ruff, was a constant irritation to him. Wilhelm's house had not been lived in for a few years and his neighbor was having a hard time getting used to having it occupied. He admitted that Wilhelm and his family were not doing anything out of the ordinary. Wilhelm went to visit him one day and tried to discuss the matter. When he left he felt as though he had not helped the situation one bit and he had no idea what was bothering the man. He did learn that Ruff had moved to Shinufka many years before and had moved twice within the village. He was married and had two adult sons, one

House in Shinufka. Did the Jess/Rode family live in it?

of whom was drafted into the Russian Army. The other had moved to Kiev two years before and he rarely heard from him.

> *When visiting the village in July 1996 we met with several villagers. They said that when the Communists were in control the regional man in charge came to visit. One of his orders was to plow up the graveyard and cut the trees so that crops could be planted there. The man in Shinufka who was ordered to do that ignored the order. He knew there were many German graves there—and he also knew the man who ordered it would not be back because of the remote location. I walked through one side of the cemetery but did not see any gravestones. At the time we visited there were six or eight homes in the village. The photo is of a home that may have been built a long time ago. Did one of our ancestors live in that home?*

They enjoyed the community, and at the first joint Church event in Julianowka they attended they met many more people. Julianna particularly enjoyed meeting people and it wasn't long till she was asked to participate in various events.

On a Sunday after Church in early December 1883, Justine announced to the family that next summer they would be having a new baby brother or sister. August was a little upset about that, but soon got over it and was asking questions about when the baby would arrive. Justine was ill toward the end of her pregnancy and called for the help of the midwife several times the last two months. The delivery of Charles (Karl) Rode July 6, 1884 was long and difficult. The midwife remained on call for several weeks while Justine worked to gain back her strength. She was only able to care for the baby for a short time each day and then she had to rely on Julianna to take over. Her condition slowly deteriorated and eventually she spent most of the day in bed. The only person with any medical training, the midwife, suspected that Justine had a form of cancer.

Even during Justine's illness Julianna was asked to help others. In the middle of May she was asked to be a witness to a baptism.

This is the record of that event. In the chapel at Shinufka Julianna Rode as godparent witnessed the baptism of Benjamin Hamm born to parents Karl Hamm and his wife Anna nee Kuhnert June 1885. Julianna's parents were very proud of their daughter having been asked at age 15 to be part of Benjamin Hamm's baptism.

At times Justine seemed to improve and then she would slip back and decline a little more. This went on for over three years until the afternoon of December 12, 1887 when she fell asleep and never woke up. The family was in shock, and Julianna at age 17 found herself having to take care of young Karl, as well as August who was 11. She assumed all of the household duties and did her best to hold the family together in spite of the depression they all felt. Wilhelm did all he could to comfort the family and help with what Justine would have done. He was a very sad man but he tried not show it. He knew the children were very depressed and he tried to present a brave front, hoping it would be positive for the children to see. Julianna was the glue that held them altogether.

August's grieving lasted a long time and it affected much of what he did. He was still in school and his teacher commented to Wilhelm and Julianna about it. They did not know of anything to do so they chose the Cantor at the Chapel to talk to about it. After many visits August developed a rapport with Cantor Appel and told Julianna and his father that he wanted to visit with him alone. They agreed so August went alone to see him once a week for several months. It was a year later when he told Julianna and his father that he would not see Mr. Appel anymore. They were very surprised and agreed with him that it was okay to not see him anymore. They were curious and discussed it with the Cantor, who explained that many times a person grows from such an experience and gets to a place where they feel that they can handle their issue by themself. He said that it should be viewed as a very good thing, that August may finally have accepted the death of his mother and now he could get on with his life.

August was working side by side with his father more and more. He loved the outdoors and enjoyed the animals and watching the crops grow. He was still in school and they decided that he would stay there till he was 14. He was constantly challenged by a much older boy. August kept the problem to himself. Although he had not been visibly injured, he was threatened many times away from the school, as the young fellow knew that if the schoolmaster heard about it he would be in serious trouble. The harassing continued and August bravely dodged him often as best he could on the way home. This went on for several months. One day this big boy was chasing August close to his home and Mr. Ruff happened to see what was taking place. He grabbed a club and ran to meet them. As he swung it the offender's leg was moving swiftly forward into the next step. The loud sound of the club hitting the shin scared Mr. Ruff. The ruffian fell to the ground screaming about the pain. They tried to help him stand up. After several attempts he was able to, confirming the leg was not broken. Mr. Ruff told the boys to tell him what brought all this about so finally August told the story. Mr. Ruff asked the fellow if that was true. His non-answer confirmed that it was. With the club in his hand he marched the boys over to the Rode house to tell Wilhelm what had happened. After the session with August's father, the bad boy went home. From that night on August was never bothered again and the relationship with Heinrich Ruff was very good.

September 1888 Wilhelm met Caroline Mildner one morning at the harness maker in Shinufka. They had been aware of each other, having been at Church and around the village. Her husband had passed after several years earlier from what was thought to be stomach cancer. They were interested in each other and started to meet as often as they could. Wilhelm being a student of the word recalled reading that man should not live alone, and he felt he might be able to live that biblical quote. The children quickly knew what father was up to and they began to prepare for the inevitable. Caroline did not have any children and was the only child in her family. She welcomed the chance to be in this family and maybe even have children of her own. She was 33 and Wilhelm was 50.

Wilhelm learned as much as he could about Caroline's ancestry. He was a curious man, and with the possibility of their having children he constantly had questions to ask Caroline. She began to tire of them and started to inquire about his family. He would not return answers the way she had. It wasn't that he was trying to avoid divulging something, but he was focused on her heritage to a fault. They eventually worked that out and each found out what they wanted about the other's family. Eventually Wilhelm talked to his children about his friendship with Caroline. Julianna was 19, August 13, and Charles 5. Julianna had already had some long discussions with her father about Caroline. Neither one mentioned it, however both of them knew where this friendship might end, so the discussions continued. Julianna was the lady of the house. She was worried what would happen when a wife of her father was suddenly living there. Wilhelm had no opinions and tended to not discuss issues like that. Wilhelm did not bring Caroline home to visit until long after they met. He first did it on a day when Julianna and August took Charles to visit with a young friend of his.

Their friendship continued to grow and finally together they told the children that they planned to get married soon. Their wedding day was only a week away: April 4, 1889.

Life changed for everyone very quickly, starting out with the realization that they would have to find a way to settle their differences. Julianna had the most difficult time adjusting to the change in the household. She told herself that she would not let any minor disagreement become a big one. Under no circumstance would she show disrespect to her father's new wife. It was a huge adjustment, but eventually things smoothed out between them. Caroline wanted so bad to get along with Wilhelm's children. Not having had children she realized that she had a lot to learn when it came to parenting. She wanted to start having a family and Wilhelm seemed to want more children also. As time moved along the harmony in the house became very comfortable. Caroline did her very best to take the extra step to see that the harmony in the house continued. Caroline merely 14 years older than Julianna, finally crossed the threshold where she treated her as a fully grown woman. There was a lot to look forward to in the Wilhelm Herman Rode home.

CHAPTER 6

— 1888 —

Third Move: To Julianowka

The two wagons moved well on August 28, 1888, covering a third of the distance on the first day. Traveling alone was much more intimate and Michael enjoyed not having the responsibility for a long caravan. Though he felt free, still his heart was heavy to leave the village where his dear wife had died. He tried hard to keep looking forward, hoping the pain would lessen as time went by.

Ludwig, on the verge of 20, was a veteran team driver and a real wagon master, constantly checking the wagons whenever they stopped. He knew well the cost of trying to put off maintenance. Michael relied on him, and paid him a compliment when he thought he had done an exceptional job.

Anna was busy watching Pauline and Heinrich who was a good traveler, content in the wagon until it got near the noon or the evening stop. When they stopped he let loose to burn off some energy. Pauline at 10 was more subdued and content to be close to Anna.

Late afternoon on the third day they turned left to approach the village of Wladyslawowka. From there they went southeast less than a mile to arrive at Julianowka. The whole village knew they were coming. There were many welcomes as they moved toward Uncle Ludwig's house. When the Riskes came out to greet them, it was a very happy time. The greeting was especially exciting to the two youngest children. It was some time before Michael and Uncle Ludwig moved the wagons to a place behind the house and took care of the horses. There was so much to talk about, they continued over their supper. Michael asked if the Wunnik family lived nearby. Ludwig said they were at the far end of the village for only about a half mile from Ludwig's house. They were very happy to hear about their arrival. After a long day and a long night it did not take any encouragement to get the children to sleep.

The next day Ludwig led the Jess family to their new home. There was a whirl of activity, with Anna the force behind it. The first wagon, mostly household goods, was unloaded. The second wagon had some household items, but the rest were tools and items for the horses and cows. Michael's prize silage shredder was on that wagon, and he saw to it that it was very carefully unloaded. It did not take long to unload everything and place things in their permanent spot.

Michael and the children were anxious to see the Wunnik family. They were preparing to go find them, when the Wunniks' wagon pulled into their yard. There were many hellos and greetings. Someone later remarked that it was as if they had not seen each other in decades. Everyone was anxious to catch up on the news. The Wunniks now included Ferdinand 45, Julia 42, Ferdinand 22, Johann Julius 19, Gustaf 7, Wilhelm Otto 5, and Herman 3. Ferdinand told them there was a schoolhouse that also served as a Chapel. As in other villages, the schoolmaster was also the Church Cantor who conducted services. Pastor Heinrich Wassem, headquartered in Zhitomir, was the priest for the whole parish. He would come by the village two or three times a year to sanction the acts conducted by the Cantor, lining up all newlyweds and marry them all at one time.

Pauline had attended school in Sablotsche. Anna planned to enroll her as soon as she could in the Julianowka school—though at that time many families did not give their girls even the basics of reading and writing. Though Michael and Krystyna could not read or write—facts that Pastors noted on Church documents for marriages, births and deaths—Ludwig was lucky to have had four grades of school in Bielsko and some in Karolinow.

Michael and his family felt at home as soon as they first entered the village. After several months their feeling for the village was even stronger. They were happy with the Church, school and their many new friends.

They soon learned about the villages close by. Once or twice a year the Churches from Shinufka, five miles to the east, and/or Kurdyban, a half mile south of Shinufka, would get together with the members of the Lutheran Church in Julianowka for a social day. These days typically started with a worship service, then food serving would go on for a couple hours. The young people would be involved playing games and the adults might play "Game of Bones" using actual horse ankle joint bones sawed square so the bone would stand up. Ten joint bones were set close to each other facing a line of ten joint bones 33 feet away. Each team tossed a bone at the opposing line to knock a bone over, away from the area of play. The winning side knocked over the opposing line first.

There was also a fall festival held at Julianowka. The Church members of the Chapels at Shinufka and Kurdyban were included, making it a large joyful crowd. Johann Julius Wunnik arrived escorting a lady named Maria Kaminoski born in the village Marianowka, Podlubitz, Lutzk County. She was the widow of Gottlieb Schendel, who was born in Rzasnie, Radom Powiat, Poland. In this community of close villagers, whenever there was the prospect of a wedding the three communities came together to celebrate. The talk among the families was that Johann was very serious about her and was wanting to propose to her. Her parents were in agreement, as they respected Johann. Maria was frail, and some people thought she did not look healthy. They were enjoying the day, and some of the more chatty people opined that he was there with her to show her off.

The wedding bans were posted on Sunday September 11, 18, and 25. There being no objections, they married October 4, 1888 along with several couples when Pastor Wassum came to the village on his semi-annual visit. Johann was 19 and Maria was 29. They settled in Julianowka and during that summer they both helped Johann's father with his farming. In spite of Maria's health, the Wunnik family liked her very much and were supportive of the marriage. Her health continued to be an issue and Johann did whatever he could to comfort her and improve her condition. It was helpful having his parents and siblings nearby. The winter went well for Johann and Maria and they made plans to help his father on the farm that spring, but when the time came Maria was too weak to help in the field, though she helped Johann's mother a few hours a day. Throughout the summer Maria became weaker, and concern made its way through the family and the village. Aunt Krystyna was with her much of the time and did her best to comfort her. With her interest in health and home remedies, she came as close to being a nurse as anyone in the village. By the middle of November, Maria was bedridden and suffering. She was very sick and Johann knew that she would not live much longer. December 5, 1890 Maria died. The villages came together to support Johann as Maria was laid to rest. Johann, only 21, was devastated. He had seen a lot of death as a child in the Gostynin Parish in Poland where he was born. He thought about how different it was when it happened to him rather than someone else. He soon learned that grief would be with him longer than he first thought.

The tragedy in their lives did not stop with the death of Maria. Ferdinand Wunnik unexpectedly died in his sleep in the early morning of February 2, 1890 at age 46. Julia and her son Johann had both lost spouses within two months. A pall hung over the Wunnik house and the grief was shared by the community. Anna, having experienced similar deaths in her family, gladly made herself available to the Wunniks, who lived within walking distance, wherever she saw a need. Johann, living in his own place, now spent a lot of time at his mother's home and appreciated Anna helping her too, often telling her so. Michael stopped by several times a week and was happy to see the help that

Anna was giving. The Wunnik children had taken off time from school and Anna helped prepare them to go back. She talked to them about their father's death, as she knew from experience that their feelings would need to come out—the sooner the better, she felt, based on her experience. Anna often talked with Johann, and she was surprised at how often he stopped by when she was there.

After several months she came by less as school was soon ending for the year and she felt that Julia was doing well enough to take care of the things that were a priority. Five months after Ferdinand's death Anna's visits were once a week, and for only a few hours. If she missed a visit Johann showed up at Michael's house with the excuse of checking on everyone. However, most of that time was spent visiting with Anna—who was always busy catching up on work after having been gone helping his mother. On Johann's third visit Anna realized he was coming only to see her. This made her very uncomfortable and told him to let her know if he intended to visit in the future. Her responsibilities included being mother to her own siblings. Having the interest of a man was not something she had thought of. She saw Johann at Church and some social events in the village, but he seldom stopped by the house after Anna called him on it.

Ludwig happened to be at the house only a couple times when Johann stopped to visit. Ludwig did not like that idea, though he did not discuss it much with Anna.

Ludwig moved about quietly. He had developed many friendships in the village and spent time with his buddies, men his age. They talked about their work and about moving to America, based on a couple of reports they had heard from letters from villagers who had moved there. Most of these fellows whose families had moved several times—adventures they all recalled with fondness. They were ready for more adventure in a new land, but their closeness in the village was something they would hate giving up. They chatted about the young ladies in the villages, and looked forward to Church events for that reason. Only one of them did not want to leave Julianowka. Moving to other countries was a dream—but none of them really thought it could ever happen.

Now that Pauline was 9 she was a big help to Anna, especially to prepare the food crops for the long winter. Though not many parents let their daughters attend much school, Pauline was happy that she would go this fall. Anna regretted not having that much education, but she knew she had been needed at home.

Michael was happy. He never once regretted the move they made. He noticed Johann's interest in Anna, but had no particular feelings either way about it, although he and Ludwig had discussed it several times. Ludwig did not hesitate to express his negative feelings toward Johann. In responding to why he felt that way, Ludwig told his dad, "I don't know why I just feel that way." Michael had visited a couple times with Julia, and they enjoyed trading stories about their families. They talked a lot about their respective communities in Poland. Julia said it had been very hard to leave, as their families had been in a small area of the Gostynin Parish for many generations. She was happy they had moved, but she missed the relatives and neighbors she had known all her life. She was struggling since Ferdinand's death, especially with the farm. Before there had been wonderful village help and advice, which she needed. Her son Ferdinand was working in Zorniv, east of Julianowka, and was not able to be of much help to his mother. Johann's interest was in working with tools and could provide more than farming.

The joint-village Church events were appreciated by all. Everyone tried to attend, and it was a good place to renew old friendships and meet new people. Michael and his children went to the fall festival in Shinufka. Michael and Ludwig watched some men playing "Bones," and afterwards they chatted with one of the players about the game. He introduced himself as Wilhelm Rode. He and Caroline had recently married. Upon meeting his daughter Julianna, who was 20, Ludwig began talking to her. Moving a few steps back removed them from the ears of their families. They visited all afternoon and agreed to meet again as soon as they could. All of a sudden just another Church event had brought some real excitement to Ludwig's life. He even surprised himself, as he related the visit to his father on the way home. Anna asked several questions which Ludwig tried to ignore. He told himself to calm down a little. He hoped he had made a good impression on Mr. Rode and her brother August.

Over the next few days Ludwig thought constantly about what he would have to do to make travel to Shinufka possible. His thinking changed radically after that meeting at the festival. Michael commented that he had more spring in his step since returning from Shinufka. Of course Anna had to tease him a bit and try to make his life a bit miserable. After all that is what sisters are for, she said.

Ludwig was preoccupied thinking about Julianna. He now had to figure out a way to get to Shinufka for a visit. He talked the family into attending services in the Chapel at Shinufka. They went a month after the festival, and Ludwig was an excited guy when he finally saw Julianna. They stayed within sight of the family, and this time they talked about their families and how they both happened to end up in the same area. They had so much to talk about that Ludwig was almost babbling, trying to get out everything he wanted to say, including that for a long time he had dreamed about going to another country, maybe America or Canada. Julianna was very surprised and Ludwig wondered why. She said that her father had also talked about it for as long as she could remember. She said her father had heard stories of vast parcels of land being available, with good soil and water. She said that he and her mother had talked endlessly about it. They had some friends who had moved to America and reported back many good things.

Ludwig was able to elaborate about his driving the team whenever they moved. Julianna was amused and impressed that he could do that, starting at such a young age. She told him about her father's recent marriage and the problems that she faced in the house with his new wife. She felt displaced and in a way unappreciated for all she did to help raise her siblings after her mother died. She was not angry at her father for getting married, just upset at the circumstances that came together to create undesirable issues. She knew she could not expect her father to remain single. He had a right to companionship, and she was certain that he was very concerned about her and her brothers. Ludwig expressed his understanding regarding her situation and opined that he might be facing a similar situation someday. They knew the time to leave was approaching, and they had wandered out of the sight of their parents. They had walked by a barn and stopped to rest against it. Ludwig reached over for Julianna's hand. As he was stretching his neck to give her a peck on the cheek, Wilhelm came around the corner. Ludwig said they had been looking for him, for it is time to go home.

Ludwig was doing most of the farm work and Michael was happy that he could. Michael had some minor back pain, and he welcomed a break from work. He also took time to visit with Julia Wunnik. He visited often, and they seemed to have a lot to talk about. She was still overwhelmed with all that faced her each day. Michael was able to give her some moral support, make suggestions regarding crops to plant, and advise her which cattle should be kept and which should be sold or traded. She appreciated it and followed closely what he had to say. They seemed comfortable and continued the friendship. They had known each other for a long time, though they had not spent much time together until now. He was aware that her German Lutheran roots were very deep and that her extended family in the Gostynin Parish was very large. Michael was a plain, simple man with a large heart. That appealed to Julia and she tested him many times in her quiet unsuspecting way. She was a happy lady whenever Michael was visiting, and she always looked forward to his next visit.

When Michael was visiting with Anna he mentioned that they had been in Julianowka for two years. So many things had happened and in some ways it seemed like they had been there longer. Heinrich at seven was in school and enjoying it. Anna was concerned about Heinrich not knowing his mother and her being the mother figure for him. She talked about it with her father so they would both be aware and mention his mother to him so he would know something about her.

Ludwig visited with Julianna whenever they could. Since meeting her, Ludwig was a different man—more focused in what he was doing, with less time for his group of friends in the village. He cared so much for her. He felt that she was the one, so he had to find a way to spend more time with her. The distance was an issue in their relationship, which many years later Julianna mentioned this to her daughter Lydia.

A ten mile round trip was far enough that it would not be made often. It was a good incentive to have the wedding sooner.

When Michael visited Julia, it was as friends who had both lost their spouse. They both benefitted from their companionship and it seemed they both realized that there was a future for the two of them together. Johann got along very well with Michael and Michael knew what his intentions were with his daughter Anna. Michael was all right with that.

Johann was showing up more and more at the Jess home. Anna was beginning to warm up to him and did not put restrictions on his visit, though whenever Johann appeared Ludwig would display some unkind behavior. No one knew why he was antagonistic regarding Johann. The family thought it was his way of displaying protection for his sister whom he always held in high regard. He just was, and it was the topic of several discussions over the evening meal.

No wonder the time was passing quickly. Their lives were full and some of the suffering that had fallen to them was less painful. Their memories were good and the experiences they had were profitable in that it made them all better and stronger people. They enjoyed living where they were, and other than the wanderlust that Ludwig had talked about, Michael felt they had found a home.

CHAPTER 7

— 1891 —

The Families Form

The air was heavy with anxiety at the Wilhelm Rode home July 18, 1891. Caroline was being attended by the midwife who helped deliver their first born, Julius Richard Rode, late in the afternoon. There was happiness and some mixed feelings after the new baby arrived. Julianna prayed that she would be able to keep the relationship with Caroline congenial. No matter how hard Julianna tried, there was always a bit of tension in the air. She also knew that she would not be in the house much longer, as she was planning her own marriage to Ludwig.

Life changed dramatically in Wilhelm's house. Now that his second family had started, Wilhelm wondered if these two families would be able to come together and live as one. It would be years before he would have an answer. All he could do now was tend to his farm and pray that all would be well. His farm was not producing as well the last couple years as it had when they moved to Shinufka. The rains had not been coming like in the past, and people in the area were very frustrated. But all he could do was to plant his crops and pray for rain. He was a very spiritual man, considering himself a Lay Minister. He had conducted Sunday services several times over the years when Cantor was ill. This was a contribution that Wilhelm enjoyed, and he told Julianna that he felt that was his real calling. He especially enjoyed getting into a discussion about religion with members of the clergy, though he rarely had that opportunity. When he did, he felt like he was doing what he did best. He knew he would till the soil for a long time, so he satisfied his religious interest by talking with people who enjoyed the same thing.

Ludwig finally approached Michael to tell his father about his strong feelings for Julianna, though Michael had known for a long time. Ludwig wanted to follow the tradition of discussing it with his father, and they spent a lot of time alone talking about his intentions. Michael was very much in favor of the relationship and encouraged Ludwig in his quest. He asked Ludwig about his plans after they got married, should she accept. Ludwig said that he wanted to leave to another country. He had been talking about it for years, and he considered this a stepping stone to that end. Michael asked what he would do when he got to the new country? Ludwig's only answer was that he would want to have a farm. He said he enjoyed that work and he thought that he was very good at it. Michael gave him his blessing and Ludwig appreciated their time together.

They also discussed Johann's more frequent visits to Anna, and Ludwig did not hesitate to express his opposition. Michael's attempt to dissuade Ludwig's feelings fell on deaf ears. His father realized he was not going to change.

Ludwig visited Julianna and told her about his discussion with his father. She was impressed and said she thought that meant the relationship between them was very strong. They continued the discussion about his relationship, and without having given it a thought he asked her the question. Her response was: yes of course—and why did it take you so long? As they walked they came upon a wagon. They both slumped against the wheel and laughed. Julianna said it reminded her of the day that her father caught them leaning against the barn. Ludwig told her that he would talk to her father and ask for her hand. She promised she would not let on until that was done, though Ludwig was not about to delay this matter. They went back to the house, but Wilhelm was not there. Caroline said that he had gone to visit someone in the village. Ludwig went looking for him. He had some ideas of where he may be, but he was not in any of those places. With each step Ludwig grew a little more anxious. He had spent a couple of hours looking and it was time for him to go back to Julianowka.

When he returned to the house, Wilhelm was there and had been since a few minutes after Ludwig went looking for him. Ludwig asked for a few minutes with him and Wilhelm granted it. While still a little short of breath Ludwig got right into his rehearsed lines and asked if he could marry his daughter. Wilhelm's tone indicated that he was not going to make it easy for Ludwig. He wanted to talk about how Ludwig intended to provide for his daughter. He asked him what he wanted to do long-term. Unfortunately Ludwig brought up his idea of moving to another country. Wilhelm talked about how that would split up the family and he thought he should plan on staying where he was. Of course if Ludwig would promise to ask Wilhelm and the family to join them, he might look differently on that idea.

After a couple hours of discussing everything that Ludwig did not want to discuss, Wilhelm gave him his blessing. Delighted, Ludwig and Julianna and her father had a brief discussion about the proposal. It was now dark and Ludwig had to start the trip back home. He was thankful for a bright moonlit evening. He made it back without incident and was bubbling as he told the news to his father and Anna. Anna was very happy, as she had liked Julianna from the first time they met.

The wedding party in two wagons left about 4 AM on the morning of November 12, 1891 to cover the 30 mile trip to Rozyscze. In the first wagon were Ludwig, Julianna, Michael, Anna, Pauline and Heinrich. In the second wagon was Wilhelm, August and Charles. Wilhelm's wife Caroline stayed at home with newborn Richard Rode. With his father two feet from him Ludwig was not going to say much. They did discuss how life would start out for the newlyweds. Years later Julianna told her daughter Lydia that she wore a plain skirt and a light colored blouse for her wedding. Times were tough, but the young couple was full of optimism about the future.

Ludwig told his father that when they moved to Shinufka he was going to work for Julianna's father. Michael had not heard that they planned to move to Shinufka, and there was disappointment in his voice, though the conversation was very casual, and mostly about relatives. The trip was long and they arrived in time for a late afternoon ceremony at the Evangelical Lutheran Church. This was their first visit to it. It reminded Michael of his first visit to the beautifully decorated Lutheran Church in Lublin.

Following is the translated marriage record written in Russian:

> *Ludwig Jess of Julianowka Kreis Dubno. Son of settler Michael Jess and his wife Chrystyna born Riske; born in Bilsk, Gubernia Lublin: Julianna Rode of Julianowka Kreis Dubno, daughter of settler Wilhelm Rode and his wife Justine born Gering; born in Chmielewo Gubernia Lomza. Both Evangelical Lutheran Confession.*
>
> *Wedding bans were posted October 13, 20, 27, 1891.*
>
> *Married the 12th of November 1891 in the Church of Roshischtsche*
>
> *By Pastor Kerm[2]*
>
> *Ludwig unmarried 23 years*
>
> *Julianna unmarried 21 years*

Ludwig and Julianna lived in Julianowka until the end of 1891. The first part of January they moved to Shinufka and made their home a short walk to Wilhelm's. Since Wilhelm needed help working his farm, Ludwig was hired to help him. The move also helped as Julianna was able to visit regularly with her brothers August and Charles—it had been her concern that she not lose touch with them. Her brothers were very happy when she and Ludwig moved to Shinufka.

Ludwig's work was to repair the farm machinery and tools that were used on Wilhelm's farm. He also did some work on the harnesses.

---

2 Pastor George Friedrich Kerm was Pastor of the Rozyszce Lutheran Church from 1879–1903.

What he could not repair he took to the local harness maker. There was enough work to be done to keep Ludwig busy most of the time.

Ludwig continued to dream and talk about someday moving to another country. He did not mention it around Wilhelm, as he recalled that it was a sore subject with him, though he would mention it often with Julianna and she did not question his dream. Michael, however, encouraged him to keep his idea.

Much to the surprise of Ludwig, Michael arrived the middle of January 1892 for a visit. Ludwig and Julianna were very happy to see him. Ludwig and Julianna noticed that the casual conversation lasted much too long. Michael stuttered a bit and finally blurted out that Anna was going to marry Johann Julius Wunnik. Without taking a breath, and with a sweaty brow, he told them that he was going to marry Johann's mother Julia Kuehn Wunnik. This caught Ludwig completely by surprise. Ironically he did not mind his father marrying Julia and he even said so, but he still did not want Anna to marry Johann.

It was a cordial visit and did not get out of hand. After the discussion about the upcoming marriages, they had some casual conversation and then Michael left to go back to Julianowka but still worried about Ludwig. He was so proud of Ludwig, but it bothered him that he was upset. He decided to relay the message to Julia the next time they visited. He felt it would be better if she knew, in case Ludwig slipped at a gathering and brought up the subject. With the family on the way to getting bigger, Michael especially wanted everyone to get along. He had heard stories of families not getting along, even turning to violence, and he would not allow that to happen.

Anna Julia Jess and Johann Julius Wunnik, and Michael Jess and Julia Wunnik were married the same day in a joint wedding ceremony on April 22, 1892 in the village of Iwanowka, three miles from Shinufka. Anna Julia was 26 and Johann was 22.

The ceremonies were held in the schoolroom which also served as a Chapel, conducted by Pastor Wasem[3] who was headquartered in Zhitomir and whose name appears on several family documents.[4]

Now that the Jess-Wunnik families were tied closely together, Ludwig decided that he would do his best to welcome Johann into the family. Ludwig and Julianna went to Julianowka on a sunny Sunday the middle of May. They had not seen Michael and his family since the wedding. Michael was particularly happy to see them, and welcomed them as a couple. Heinrich and Pauline had wondered why they had not visited, and they were overjoyed. Heinrich, now nine had many things to tell his brother. Pauline, now 12, was anxious to visit with Julianna as she had become very fond of her. As soon as Ludwig felt he had everyone's attention he said that Julianna had something to tell them. Julianna was blushing and taken by surprise, for she thought Ludwig was going to do the honors. She finally was able to tell them that a baby would be arriving at their home. There was much excitement that occupied the conversation the rest of the day. Finally, early evening Ludwig and Julianna left for Shinufka.

Ludwig was confident that he was well prepared for his own place. His father had prepared him well to farm land and raise some livestock. Ludwig was still working for Wilhelm, but also looking for land with a home on it. People were moving to other parts of Volhynia and mostly to other countries. Ludwig had looked at one farm at the far end of the village and over a little hill. But with the baby coming he wanted to be in the village with neighbors on both sides. He was anxious to live in his own place, but he would wait until the right one came along. Julianna was a very excited future mother. She was happy to tell her brother August and Charles the news. They realized that when the baby arrived

---

3   His gravestone is in the German section of the Zhitomir cemetery. His grave had been desecrated during World War II, either by the Russians coming from the east or by the suspicious Germans coming from the west. Johann's name was spelled Wonnek on the marriage record and Anna was listed as Julianna Jesse—and both of their birth record locations were incorrect as noted.

4   Anna Julia went by Julianna during her life and Johann Julius went by Julius during his lifetime. The marriage record that we have of Anna and Johann's marriage was obtained in October 22, 1943. It has the Nazi stamp on it and the implication is Wilhelm Wonnek obtained it to prove his German heritage. The record was obtained from the Zhitomir archive. The Wunnik family began spelling their last name with slight variations: Wonnek, Wonneck and Wonnick.

they would become uncles. Ludwig told Julianna that he was hoping for a son who would help him when they moved to another country. Julianna replied that she was sure that she was going to have a girl. They were a happy couple and there was not much conversation that did not include the baby. Julianna received preparation help from Caroline. She also got promises from brothers August and Charles that they would help with the baby because they knew that it would be a boy.

One day when Julianna and Ludwig were talking, Julianna said if it is a boy I want him to be a Minister, but Ludwig just wanted him to follow Ludwig's path, helping on the farm when they moved to another country. Julianna could not fathom moving to another country. She even started to challenge Ludwig's thinking about it and wondered why they couldn't be just as happy where they were. Finally when Ludwig had talked about it a little too much, she made him promise to not discuss it again until after the baby was born.

It was summer time and there was not much work for Wilhelm till the middle of August, but Ludwig was able to get a job with the local harness maker till it was time to help Wilhelm harvest his crops. Ludwig had always been interested in leather and the process that turned it into a harness. He was very happy about his temporary work and he knew that what he would learn would come in handy in the future. He also thought that it would be a good trade to know and use to barter. He was interested in anything he could do to help him provide for his wife and family. His work at the harness maker included repairing harnesses and some bridles. He had always been good with his hands and enjoyed learning. There was a crude forge in the shop for forging new iron harness parts and reshaping iron rings, clips and whatever else was brought to them. He branched out into something new and was proud of what he had done. His pay was very little, but that was the last thing on his mind. He was learning something new, and he realized the value in it. His boss observed his interest in forge work and let him work on shaping a ring that had been built. It wasn't very long before he realized it was not easy and would take a lot of time and work to learn the basics. Whenever work was slack and the forge was on, Ludwig would try to shape pieces of iron into rings and angles. He would hammer pieces of metal into chisels, even rough knives. As long as he could practice he was happy.

Ludwig almost lost his job one day when a friend of his father's came in to have some work done on some badly torn harnesses. The story was that the man foolishly bet a neighbor after Church that his team and wagon could go faster than the neighbor's. The race was going well, the man was winning, but the horse on the right tripped on a piece of log that was in his path. Because of the speed they were going, much damage was done to the harness on the horse that tripped, and some was done to the harness on the other horse. He not only lost the bet, he now had to get his harnesses repaired as soon as possible because he had to go to Kurdyban for a funeral. The problem for Ludwig is that the man started telling his boss that he was going to leave next spring for America. Ludwig heard that and he started asking the man questions. He couldn't stop talking about the trip with the man, even after his boss told him for the third time to get back to work. He finally did and they did get the harnesses repaired, but not in time for him to get his family to the funeral. Ludwig received a stern warning about his action that afternoon, and he was very concerned about his job, even though he would only be able work a few more weeks.

Ludwig left his job in time to help Wilhelm with the harvest and to get ready for the winter. Wood had to be cut, hauled, sawed into stove length and piled. Ludwig had a lot of experience, and Wilhelm welcomed his being available to help. Wood was available nearby and the sooner they could bring it in, the drier the sun would make it.

Ludwig was getting anxious about the arrival of their first baby, feeling the heavy responsibility. Every day he realized that his life had changed the day he got married, in more ways than one. He felt the weight and he also enjoyed it, as he felt his father had done a good job preparing him for this time in his life.

The first Saturday afternoon in September 1892, he and Julianna went to visit Michael and his wife Julia. The conversation started out in the usual manner, talking about family and some of their travels moving from place to place. It wasn't too long before the four of them separated by gender. Michael and Ludwig went for a walk and soon

Ludwig mentioned the *good* weight of responsibility that he was feeling. Ludwig was feeling much better. He even felt good about calling on his father for help and support, should he need it any time in the future. The four of them enjoyed the evening meal, then Ludwig and Julianna went back to Shinufka. The ride back home was all conversation about the afternoon. Julianna was delighted that Ludwig and his father seemed to get along very well. They had always gotten along, but now they seemed to be much closer. Julianna felt that the new baby arriving had Michael looking forward to his first grandchild. It was a trip that they were both glad they had taken.

Ludwig's work for Wilhelm was going well and Julianna was happy that the two of them got along well. After Ludwig's promise to Wilhelm, he did not mention moving out of the country again. It would not be long before the cold weather and snow would end Ludwig's work. Then they would be waiting through a long winter, broken up by the birth of their baby.

One day Julianna brought up the question about what to name the baby. She said she wanted to have names ready for either gender. She said that if the baby was a girl she should be named Emilia, a name she loved. Julianna said that if a boy was born she wanted him named Ludwig. That created a rise out of Ludwig and he shouted his opposition to having a namesake. Julianna tried her best to pacify him, and she said that he could be called Junior or Sonny. Ludwig said he liked the name Jesse so he would be called Jesse Jess. That did not resonate with Julianna. They agreed to disagree on names, to think about it and decide later. There would be plenty of time to discuss a name before the baby arrived. Ludwig started thinking seriously about names and he said he wanted a name that sounded strong.

Ludwig and Julianna contacted the midwife and agreed on when she would visit and how often, beginning the middle of November. Ludwig offered to pay for her services with firewood. She was elated about that, as her husband had been too sick to bring in the wood the winter. Now it was time to wait.

One day when Michael was visiting, he listened intently to the discussion of names. He thought Emilia was a fine name for a girl. Then he suggested a name with strength: Julius. Julius Caesar was a strong man of some type. He thought Julius Jess sounded very good, even though some people might call him J.J. Both Ludwig and Julianna's eyes lit up. "I think we've found the right names." Tension was now gone and there was room for other discussions.

Baptismal Certificate

1. Julius Jess, and in the church book
it is written Gesse
Born the 1st of January and baptised
also the 1st of January 1893 year
Son of father Ludwig Jess
whose spouse is Mrs Julianna born
Rohde and baptised in Colony
Schinufka, the verification fee
is paid

Christening record for Julius Jess, January 1, 1893

CHAPTER 8

– 1893 –
Julius Is Born

Christmas was not as relaxing time as it usually had been. The air was full of hope and anxiety. As the end of the year neared, Ludwig was approaching his 25th birthday, the day he went to ask the midwife to return with him and stay a few days. Julianna was beginning to feel the time was approaching and was comforted when they arrived. Final preparations were made by the midwife, and Julianna was comfortable but very anxious. Ludwig had settled down and a calm came over him. The last day of the year was very cold and windy. Ludwig kept himself useful keeping a good fire going in the wall heating box. They were all warm and comfortable. The anxiety level, however, reached to the heavens. Ludwig said out loud to no one in particular, "That baby has to be born." Little did he know that years down the road a family birth to him would be almost like any other day.

Early morning January 1, 1893 Julius Jess was born, but he was very sick and not expected to live. Ludwig immediately left to fetch the Cantor. The baptismal certificate shows that Julius was baptized the same day that he was born. Many thanks went to the Cantor for coming out on a cold day. Julianna was well prepared, having helped raise her two younger siblings, so she and the midwife were on constant alert to do what they could to strengthen Julius. His mother said several times, "If we can pull him through the first day, we have a good chance of saving him."

Father Ludwig now had another reason for anxiety, and he had plenty of it. Although it was a long distance, he traveled to Julianowka to visit with his father, Pauline and Heinrich to tell them the news. He only stayed about an hour so he could get back to Shinufka. As Pauline and Heinrich were saying goodbye, they realized they were now an Aunt and an Uncle.

The next day Julius was a little stronger. Everyone in the house was cautiously hopeful. On the third day of Julius's life he was stronger, and that evening the midwife went home. But Ludwig was not about to relax, and he kept asking how Julianna knew he was getting better. Finally his wife told him she knew what she was doing. And in a very curt voice she suggested he go out and chop wood. Ludwig got the message. But he did not chop wood. He went to their neighbor Albert Rauch a few houses down to tell them the news. He was warmly welcomed and invited into their home. Albert suggested that they celebrate by having some of his special rhubarb wine that he had made last fall. They had a glass and both agreed that it was a special occasion so they should have one more to celebrate. Ludwig stared into the glass for a few moments. Albert commented later that he thought Ludwig was in a trance. Ludwig realized his mood would change if he continued to visit with Albert. After that second glass Ludwig knew he should go home. He expressed his appreciation for visiting with him during this stressful time. He went home and he began to tell Julianna about the wonderful time he had at the Rauch home. She said, "Ludwig, I can tell you had a fine time as your face is all red and you smell of that strong wine everyone in the neighborhood knows about." He realized the best thing he could do was to sit down, be quiet, and maybe doze off for a little rest.

Two weeks later Julianna was sure that Julius was going to grow into a healthy young man. Finally they could relax a little. Ludwig was still looking for some land and he was also talking with his father-in-law about working for him again. Ludwig's good reputation had spread and he had three men ask him about working for them. These were established Germans who had owned their farms for many years. He told them all he would think about it and discuss it the next time they met. Ludwig did not like this dilemma, for the three farmers had promised him more than Wilhelm had for the same kind of work. He did not want to leave Wilhelm for extra money, but he had to consider his family. He decided to not think much about it, in the hope that when he got back to the issue an answer would come to him.

With spring fast approaching, Ludwig made his decision to secure a position with one of the farmers. Then he went to talk to Wilhelm. He quickly and clearly told Wilhelm that he had chosen to work this year with another farmer in the village. Wilhelm was very agitated about Ludwig's decision and he let him know it. He said his main issue was that he had given Ludwig work when he really did not need to hire anyone. Ludwig said he understood why he felt that way, and he attempted to smooth things out, but only made matters worse. He left feeling very unhappy and wishing he had not made the decision he had. He told Julianna about the conversation and she said that the bad part about it was that her father tended to carry a grudge. She was concerned about it, and she decided that in a couple days she would bundle up the baby and visit him. Wilhelm was very happy to see Julius and Julianna. Eventually they talked about "the event," and Julianna related how her husband felt and Wilhelm said that, regardless, they all had to get along and he would work toward that goal. Julianna left feeling the visit had been worthwhile, though she was concerned that he might not carry forward on his promise.

Ludwig had a few weeks till the weather broke. He was in a quiet, reflective mood, almost stumbling when he walked—a few months over 25 and a proud father. Julianna read his mood and knew it was best to not disturb him. He was thinking and wondering. He had to get his own land but he had just committed to working through the summer season. He would do that—it was another step toward building his character. He lived to make his word mean something. Next to his family, this was most important to him. That was the man that he wanted his son Julius to become—hard working, loving his family and his God, and a model member of the community. He had thought of those things for the last few years, and since the birth of his son he had thought of little else. He had to think about the long life ahead for him and his family.

Ludwig continued to think of moving to another country, thinking there had to be somewhere with more opportunity, meaning available land. But he could only consider it and not let it take over his thoughts. He had no information and whenever he heard of someone arriving from another part of Volhynia or moving out of Volhynia, he would find a way to get next to those people to talk to them. He spoke with the Cantor, who invited him into the schoolroom and showed him a map on the wall. He pointed to where they were and then he reached way to his left and showed Ludwig the continents of North and South America. Ludwig stepped back. He felt faint. He had no idea that those places he had thought of so often were so far away. He thanked the Cantor and left almost more moody than before. Yet he was driven. He could go to any of those places, as he knew many of the people who had left with those countries as their destination. He soon got back to being his old happy confident self. Julianna had read him correctly and quietly smiled to herself as she went about caring for her family.

On May 10, 1893 Ludwig became an uncle when Anna gave birth to a girl, whom they named Bertha. She was born in the village of Alexandrowka, a short distance south of Dubno. He congratulated her and Johann, hoping he would somehow be able to create a rapport with Johann. Out of the thinking mood he had been in, if he was to be true to himself he would have to make the effort. Anna appreciated his effort and Ludwig felt he would have many more opportunities.

He was working his job in June when he made up his mind that he would start talking to his father about moving. His father was happy, saying he would never leave Volhynia. Ludwig would have to create the desire in him to move, which would take a long time. He decided this would be his main goal until it was accomplished, whenever that might be. He continued to talk to people in the village, but he did not want the villagers to think he was obsessed with the subject.

After he had made the decision his thinking was more clear. He also paid attention to doing things or not doing things that would prepare him for the day when they would leave Volhynia. Julianna commented that he seemed to be feeling much better lately. Relief is what he felt—he now had a purpose in life. The move would be unlike any of the three moves that he had done, so it would have to be well planned with preparations for unforeseen events.

September 11, 1894 Ludwig and Julianna became the proud parents of another son. They both agreed they would name him Ferdinand. The family was growing, but Ludwig was very aware that this would not deter him from planning his dream. While they were enjoying the first few days of Ferdinand's life, they realized that he was not as healthy as they originally had thought. They watched him carefully and sought health advice in the village. The general feeling was that he had some lung trouble and it needed to be carefully watched.

About three weeks later Wilhelm arrived at the Jess home with the news that Caroline had delivered a healthy boy named Fred on October 1st. There was much talk about babies, but there was some tension between the two men. Ludwig did what he could to ease it, commenting that it was probably rare for a man's father-in-law to become a father the same time as his son-in-law. The tension was low level and did not seem to get in the way of a cordial afternoon.

A neighbor of Ludwig's came over one day when he was out in the yard. After discussing the weather and the children, the man asked Ludwig if he knew anyone who had a silage maker, Ludwig's eyes lit up as he thought of his dad's. Being that it was still early in the day, they decided to harness the team and go to visit Michael. Ludwig knew that his father was not using the silage maker and was almost certain that he would want to sell it. It was a quick bumpy ride because they pushed the team more than they should have. After the introductions Ludwig brought up the subject of the silage grinder and said that his neighbor wanted to buy it. Michael exploded with anger and told Ludwig how disgusted he was that he would even think of such a thing. He said he would never sell it and might even want to be buried with it. He also told Ludwig that he was very disappointed that he did not even bother to discuss it with him before showing up with a buyer. Ludwig excused himself and went to say a quick hello to Pauline and Heinrich. After a few minutes he went back out and apologized to his father. He and his neighbor left and headed back to Shinufka. Ludwig was very embarrassed, and whatever he had said did not mitigate the uncomfortable situation. The neighbor understood, for he knew his intention was honorable.

Anna and Johann came to visit a couple days before the New Year with Bertha and their new son Daniel. Ludwig tried to make them feel welcome, though it was difficult to not show his discomfort. They enjoyed seeing the new baby and they liked the name they had chosen. Ludwig hoped his sister was happy. During the several hour visit Ludwig and Julianna did not sense anything in Anna and Johann other than a happily married couple. That made Ludwig feel better.

Their families were growing and now their peers were married and having children, though most were having a difficult time providing for them. It wasn't for lack of desire—it was for lack of opportunity. Most of them had small farms and grew the food that was needed to get them through to the next season, which took a lot of time and energy. Some of them had to learn how to use root cellars in winter and how to store ice through the summer. Most had good training growing up, so the tasks were not new to them. Some did something extra that they could barter, and everyone seemed open to that.

Ludwig was always looking for an opportunity. One day he bought a team from a family that was leaving Volhynia. When he had a chance to resell them to a man in the village, he could have reaped a very nice profit, but he did not jump at the offer saying he would give it some thought. When he saw the man the next day, he lowered the price. The proud owner of the team was very happy—and as Ludwig guessed, the man spread the news to anyone who would listen. Ludwig had carefully thought that out. It would be many years before he would have an opportunity to emigrate, so he was carefully building his reputation in case he needed a little help when he was preparing to leave. Years before Michael had counseled him about leaving a good trail that he would be proud to look back on. When those conversations came back to Ludwig, it was like he was hearing it for the first time, but he was ready to listen. He had heard someone say that when someone wants to learn, a teacher will appear. He was grateful to his father—he was building his character and Ludwig felt so good about it.

A year later Ferdinand's health was the same. He had not gained much weight and his breathing was worse during the summer months. Julianna thought that he was allergic to certain weeds and crops they were growing. She was concerned and vigilant, always trying to get help and advice. Several ladies in the villages offered home cures and suggestions about how to place Ferdinand in a certain position for sleeping.

It looked like the crops this year would only produce half of the normal yield. Ludwig was glad he had several hogs and a lot of chickens they could butcher when needed. He was happy to hire out for the next two years. Even though his pay was not much it helped cover the family needs.

Wilhelm and Caroline added another son to their family during the summer of 1896. To Julianna, as an adult in her mid-twenties, it seemed a bit strange that her father was starting another family with ages close to her family.

Her third son Emil arrived early on October 11, 1897 about a mile west of Schinufka in the village of Gonczarycha in the home of the midwife, preferred because of Ferdinand's health. A very healthy robust fellow of good weight and breathing very naturally. There was much joy in the home, but unfortunately it was very short lived. A few hours after the birth, Ferdinand started a breathing episode that was labored. The midwife, at the direction of Julianna, prepared a steam apparatus to help ease his desperate situation, but Ferdinand was not to be helped. Within a couple of hours he was gone. This happy-tragic family lore would be passed down through the generations of the Jess-Rode family. It was difficult to prepare for the burial of Ferdinand. Ludwig told Julianna he would take care of it and not to worry. He wanted her to rest and not have any other concerns on her mind. She grieved heavily and went through the process of questioning what she could have done differently. She understood that he was born weak, but she thought maybe she did not try hard enough to save him. Julius was especially upset about the death of his brother. He even felt cheated because he had not been able to play with him, and now he had died. His parents tried hard to involve him in doing little things for Emil. They would even let him hold Emil, even though he was only a few days old. This did help Julius. They kept him involved in caring for Emil, and as time went by it became a natural thing for Julius to be there for him. It was too much for Julianna to go through, and Ludwig did what he could, talking to her and inviting her to go to Church at the village Chapel. Even though it was winter time he got the team ready for the short ride each Sunday. She appreciated his effort, and even though her heart was very heavy she felt so much better after each Church service. Mixing with the congregation and the occasional visit by the Cantor was a big benefit to her.

In the fall of '99 Julius started school. Emil was two and very upset that his protector brother was leaving every day for many hours. It was a hard adjustment for both Emil and his mother. Julianna had not realized how much she had relied on Julius to help around the house. She missed him.

Beside dealing with Julius going to school and handling Emil's emotions, she was planning for another child to arrive in the next few months. Ludwig was realizing that he was going to be the head of a large family if these births continued. He was happy with his family and proud that his oldest son was in school. His own schooling was limited in Bielsko. Comparing his age when he was driving a team and wagon when they left Bielsko, he realized that Julius was only four years shy of that age. Would he be capable of driving a team for many miles in a few years? He might be able to, as he looked like he was going to be a tall man. Ludwig had a lot that he could dream about as his family was growing.

Ludwig instigated discussions among the families about moving to another country. Michael found out how he could get a copy of Pauline's birth record from the Evangelical Parish in Chelm. With the help of a literate villager, they ordered the record. He told Ludwig that just in case they decided to emigrate someday, he wanted to have all the papers ready. That was a big surprise to Ludwig, and he had trouble containing his excitement for a few days. The next time they met there was a lot of talk about moving. It began to look like Wilhelm's and Michael's families could both be interested in moving whenever Ludwig was ready. This interest spread through the families. Anna wanted to go, but Johann did not. (In the end they stayed in Julianowka.)

The bans had been posted and on October 6, 1899 August Rode and Pauline Jess were married in an outdoor ceremony with 14 other couples. Many had waited many months for the Pastor to arrive for his semi-annual visit. While there, the Pastor held a worship service and blessed many of the acts performed by the Cantor.

August and Pauline were both very enthusiastic about the possibility of moving to another country. Bits of information arrived by mail from former villagers who wrote about their new lives. This information would be food for discussion for weeks. As time went by most were fully convinced that they should move to another country.

Amidst the discussions, on January 6, 1900 Ludwig and Julianna became the proud parents of a robust son whom they had decided to name Heinrich. They were very thankful for a healthy growing family. When Julius was not in school he was a lot of help to his mother, though she knew that in the next year or two he would be spending all his extra time outside with his father, a tall man whom Julius followed whenever they were together. He tried to mimic his steps, but soon went back to his regular stride—it was tiring to mimic his father. Ludwig was gentle with his children—which did not mean that they were not well disciplined and respectful. Ludwig had learned that showing respect would get a person further in life than trying to boast and falsely impress people. He taught his children that, and told his father that if that was all they learned from him, he would feel he had done a lot for them. Julius at seven was full of energy, and Emil at three tried to follow along and keep up. He was not big enough, but most of the time Julius tried to include Emil. Julius had a very serious side to him and a lot of the time he appeared to be withdrawn, perhaps moody. He wasn't—he was simply deep in thought.

That summer Ludwig had several visits with his Michael, Wilhelm, and the newlyweds August and Pauline. The conversations were serious about moving out of Volhynia. Most of the discussion was about going to Canada or the United States. Mexico or South America seemed to be too much of a trip to undertake. In May 1901 Ludwig, Michael and Wilhelm decided that they would leave the following year.

During the summer of 1901 Ludwig was visiting with his Jewish friend Karl Schulz, a Shinufka villager who owned a store and also conducted a small loan business. Ludwig told him about the plans to leave Volhynia and travel to Canada or the United States. Much to Ludwig's surprise Mr. Schulz announced he and his wife were leaving for Canada the following May. He asked if Ludwig had put in for tickets and asked if they had passports. Ludwig said they did not have passports and had not thought of getting tickets ahead of the travel dates. Mr. Schulz said that they could travel under the passport of him and his wife. He also said that there was plenty of time for tickets, which could be obtained from an agent in Rovno. He suggested that they meet again soon, and Ludwig was to have a list of everyone traveling. Ludwig asked him what his fee would be for arranging the ticket purchase. Mr. Schulz said that he would not charge them anything. This was an opportunity for him to pay back to Ludwig for all the good deeds he had done for the villagers who held Ludwig in high regard for his willingness to help people in need. He would gladly help.

The agent in Rovno would travel to Warsaw when he had a large enough list of tickets to buy to make the trip worthwhile. Along with the tickets, the agent would obtain a one year pass on the CPR railroad so people could explore and travel wherever they liked without having to worry about tickets. The agent would also arrange for help along the way if a need arose. He would also assign them a name and a town of someone they were to meet when they arrived. These people would help them find relatives and other Germans in the area.

The ticket purchase process would be a long procedure and require two or three trips to Rovno by Mr. Schulz. If Ludwig wanted to accompany him on one or more of the trips, he was welcome. Ludwig said that he would gladly go with him if it could be arranged with his busy life. They decided to keep in close touch and advise each other of anything new regarding their departure. Ludwig was suddenly realizing that it was complicated to make this long journey. He felt overwhelmed and at the same time relieved that he had made the acquaintance of Karl Schulz.

There was much excitement in both the Jess and Rode families. There was also fear—mostly among the women. The men had not shared as much as they should have, and that caused the women to question the reason for the move. The men had not told the women much about the letters that came back from people who had emigrated in the past years. Most of those people had successfully found work, mostly with established farmers. They all seemed glad that they had moved, and kept urging others, saying there was room for more people willing to work. Michael and Wilhelm expressed surprise at the number of people from their respective villages that had migrated. Michael encouraged Ludwig, who had been the leader all the time, and now Michael was getting excited about moving. The men realized they needed to share with the women all the details they knew.

Among the conversations Ludwig advised that there was going to be another passenger on the ship—Julianna was pregnant and expecting near year end. There was a lot of good news—in fact all was going well, except the crops. Yields were down and it was a struggle to produce enough for their own use, much less for barter. The farm animals, their main source of extra income were faring well.

Pauline gave birth to Emily on Christmas day 1901 in the village of Shinufka, so it was not until the middle of January that the rest of the family heard the news, since snow and cold prevented much travel. Wilhelm and Michael were very proud, but realized they would have to make provisions for traveling with a baby. Michael had been through several moves and was considered quite experienced.[5] Wilhelm had one long-distance moving experience and was willing to share that.

In early March Ludwig stopped to visit with Karl Schulz. He asked if they had their passports. Ludwig expressed surprise—they did not have them. Mr. Schulz reiterated that they could travel under his passport, which would be accepted at the various check points. Ludwig asked the question that he dreaded—what would he charge for using his passport. Mr. Schulz reminded Ludwig that there would be no charge. Ludwig thanked him several times and left feeling a weight was lifted off his shoulders.

They were all beginning to feel the reality of moving, busy selling what could not be taken. Michael tried to convince his family that he could take his silage grinder, but they had a hard time thinking he was serious. Finally they insisted that the two huge iron wheels were too big and too heavy to move. Eventually he said that he would sell it, as there were several people interested in it.

The planning was getting very intense, and Ludwig involved Julius who was nine and tall for his age. He had him help make boxes to put their precious items in for the trip. Julius was getting very excited about the trip and jumped at the chance to help whenever anyone asked. Emil was five and wanted to be involved, so small jobs were saved for him. Julianna was very pleased that her father and Caroline were going to be moving with them, as well as her brothers Charles and August along with Pauline and Emily. After hearing that all of her family was leaving, Julianna felt happy.

Ludwig with Karl Schulz made arrangements for two teams and wagons to transport the families to Kostopol, a distance of about 40 miles. There they would board a train for Gdansk, Poland with a change of trains in Warsaw. In Gdansk they would board a boat which would travel from the Baltic Sea between Denmark and Sweden into the North Sea, then continue on to Hull, England. They would take a

---

5 In later years Emily talked constantly with her mother Pauline about the family history. When Emily was in her late eighties, it was the vast information in her head that helped answer many questions. What she said turned out to be true, as records were discovered. Without her having provided vital information, many gaps in the family history would still exist.

train from there to Liverpool and wait to board their trans-Atlantic ship.

Mr. Schulz made the final trip to Rovno to get the tickets and all the necessary paper work, but he came back with bad news. Michael, his wife Julia, and his son Heinrich could not get tickets for the same ship. They were to leave several days earlier and would cross the Atlantic on the SS Sardinian. This was a huge disappointment for everyone. It could have been much more complicated, but fortunately Mr. Schulz had secured those three tickets and arranged for them to travel under the passport of someone in a nearby village.

All was taken care of, but for another wagon to take Michael, Julia and Heinrich to Kostopol three days earlier. Michael quickly arranged for Julia's son Johann to take them. Then as soon as he returned to the village he would take the large group to the train station.

The Wunniks were not moving with the Jess/Rode families. They did want to emigrate, but expected to move in the near future. Anna and Johann Wunnik were not thinking about emigrating. They were getting by where they were, with Johann able to provide for their growing family, though his older brothers were definitely wanting to move. They had heard from families in Manitoba that there were opportunities for jobs and land. They hoped to follow to near where the Jess/Rode families would settle.

Johann decided to leave a day earlier to allow for his return to pack up the large group and take another trip to Kostopol. Michael, Julia and Heinrich boarded the wagon and quietly left the village very early, having said the necessary good-byes the night before.

Johann returned from the Kostopol trip and reported all went well. He saw them off on the train to Warsaw and now he was ready for the next trip.

The emotions varied from anxiety to sadness to great excitement. The older members of the group knew that they would never see some of the villagers again, though they felt that eventually they would see their relatives who were planning to move in the next few years. There were no community goodbye parties—the villagers knew from past experience that the parties were too sad. People quietly said their good-byes, and some of them from experience did it weeks ahead of the departure.

Ludwig, the group's appointed leader, was very busy working out last minute problems, issues, schedules and anything else that someone felt he could handle. He met several times with Karl Schulz who was confident that there would be no problem with his newly acquired relatives. He seemed to know how the processing went at each of the passage points. Most of the Jess-Rode adults were concerned about the passport issue. Ludwig was not. His many visits with Mr. Schulz had convinced him that it would not be a problem. Ludwig tried to calm the rest of the travelers but finally gave up, realizing that some people would worry no matter what. Mr. Shultz, traveling with only his wife, was really looking forward to the trip—and he would enjoy the company of familiar faces. Ludwig decided to give Julius his job a little early—he was to watch Emil and Heinrich so that they did not fall overboard when they were traveling on the big ocean, as well as on a smaller boat on the Baltic and North Sea. Ludwig talked a lot to him about it, and at age nine Julius was feeling that he had a very important job.

Johann would drive one team and wagon and Ludwig's neighbor Albert Rauch, who had bought Ludwig's team and wagons, would use those to take them to Kostopol.

Ludwig wisely sought the experience of Mr. Schulz and made sure that he was in full agreement with any decision Ludwig made. They decided to leave Shinufka the middle of the morning on the appointed day. He felt the extra rest would be needed for everyone, and the timing would put them close to the one train a day leaving Kostopol.

Mid-morning the 30th of May, 1902 the wagons started to roll. There was waving of arms and loud good-byes as the wagons with the Schulzes and fifteen in the Jess-Rode family pulled out of the village of Shinufka.[6]

---

6 [7] Wilhelm, Caroline, Julius Richard, Fred, William, Christine and Charles
　[3] August & Pauline, Emily
　[5] Ludwig, Julianna, Julius, Emil & Heinrich
　15 emigrating

CHAPTER 9

— 1902 —

Fourth Move: Emigration

The emigrants made good distance that first day. They would camp out and get an early start the next morning. Everyone in camp that night was very quiet. The mood was gloomy and there was more than a few teary eyes. Julianna was very upset—it was much more difficult to leave than she had thought. Ludwig tried to cheer them up as they ate, and finally realized each one would have to work it through their own process. By this time tomorrow night they would be close to Kostopol.

Karl Schultz was a fine man to have on a trip. He not only was right there to help whenever the need arose, he also knew the road very well, having traveled it many more times than Ludwig had realized. Mr. Schulz's wife Emilie was getting along well with Julianna. They never ran out of something to talk about. All this pleased Ludwig, as he had asked them to ride in his wagon though he did it with some reservation. He felt he did not know Mr. Schulz that well, but then he realized it was one of the better moves he made in placing people in the wagons.

The trip put them in Kostopol several hours ahead of the train's departure. They unloaded at the train depot and chatted with Johann and Albert till it was time for them to return to Shinufka. Again it was a round of saying goodbye, and for Julianna it was a much better experience than leaving Shinufka. Ludwig thanked Johann several times, making sure that he left him with a positive feeling. They departed saying it may be a long time before they would meet again. Ludwig was glad that from now on they would be traveling on other modes of transportation. He would simply be a traveler, which would be hard enough, but he no longer would have to be in charge.

They boarded the train early afternoon on May 31st. The train was slow and made numerous stops and there would be a long layover in Warsaw waiting for the train to Gdansk. They had food which each family had prepared, and when they got to Warsaw they bought drinks. For most of them this was their first train ride. Julius was fascinated. Anything mechanical captured his interest and he did all the looking he could while the train was running. Emil was close behind him, so he had to watch that Emil did not take a wrong step. He was already getting into protecting his two younger brothers.

In Warsaw people looked at them waiting in the station. It was more than a look—it was a quick stare. Julianna was bothered, but understood they were in an area they had not been before. She and her step-mother Caroline talked about the experiences that were rapidly unfolding. Caroline had not wanted to move—she had cousins in Volhynia whom she had only seen a few times, but felt she was leaving them. Wilhelm spent a lot of time convincing her it was the right thing to do.

They were not allowed much baggage. Their few valuables and documents were held close, and it was Julianna that took care of their family's papers. Their belongings fit in some small trunks and boxes that Ludwig had built with Julius's help. Everyone was settling into the traveling routine. The schedule that Ludwig had set was turning out to be very realistic. The trip to Gdansk would be long enough, but after crossing the Atlantic, they would have a train trip four times as long.

Wilhelm's four sons were the most animated, discussing the experience. They talked about what they would do when they reached their destination. Young and full of energy, they let their imaginations run wild, which helped sustain them on the long trip to their new world.

They talked about the boat ride from Gdansk to Hull. Wilhelm thought the boat ride of several days would be good preparation for their trip across the Atlantic. He said it would be a long trip and could be rough at times. He did not say out loud that he was scared of the trip across the Atlantic. He hoped he would not get rubber legs as they were boarding the ship. That would be a huge embarrassment for him, especially if he showed weakness in front of his family. He was strong and he knew that all would be well, as the enthusiasm about this being "the big part of the trip" would surround the group.

Mr. Schulz was able to describe the type of boat they would be on for the next leg of the trip. That was helpful information for purchasing food supplies. It would be small and cramped, probably filled to the maximum, and take a few days. Their traveling in Poland and Volhynia was focused, not the free feeling to take in the changing landscape as they moved from one place to another. If they did allow their minds to wander, they would look at the land as the opportunity it could provide whoever ended up owning it. Mr. Schulz had a good idea of what they would be seeing. The first part of the trip would be close enough to the shore so they would be able to view parts of Denmark and Sweden. As soon as they boarded the boat and it pulled away from the dock everything would be new.

Food preparations had been made for the trip. Mr. Schulz did a final check with those carrying the tickets. Some of the group had to adjust their ages to fit in with Mr. Schulz and his wife, for they were going under the pretense that they were all his relatives. After Mr. Schulz was satisfied that everything was in order, they boarded the boat for the next leg of their trip.

The boat was small and grimy. Dirt was everywhere, and an embarrassed Mr. Schulz said that he would do what he could to help get their area cleaned up. The vessel was moved by a very noisy engine spewing smoke that was not all directed away from the passengers. These travel pioneers felt that it was just that way, and did not complain. Now they are on the way and would soon be sailing on the North Sea, headed for England. The world was opening up to all of them. Ludwig was the most excited and emotional. It was he who had started dreaming about this day years ago. He had wanted to move to another country years before he told anyone about it. Now it was happening and what he thought would be a grueling trip was turning out to be enjoyable. He hoped that this move would turn out to be the right move not only for him, but for his three sons. He was concerned about them, and he did all he could, considering their youth, to teach them things he felt would be good life skills.

Ludwig talked to his father-in-law Wilhelm about the future. He said he wanted to find some good productive farm land. As soon as he could after they reached their destination, he would start looking for work. He told Wilhelm he would do any kind of work, so he could save up some money, but would continue to look at farm land or any opportunity that would eventually get him and his family on the land. He appreciated having an in-depth discussion with his father-in-law, and suggested that they chat again during the trip.

Wilhelm was concerned what his sons, full of energy, would do on this small boat. He reckoned they would learn to deal with it, for there were no other options.

They sailed past the north shore of Germany, past Denmark and Sweden. Their direction would change after they passed Gothenburg, Sweden and turned out into the North Sea. The boat went southwesterly into the North Sea and the western side of Denmark faded away. They were on the open sea and headed for Hull.

The passengers gave out a yell when they saw England. They were ready to get off the boat. The trip had been tiring as well as educational. Julius had done a good job of taking care of Emil and Heinrich. He proudly held onto them as the boat pulled into the harbor. It seemed to the passengers that it took forever for the boat to get tied to the dock so they could unload. Though they were all anxious to get off, they still faced a longer ocean trip, but did not seem to mind. Even though it might be a tough trip, their goal of being in a new country would be that much nearer.

They all left the boat together and Mr. Schulz checked back to see that they were all behind him. He had advised them well, for they all fell in to place. They went through the Hull checkpoint and were told where and when they would catch the train for Liverpool. The train scheduled for noon departure would not be leaving due to mechanical problems. The next train would leave in the morning. They would camp out in a huge building used for processing travelers. Baby Emily would have to be cared for, and they would have to find some benches, tables or anything that would let them prepare a couple of meals. They did find enough to make do for several hours. Ludwig was especially helpful to Julianna. He was concerned about the stress of the trip on her condition, so she and Ludwig finally decided to tell the group that she was expecting another baby in November or December. This was a surprise to the group, and now everyone was wanting to help. This changed the tone of the group and a calm settled over all of them. They knew they would get through the trip, and Julianna felt better that she had let them all know. They got through the night and prepared to board the train for the trip to Liverpool, 125 miles away on the other side of England.

When all the passengers had boarded and the steam whistle sounded, Ludwig said loud enough for his family to hear, "We are getting closer." It was a happy moment for him and probably no one felt it like he did, having dreamed a long time about moving to another country. Ludwig sat with Wilhelm and talked about settling down and having a good productive farm. Wilhelm was now 62. He said he wanted to take time to find one acceptable place and stay there for the rest of his life. They both talked about how they were glad they finally had made the move even though they knew that there would be some tough times ahead of them. Wilhelm said he was concerned that his granddaughter Emily would stay healthy during this trip. She had some minor stomach trouble, but appeared to be okay. She was his first grandchild and he was understandably concerned. Ludwig joked that he was bringing along another person but was not being charged for it. He had a good relationship with Wilhelm and he did what he could to keep it that way.

The train was comfortable, and with the family seated close together it was easy to visit and get to food when it was wanted. The view was enjoyable and they compared it to the terrain back home. Ludwig commented that his heart was and would always be in Bielsko where he was born. He enjoyed all their other homes and he learned a lot in each place, but he hoped to find land similar to what his father had farmed in Bielsko. By winter time he would have four children, a big incentive for him to find the right place.

Mr. Schulz did not say much about what he was going to do when he reached his destination. Most of his conversation was concern for the group and advising them what to expect next. Ludwig was very happy with the leadership that Mr. Schulz provided. He obviously had traveled some.

The train lumbered along and made several stops along the way. It was mid-afternoon when they approached Liverpool. All of a sudden they would be in the midst of many people with the same goal as theirs. They finally reached the station. It was time to gather up all their belongings and leave the train. They were not scheduled to board till afternoon the next day. They would have to find a place to park after Mr. Schulz had checked the emigration office to see that everything was in order for them to board.

They settled again as they had in Hull. They were early enough to claim a corner in a big hall. Mr. Schulz met with them after they got settled down. He thought the trip had gone well, but he warned them that the Atlantic waters could get very rough and there might be some seasickness. He did not want to scare them, just warn them so they would not be surprised. He also said to them, "We've come this far. Now you can choose to go either to America or Canada." They shrugged their shoulders and chatted briefly among themselves. Caroline asked Mr. Schulz where he was going. He said he was going to Canada. They had talked among themselves about Canada, so Ludwig spoke up and said "we're going to Canada too." It was a moot conversation because they were going to meet Michael, Julia and Heinrich in Winkler. The conversations went late into the night but finally they were all able to sleep for a few hours.

On June 10 they were ready to board the SS Lake Champlain. The dock was a mass of people hours before, milling about, adjusting their possessions. Ludwig noticed that as boarding time came closer, most people's expressions changed. There was joy and apprehension on the docks. It was the first ocean crossing for most of the people so apprehension was understandable. Mr. Schulz handed out boarding passes for each family. He arranged their boarding order so they would fit in with him and his wife as a family. The Jess/Rode families waited for his signal.

Boarding was a very slow process, but Ludwig wondered why everyone was crowding onto the gangplank. As long as they were in line, the ship was not going to leave without them. After they passed the man accepting their passes, they breathed a big sigh of relief, even though Mr. Schulz had assured them that there would be no problem. They were guided to the lower part of the ship to a giant room whose sides were lined with twin bunks. Most of the center was taken up by tables for eating meals. A few bunks were placed perpendicular to the sides of the ship—difficult to sleep in because the movement of the ship would roll the person trying to sleep unlike the other bunks that moved with the ship. Luckily their spot was near the center of the boat, so they would feel less movement if the weather got rough. Mr. Schulz told them the next move would be to start hanging sheets or blankets to provide separation from other families. In a couple of hours the whole lower level was divided up into rooms. Most "rooms" shared a porthole, though some had their own.

The SS Lake Champlain was large: 446 feet long and 52 feet wide, a third longer than a football field. Gross weight 7,392 tons, four masts, twin steam engines capable of 13 knots, and one funnel, the smoke stack large enough to handle all the engine exhaust and tall enough to keep it from falling on the deck.

The ship's accommodations included first cabin, second cabin, as well as steerage where the Jess/Rode family was settled. Mr. Schulz, age 60 on the manifest, and his wife Emilie, 30, also traveled in steerage. This ship was the first merchant ship to be fitted with permanent wireless telegraphy apparatus, though the emigrants from Volhynia probably were not aware of that up-to-date luxury.

As the ship was leaving port many of the passengers were on deck to watch, while lucky third class passengers claimed a port hole. It was exciting to be on the last half of their journey, though for the next 8 to

10 days they would only see water. As they watched the harbor disappear, sadness came with thoughts of never again seeing many friends and some family. Several hours out, the ship slowly turned south into St. George's Channel. Julius was having the time of his life wanting to explore all the nooks and crannies, but he kept true to his promise and took good care of his brother Emil. Julius kept going, and sometimes Emil had a hard time keeping up with him, but he always saw to it that Emil was close enough to be in no danger.

During the night the ship left St. George's Channel and headed out to the open sea. Early the first morning out, anyone on deck would be having their last glimpse of what would become for them foreign soil. That first morning was devoted to more settling in and getting acquainted, especially for the mothers.

Ludwig was concerned about his father, his father's wife, and brother Heinrich. It happened so quickly that they could not travel with the group. His big hope was that they would have a trip with no problems. He thought of the people back in Shinufka, but there was no turning back. He promised himself he would look ahead and not get caught up in the past.

By 1870 most sail ships had been replaced with steam engine ships. Crossing from Liverpool to Quebec had taken from a month or even six weeks, some of the smaller sail passenger ships taking up to 100 days. Under sails, there was much sea sickness for the passengers in steerage. Diseases like cholera and typhus frequently reached epidemic proportions as infection spread throughout the confined decks, and there were frequent deaths among the newborn and young children. Many sad sea burials took place and the ship's crew made small coffins for deceased children. The SS Lake Champlain was a giant step up, and by then many laws had been put in place to protect the passenger and to allow for proper food and food preservation. The Jess/Rode group had brought dried and smoked food to supplement what was available.

The steam ships cut the travel time so much that even if someone did get sick half way into the trip, they knew they would soon be in port. Even with the modern, large ship the Jess/Rode group still had to contend with sea sickness, which most of them did experience it some-

SS Lake Champlain. Jess/Rode Family crossed Atlantic in ten days.

time during the trip. Pregnant Julianna had her share of mild sickness due to her condition. She was experienced, having had four children, so she felt confident that she would not run into serious illness during the trip. Many emigrant ships experienced births and deaths. When a girl was born there was pressure from the Captain to give the child the ship's name, considered a high honor by the Captain. Depending on the name of the ship it may not fit because of the length of the name or that the ship's name did not fit with a human being. Often the compromise would be to use the name the parents had picked out as the first name and use the ship's name as the middle name. Julianna was thankful her baby was not due until long after the ship would pull into the harbor, another decision she could avoid.

On the ship manifest for the SS Lake Champlain the following was listed:

Adults:	831	First Cabin:	33
Age 1–14:	237	Second Cabin:	52
Infants under age 1:	69	Steerage:	1102
Total passengers:	1137		

The SS Lake Champlain made six crossings in 1902: May, June, July, August, October and November. With these many trips by just one ship it is easy to see that from 1830 to 1930 nine million people could emigrate out of Europe. Hull, Liverpool, and other receiving and sending ports were in constant building and revising mode to accommodate the huge numbers of people that used them. Having trains ready to accept passengers after the ship unloaded and processed them was necessary to be able to get the passengers loaded and underway to take the strain of too many people in the port. Some people waited on the docks for as long as 10 days. At least a roof and food had to be available to accommodate them. Because of their location Hull and Liverpool were prominent ports and had very heavy emigrant use. On the return trip across the Atlantic, some of the emigrant ships would reconfigure the steerage section to haul cargo, delivering it to a port other than the one they left with emigrants onboard. They could unload at other ports as long as they would be ready to leave their port on time with emigrants ready to cross the ocean to fulfill their dreams.

It was not easy for the Jess/Rode family to adjust to living in steerage. The double bunks were so close, though the sheets and blankets provided some privacy. Ludwig saw it all as another opportunity. The first day out he started to get acquainted with those closest to him. He planned to meet three or four new families a day. He very soon learned that most of the Germans were going to Winnipeg. From there they would scatter across Canada, with a few settling across the border in the United States. He would discuss his findings each day with Wilhelm, and soon they understood where most people were going and what their aspirations were. Ludwig was learning about the productive farm land around the Winnipeg area. He also found out that there were many jobs available for people new to Canada.

He became much more optimistic about his future than he had even been. He kept meeting new people each day, and after a few days he was warmly greeted as he moved about the steerage area. One day he found it hard to move on to meet new families, as those he'd already met wanted to visit. One of those families was going to an area south of Winnipeg, to the town of Winkler. A brother had migrated there 10 years earlier, after years of suggesting his brother join them, he was now making the trip and was very excited about it, but they did not know much about the town. He was going to work for his brother on his farm. His plan was to buy some land as soon as he had a little money saved up. He and his brother would help each other, and he had big hopes they would both prosper.

Ludwig continued meeting with new people. Many like himself had yearned for years to leave the old country and move to another. He began to feel more at home with their venture, and after some encouragement his father-in-law began to move about. Ludwig soon learned that Wilhelm was meeting many people, with his talent as a Lay Minister. He spent most of the time having religious discussions. That was okay, as long as he wasn't overbearing or spending too much time with uninterested people.

Ludwig encouraged him to try to have discussions that would help them find homes when they reached the Winnipeg area. Julius followed his dad around and just listened. Sometimes the new friend would ask him a question that gave him a chance to say a few words, mostly about his job taking care of his younger brothers. Ludwig found out that most of the couples his age had families about the same size. These people were moving because of more opportunities for their children, for conditions had forced them to seek a better opportunity for themselves.

Five days out the crew informed them that they were half way to Quebec. Julianna commented that even though their quarters were very tight in steerage, she was surprised they were half way there already. When Ludwig was away meeting people Julianna met the women close to her area. She found a lot in common, as all near her were German. They had all lived in what is now present day Poland and most of them had moved to Volhynia as her family had.

Emil and Heinrich had experienced a lot seasickness, though Julius had escaped it. Their mother could only comfort them, as there was nothing available to relieve it. Heinrich seemed to roll with the punches, even though he was only two and a half. He was full of energy and was a vigorous explorer. He got along well with his two brothers and had more energy than the two of them together. He seemed to enjoy life more than anyone around him. His parents speculated on what he might do in life with all that energy. She calmed herself by thinking that it would not be long before they would be living where the children could run till they were tired out.

Ludwig met a family who had lived in a village a few miles out of Rovno, Volhynia. They were going to a relative who lived in Morden, a town south of Winnipeg and a few miles west of Winkler. Ben and Elsie Unger were migrating with their adult daughter Mathilda. Ludwig visited with them and soon began chatting with Mathilda. She was 20, had married in their village two years earlier, but six months after the wedding her husband went to a neighbor in their village to help castrate a strong and highly-spirited stallion. After many attempts they finally got him down. As they were working to get his legs tied together, the horse kicked loose, got on his feet, reared up and came down on all four feet. He spun around, pulled his left hind hoof forward and kicked hard, striking Mathilda's husband in the chest. Ludwig was very sympathetic and complimented her on how well she was holding up. He enjoyed meeting the three of them and said he would stop by again soon. Ludwig enjoyed meeting that young lady and he was anxious to return and visit with them again.

Ludwig and Wilhelm talked about where to settle. The agent had passed along to Karl Schulz the name of a German immigrant in Neche, North Dakota who helped guide new immigrants with no arrangements. Neche was a mile from the Canadian border, southeast of Winkler, and many Germans lived there. They decided that they had very good information from their new-found friends on the ship, maybe better information than the contact in Neche.

Ludwig, Julianna, Wilhelm and Caroline discussed what they had learned. Ludwig was in favor of going to Winkler and finding a place to settle, so he could start to look for work. Wilhelm agreed that they should go to Winkler. Caroline and Julianna both liked the fact that it would put them closer to finding a permanent home. They decided in the meeting that Ludwig would go back to the people going to Winkler and ask if they could follow them to the town. They would not visit the contact in Neche, confident that they were on the right course. Karl Schulz told them that he was going to stay in Winnipeg. He had no advice to give them and he wished the very best for them. They appreciated all that he had done for them and after they left the train in Winnipeg that would probably be the last time they would see him.

As the ship got closer, they were very tired, but it was a good tired. August and Pauline kept close to themselves tending baby Emily. They were brought current on all that Ludwig had been discovering about their future in Canada. Wilhelm visited with them constantly and enjoyed seeing his grandchild being taken care of. Julianna and the family felt good because they had a plan. Ludwig had met so many people and it was expected by many of those people that he stop by each day and at least say good morning. He typically spent time with them and he enjoyed it, as it gave him something positive to do each day. He did hurry some of those conversations as he got closer to the Ben Unger family. He liked to hurry the conversation with Ben and his wife so he could visit with Mathilda. She enjoyed the attention, though the conversations were in the presence of her parents. As he returned to his space that day he asked people if they had been seasick. He was surprised to find that most people had been, and about half had other illnesses—flu, headaches, dizziness, and aching legs from lack of exercise were the common complaints. There was not any outbreak of terrible diseases like typhoid, cholera and dysentery.

Ludwig enjoyed coming up with ideas so he could have a common subject to discuss with the people. Wilhelm's sons did not enjoy the trip. They knew they had ten days in cramped quarters and most of the time they tried to amuse themselves and each other with chatter and some games that they had played growing up. Wilhelm did what he could to placate them. He knew it would be tough on young boys. Julius and Julius Richard (Dick) Rode managed to spend some time together, even though Julius was taking care of Emil. Wilhelm felt that, with the plans they had made, his boys would soon have all the room they would need to run. Even he was a bit giddy about the possibility of getting settled soon. He wanted to find one place and settle down. He knew that his daughter and Ludwig might want to keep searching till they found their dream location. He also felt that August and Pauline with baby Emily would follow Ludwig if he chose to move on. As a deeply religious man he seemed able to deal with challenges that came his way: he had trust, and it usually kept him happy and at peace.

The word was being passed through the ship that land would soon be sighted. When Julius heard that, he stayed at a porthole as he wanted to be the first of the family to see it. Julius watched for several hours, letting out a loud shout when he saw land. A good feeling went through the group and now they knew that they would soon end this leg of the journey. In a few hours they would pass through the Strait of Belle Isle as they entered the Gulf of Saint Lawrence. On the right side was Newfoundland, the fourth largest island in Canada, rich in history since Leif Eriksson's visit in the 11th century. They would cruise beside this Province for about 50 miles then sail beside the Province of Quebec to Quebec City. The portholes were all crowded as immigrants wanted to view their new country.[7]

Ludwig watched through the portholes, but it was more important to him that he visit with his new friends, gathering needed information. He visited again with the Ben Unger family and they talked about their eventual living in the Winkler-Morden area. Mathilda spoke to Ludwig about her desire to help her parents get settled. She was young with no particular aspirations. She enjoyed visiting with Ludwig as they had shared stories about each of their family's deaths.

About 200 miles from Quebec, time seemed to slow down as the ship was slowing down. Their only interest was to get to port and disembark. The whole family was anxious. Even Ludwig, who was always calm and jovial, was shouting orders to his family about leaving the ship. It was his way of dealing with the anxiety, and the rest of the family seemed to know it.

Mid-afternoon on June 20, 1902, after 10 days at sea, the ship's captain started to position the SS Lake Champlain to dock. The Jess/Rode family was ready to leave the ship and touch the soil of their new country.

---

7   The next day they sailed by the island of Anticosti. The island is sometimes called the "Cemetery of the Gulf," due to more than 400 shipwrecks off its coasts. It sounds like a lot of shipwrecks and if we consider they may have taken place over a 200 year period or longer, the number becomes understandable. Anticosti Island is 3,047 square miles in size and is Canada's 20th largest island.

They were moved to a large immigration hall where they spent the night. Processing began early the next morning, then they immediately boarded the Canadian Pacific Railroad for Winnipeg, Manitoba. They were impressed with the room in the train, the fresh air, and all of the landscape they wanted.

Though the trains in 1902 could travel up to 40 miles per hour, this one traveled only about 25, so it would take three days to Winnipeg, 1550 miles. No one seemed to mind. Pauline was holding up well taking care of Emily.[8]

August and Pauline had $7 dollars when they arrived in Winnipeg. That figure was passed on to Victor several times by Rode relatives. Ludwig had sold everything they owned in Volhynia (as all emigrants did)- which allowed them to obtain a place to settle. Ludwig, Wilhelm and Mr. Schulz all agreed that the CPR railroad might be a place to seek employment. Ludwig decided that would be the first place to go. As customers of the railroad, they knew there were many trainloads of immigrants arriving weekly in Winnipeg. The more they discussed it, the more excited Ludwig became. They were fortunate in choosing the right time to arrive in Canada. They would have the summer to get situated and adequate time to prepare for the Canadian winter.

A couple hours out of Winnipeg, Ludwig got up to move around, and a conductor bumped into him. The conductor excused himself in German—Ludwig had another friend. He responded to the conductor's question about where they were headed. Ludwig was surprised to hear that there was a railroad that went south from Winnipeg through Winkler on its way to Manitou.[9] Now Ludwig was excited to board the train for Winkler. The Conductor was going from car to car announcing the next stop: Winnipeg. Everyone in the Jess/Rode group was on their

---

8 Emily (Victor's first cousin one generation removed) would grow up in Saskatchewan on her father's homestead. After two marriages, nine children and the death of both husbands, she lived in Winnipeg. Her condo in a high rise, where she died September 21, 2001, three months short of her 100th birthday, was not too far from the railroad station where she arrived in 1902. She was a wonderful lady who talked with her mother Pauline about the family. She provided information about the Jess and Rode families that Victor still would not have otherwise, even after several decades of research. It was fortunate that Victor met her and was able to spend time with her during several visits.

9 The line from Winnipeg to Manitou was put in operation December 10, 1882, according to "A History of Winkler" June 1973 by Frank Brown.

feet, laughing, talking, looking at the Manitoba scenery and trying to contain their excitement. They had been traveling since May 30th, now early evening June 23rd would pull into the train station at Winnipeg. They still had another leg of the trip, but they didn't mind as they had easily made it to Winnipeg. The train inched into the station and a tired bunch of immigrants got off. Ludwig found out the next train for Winkler was 9:00 the next morning. They had to find a place to spend the night. With German signs offering lodging, they soon were able to settle in and get back to the station to leave for Winkler. Ludwig had said goodbye to Karl Schulz while still on the train. He would be home by now, as someone was there to meet him. It was a bittersweet moment as they parted on the station platform. That was the last time they saw each other.

Ludwig was surprised at the number of familiar faces on the platform that morning. The Unger family—Ben, Emilia and Mathilda—were bound for Morden. The two families spoke briefly and exchanged "hope to see you soon" greetings. Some families were going to Neche, North Dakota, apparently to meet a pre-designated contact that would help them get settled. All looked very tired but relaxed as they waited for the train to arrive. Ludwig made sure he greeted all of them—as he had told Wilhelm he would be seeing these people as time goes by. Wilhelm's sons were the happiest of all. While frustrated with the conditions on the ship, they now could see the wide open spaces and they knew it was all worth it.

The train pulled into the station and the immigrant passengers casually boarded, excited knowing that in a few hours they would be at their long-sought destination. This serious group knew that the real task of starting over would soon begin.

The loud steam whistle sounded as the train slowly pulled out of the station. Pauline seated across from August was comforting baby Emily. What could they have been thinking as they rode across that rich soil of the Red River Valley? Julianna, 32 years old, the mother of three sons, pregnant now, with more children to arrive. Her mind was probably occupied with what was going on at the moment. Julius was full of energy, busy exploring the railroad car. Emil and Heinrich were close behind trying to keep up. Ludwig did not restrict the boys, knowing it would be a short trip. Wilhelm and Caroline were very tired and so anxious to settle. Knowing they still had a big job ahead of them when they reached Winkler.

As Winkler came in sight the immigrants began to stand up and assemble their belongings. The local people were amused by their action, though some of them must have done the same thing years earlier. As the train pulled into the Winkler station there was a variety of expressions as The Jess/Rode family prepared to exit the railroad car. There were shouts, tears, laughter. Julianna walked down the steps nursing a lump in her throat—a mixture of emotions. It would take time for her to relax in the new surroundings. The sun was hot June 24th, so they gathered in the shade of the depot with all their belongings.

Feeling a bit stunned and unsure of what to do, their eyes followed the train as it gathered speed and disappeared into the distance. Wilhelm offered a brief prayer of thanks for their safe journey. He knew that their strong faith would be tested many times as they made their way into the new country.

Ludwig continued watching in that direction and wondered where that train was going. Maybe soon he would be working for the railroad. He could only wonder for now, and that dream seemed to fill a void as he stared off into the west. Had they really traveled all these thousands of miles? Of course they had, and he had to jolt himself back to reality and realize that they would not have to worry about traveling each morning as they had for the past 26 days. What an enormous task they had undertaken. He knew he would be thinking about this almost impossible dream for the rest of his life.

For now he was in the real world and that there was a lot that needed to be done. He turned around and everyone was looking at him. Speaking almost in a whisper he said, "Let's go."

They started walking toward what they assumed was the center of town. A loud yell with a familiar ring came from their right side. Yes—Michael, Julia, and Heinrich were in town. Their calculation was correct about the day and train they would be on. The rest of the day was spent catching up and finally getting comfortable for the night.

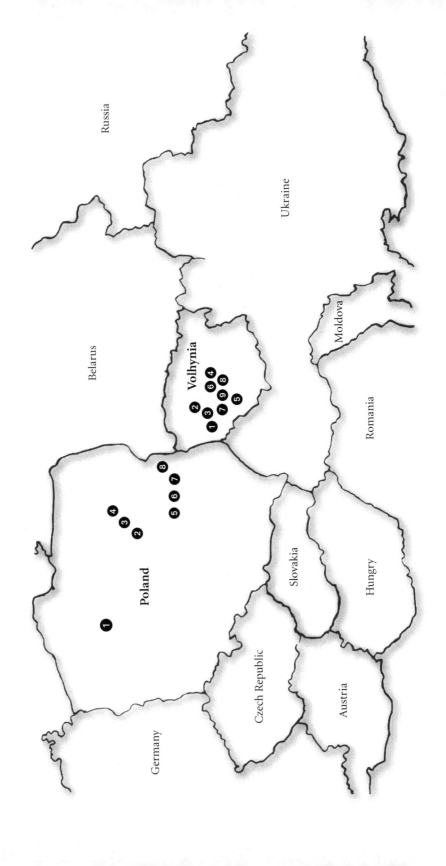

Jess/Rode Polish Volhynian Movement

Poland

1 Stara Rzeka, Kujawsko-Pomorskie
Wilhelm Rode, b. 06-12-1839

2 Warsaw

3 Pultusk
Wilhelm Rode
Justyna Gering, m. 10-30-1866

4 Chmielewo
Julianna, b. 01-18-1870

5 Bielsko
Michael Jess
Krystyna Riske, m. 01-07-1864
Anna Julia, b. 03-07-1866
Ludwig Jess, b. 12-30-1868
Rosalia, b. 01-17-1865
Rosalia, d. 03-07-1865

6 Lublin

7 Chelm

8 Arrived
Karolinow, 10-11-1878
Pauline Jess, b. 07-28-1880
Eva Jess, b. 07-28-1880
Eva Jess, d. 07-28-1880

Volhynia

1 Torczyn

2 Rozyszcze
Ludwig Jess, m. 11-12-1891
Julianna Rode

3 Arrived
Sablotche, 06-26-1881
Heinrich Jess, b. 04-04-1883
Krystyna Jess, d. 04-04-1883

4 Rovno

5 Dubno

6 Iwanoka
Johann Wonnek
Anna Julia Jess, m. 04-22-1892
Michael Jess
Julia Kuehn, m. 04-22-1892

7 Arrived
Julianowka, 08-30-1888

8 Shinufka
Julius Jess, b. 01-01-1893
Heinrich Jess, b. 04-02-1900
Emily Rode, b. 12-25-1901

9 Gonczarycha
Emil, b. 11-10-1897

CHAPTER 10

— 1902 —

Canadian Life

Julius started school in the fall of 1902. The first day the teacher asked each student their name and she wrote it on the blackboard. When she got to Julius, he knew what she wanted and he responded. She wrote down "Gess" and asked Julius if that was correct. Without knowing what she said he nodded yes. Julius laughed as he repeated the event to his family. Many documents show that the spelling did not all change to Gess immediately. The variations include Gesse, Jas, Jess, Jesse, Jehs, Jeske, Jeschke. Julius had to adjust to more than learning English, along with many of his classmates who came from the same part of Russia. Students seemed to forget what they themselves had looked like when they first arrived. Now they questioned his manner, his speech, and even what he wore. Though they should have been sympathetic, they were not. One German boy a year older, a foot taller, and 30 pounds heavier stood on the side watching all this. Julius noticed a slight smirk on his face. Whenever a couple of boys approached Julius to tease him, Willie was standing on the side watching, the smirk always there. It became very worrisome and a lot of energy went into thinking about what to do.

By November Julius was accepted by some of the boys, though there remained a small group whose mission seemed to be to make his life miserable. Julius realized that Willie was the leader. This small group was relentless—never getting physical, just keeping the pressure on. One cold afternoon in the second week of November, Julius was casually walking home. The path reminded him of Shinufka, bringing him good feelings until he noticed Willie way ahead blocking the path. He was far enough ahead to collect his thoughts. When Willie would not let him by and started to move toward him, Julius leaned forward putting his weight on his left foot. Then he threw his body back and swung his right leg forward. A swift kick with a Volhynian work boot caught the bully in his groin. He started to double over as Julius was completing a 360 degree pivot. That boot smashed into the left side of Willie's face. He lay there in agony while Julius quietly walked home, though he worried about going to school the next day.

Willie had several versions of how he got his black eye, but the word quickly spread the next morning about the truth of what had happened on the path. Much to his surprise, life for Julius was much better from then on. He was acknowledged and respected. His life in Winkler could not have been better.

November 26, 1902 a baby girl was welcomed into Ludwig and Julianna's home. There had been a lot of discussion about what to name their first girl. Julianna had her favorites and Ludwig had only one. In the end Ludwig's suggestion of Mathilda won out.

Ludwig did get a job with the Canadian Pacific Railroad a few days after they arrived. He was on a crew that checked and repaired track. Ludwig enjoyed the work and he made good use of his ability to make tools do what he wanted. Contentment was what he felt, and he knew he had made the right decision leaving Volhynia. He was 34 years old, and he had a job so he could provide for his wife, three sons and daughter. His father-in-law Wilhelm was settled and working for the municipality of Winkler six half days a week, with promise of work through the winter.

The families were told by knowledgeable neighbors that the winters would be tougher than in Volhynia, though Winkler was very close to the same latitude. Their life experiences guided their preparation in case that rough winter appeared.

Ludwig was happy that his father Michael, Julia, and brother Heinrich were in town with them. They would get together as often as time allowed. Michael and Julia liked to go to the German Lutheran Church in town. It reminded them of Volhynia, with the German language spoken.

August, Pauline and baby Emily settled into a home close to Wilhelm. August spent two weeks looking for work and found it with a Mennonite farmer who had come to visit August and asked if he would consider working for him, even though he was Mennonite. August was delighted and said he thought a Lutheran would get along well with a Mennonite. Mr. Jans was a successful farmer who bought his first piece of land a mile west of Winkler in the late 1880s. The two men got along well until one night they began to discuss children. Mr. Jans had 11 children including two sets of twins. The oldest was only 10. August detected dissatisfaction in Mr. Jans about some comment he made regarding large families, but the working relationship was long term. That first summer August was paid $100. Pauline also worked for the family and was paid $25.

Emil started school the fall of '03 and was a friend of everyone he met. At such a young age it was easy for him to pick up English. Julius guided and watched over him. Together they had covered every inch of Winkler during the summer, but now it was learning time. With a three year old brother and a baby sister their lives were full.

Bertha was born February 10, 1904. Oral family history says that one day she was in a baby basket in an entry room of the house. There were some chickens in the room excited and made a lot of noise. Baby Bertha became very excited, rose up in the crib, and fell back and died. The family felt it was the excitement that killed her. Perhaps it was sudden infant death syndrome. Extensive research has produced neither a birth nor a death certificate.

Julius now ten, walked tall. He moved quietly, always deep in thought. Some called him moody but he was not—his mind was engaged wondering, worrying and wishing. He had put in his time as the new German kid. Now he enjoyed school as his English improved. He dreamed of being a fixer who could do anything with his tools. He admired his father more every time he watched him work.

At the railroad Ludwig had to be a master with tools. One Saturday Ludwig let Julius go with him and a small crew to repair some track on the edge of Winkler. It was a cool dry day that reminded him of Shinufka, though Shinufka did not have access to other villages like Winkler had because of the railroad. Julius thought the train could take them to many faraway places. He was fascinated as he watched from a safe distance as the crew was replacing a length of track. To him the track looked okay and later Julius asked his father why they had to replace it. He liked anything mechanical and now he was developing a curiosity about trains. Often he went to the tracks when the train was scheduled to arrive, and he would watch and listen. He could never get enough of the sounds of the train, so he started taking Emil and four year old Heinrich to watch. He was surprised at the excitement shown by Heinrich who asked all kind of questions. He could not understand why Julius wouldn't take him for a train ride. Julius said it may be possible to take a train ride. He asked his father and they decided to ride to Winnipeg and back on his CPR employee pass. Heinrich was excited, as if he had never ridden a train before.

One spring Saturday the family decided it was time to butcher some chickens. Preparations were made and that meant heating a large amount of water. Julianna placed a large copper oblong boiler tub that held five gallons on the stove. After the chickens were killed they were briefly dunked in the hot water so their feathers were easily removed.

When Julianna felt the temperature was high enough she prepared to remove the tub from the stove. Heinrich was outside climbing a tree to see how high he could go. The neighbors all knew well his excess energy, as he would run up and down the street they lived on. Emil was scared because of the height he had climbed the tree, but was relieved when he came down and said he was going in the house to get a drink of water. But as Julianna grabbed the handles and turned to set the tub down on a large well built box, Heinrich came running into the kitchen and ran right into it. There were loud screams and everyone came running to see what happened. Heinrich's left shoulder, arm and chest were badly scalded. The mood in the house shifted as concern for Heinrich was on everyone's mind. Emil was sent to get a doctor, who arrived several hours later. He was a much loved young man who had been providing health care in town for several years. He stopped the pain with cold wet towels spread over the affected area and said large blisters would build up over the deeply burned areas. He gave Julianna instructions on how to drain them and how to dress the burned areas. It did not take Heinrich long before he was up and around again, visiting with neighbors and being himself. The painful recovery took weeks and the chickens enjoyed a couple extra weeks of life. Later in life Heinrich used the burn scars to prove his identity at a once in a lifetime crucial family moment.

Ludwig was pulled aside one day at work in the winter of 1905 and offered a job on the Winnipeg to Morden line as a brakeman with the CPR, which meant easier physical work and certainly a promotion. He accepted and went home that day with the good news. He remained a brakeman until he resigned to move west to file for a homestead.

The most dangerous job on the train was the brakeman. Over the next 10 years 28 brakeman died in Manitoba, but Ludwig accepted the risk. He was smart, careful and watched his every step. The brakeman at times had to walk the top of the cars in all types of weather to either set the brake on a car or release it. Most of the walkways did not have railings. Ludwig would start at one end of the train and another brakeman would start from the other end, setting or releasing brakes. Another part of his job was to go between the cars of moving trains to couple or uncouple them. An even more dangerous railroad job was to work in the yards as switchmen or yardmen.

Julianna and Ludwig became proud parents of Winnifred Alwine Gess on May 27, 1906 in Winkler. The Gess family was growing. Julius was getting along well in school and he was in confirmation class in the Evangelical German Lutheran Church. Emil was nine years old,

Heinrich was six, and Mathilda was four. The family was enjoying life in Winkler, but Ludwig knew that there would someday be another move.

By July 1906 the three families lived on adjoining lots on Railroad Avenue—Wilhelm Rode lot 19, Michael Jess's lot number was not specified, and August Rode on lot 20.

At gatherings, if someone brought up their owning property in a few short years, Ludwig answered that if they could own a lot with a house on it, why not work toward owning land?

Ludwig stayed on his job planning for the day he would own land. He was hearing about opportunities in the prairie province of Saskatchewan. Working for the CPR railroad, it did not take him long to decide to investigate. Having seen flyers advertising the availability of land in Saskatchewan he rode the train to Swift Current.[10] Chosen as a division point for the CPR railroad because it had water for steam engines, the town had a railroad roundhouse used to repair engines and to turn them to travel in the opposite direction. (The eventual demise of the steam engine took the need for a roundhouse with it, since the diesel engine can travel in either direction.) Ludwig spent every hour chatting with people and learned as much as he could in a short time. He felt at home in the busy village, where wagons pulled by oxen were loaded with buffalo bones to sell to a local merchant. The bones were stockpiled and eventually loaded in railroad cars for the trip to the fertilizer plant. Oxen wheel ruts from those trips leading into Swift Current are still visible today. Ludwig left on the next train east for the 450 mile trip home. He had talked to farmers, businessmen, trappers and wagon masters who drove many teams harnessed to large heavy loads. It took half the trip to sort out the information that was relevant. Ludwig was excited and knew that someday he and his family would be moving to the Swift Current area.

Ludwig was not concentrating on his brakeman's job as he returned to work. His memory was short on what he did at work that week, for his goal seemed a reality. The next step was to create a plan. At the end

---

10 Swift Current built their train depot in 1882. In 1903 Swift Current was recognized as a village, became a town in 1907, and incorporated as a City in 1914.

of June 1906 Ludwig and Julianna discussed moving west. She knew what her husband wanted and suggested that they invite the rest of the family over for Sunday dinner to discuss the possible move. Ludwig wondered about the reaction of the others, and prayed that they would want to move with him. Julianna did not want to move, though Ludwig never knew it. She knew what was in his heart, and she would do what she could to support it. During fifteen years of marriage Ludwig often sought her opinion. She would give it, knowing it would help him make his decision. Her life was caring for her family, but her quiet disposition was not to be taken for granted. More than one person found that out, if the intentions of her children were questioned. Even with a large family she was an active Church member. Her love of God and family were equal, and neither could not be shaken.

The families met. The August Rodes were enthusiastic about the idea and wanted to move. Michael said they wanted to remain in Winkler— they had found a home and at their age they did not want another move. Wilhelm was interested and would move in a few years. Charles Rode, now 22, was asked his opinion about moving west. The room was silent. After what seemed minutes, Charles said he wanted to move west. He added that he planned to get married next April. The tone of the group immediately changed as this was a surprise to all, including Charles's father. Some in the group had met Emily Huebner and let it be known that they highly approved of this engagement. Ludwig was in a new mood as he started work that Monday morning.

It had been confirmed, and as he had done so many times before he began to formulate plans for the move west. He had a hard time concentrating on his job that week. The hardest part was to not tell the men he worked with. He had made some good friends on the job and he knew he had to keep the move to himself. Ludwig at 38 thought more than ever about the future of his children. The next best thing he could do for them was to give them a sense of independence. He did not want them looking over their shoulder when they got into a difficult situation. He wanted them to work that out for themselves. In his mind that would in the end be a great gift for them. As he thought about moving he had another reason to do it sooner than later. A few years from now it would be more difficult for them to leave the friendships they had made. He was always thinking.

Julius now 13 would begin his second year of confirmation at the German Lutheran Evangelical Church in September. When he finished his classes in May he had good marks. One more year of school and one more year of confirmation. His formal education would end next spring and then his real education would begin. History would prove that he kept alert to all opportunities to learn. The move next year was always on his mind. He knew he had to like it and he wavered for months about it. He was an organized man who liked things to go a certain way, and when they did not the people around him knew it. He did not explode and do irrational things when he was not pleased, he just expressed his displeasure. Both of his grandfathers were pleased with him and said they always wanted to know what he was doing. He enjoyed being looked up to by his siblings and tried hard to fulfill that role. He knew that someday he would be leaving while some of them would still be very young.

Anxious was the best way to describe his last year of school. He tried to enjoy it but never reached that point. The year went by quickly and there were family events that made the time pass quicker. On April 13, 1907 Wilhelm's son Charles married Emily Huebner in St. John Lutheran Church at Rosenfeld, 18 miles straight east of Winkler. This was a two day event with people arriving by train and team-drawn wagons, as well as by light-weight four wheel buggies.

The word had spread rapidly that the Gess and Rode families would be moving to Saskatchewan in a couple months. Casual conversation at the wedding with friends and relatives soon turned to questions about the move west. Many had stories about friends and relatives who had moved west. There was a couple who were considering moving west, attracted by available land. Within a few days after the wedding, Charles and Emily began making their own preparations. The wedding was a solemn event and well attended by friends and relatives, as always. With travel still slow and difficult, a chance to see friends and relatives was always taken.

Ludwig wanted to move early. He had learned over the many moves to plan so the weather would work with them and decided on May 15th. Pastor R. Zwintscher advised the family that Julius would be confirmed April 7th. That news meant the family would all be able to move together—on the CPR railroad. Traveling by teams and wagons was not given much discussion. Any big items that could not be taken along were sold or given away. They were able to transport all their personal goods, kitchen items and even some furniture.

Ludwig had a friend in Winkler write to the land office several months earlier asking about applying for a homestead. There had been letters exchanged, but they did not know how they stood with the application. He had decided that they would go anyway, which would place him face-to-face so he could do what was necessary to get a homestead. He had been offered lodging by communicating with an acquaintance, Gustav Libke, who said they should get off at Cantaur, the first stop after Swift Current. Gustaf lived not too far from there and could provide temporary living for the large crowd. Some would be sleeping in the barn and a vacant sheep shed. Ludwig was confident that his homestead would be available to begin doing the first steps toward living on the property.

Ludwig had to concentrate on working till a week before they were to move. He was appointed the leader of the group as had been before. The appointment was by his own action, but no one challenged it. His experience qualified him to lead the group. The properties, wagons and teams had been sold with the provision that the families could use them till they left. Julianna had a huge job preparing for the trip. Where they would be staying after they arrived worried her. She relied on Julius to look after his brothers. All she had to do was to give him instructions and she knew they would be carefully followed.

The good-byes were unlike the Volhynia good-byes, for they knew they would see most of the friends and relatives again. They were only 450 miles away and with the train it would be easy to visit. Ludwig was leaving behind his father Michael and his brother Heinrich. Wilhelm and family would be following them west in a year or two. Ludwig was feeling good about the progress of the group. It would be an all day trip and a relaxing one. A lot had happened since the train ride from Quebec just five years ago, but Ludwig was not thinking about that. He was dealing with the present and looking forward from where he was, an attitude deeply instilled in Julius.

Friends and relatives had teams ready at 6:30 the morning of departure. Julius was with them to say goodbye and make all the promises about studying hard and helping at his grandfather Michael's house. They used up all the space allotted to their ticket. The help to get them to the depot and get all their baggage loaded onto the depot's wagons was effortless compared to doing it alone.

The train arrived on time, as Ludwig said it would. After his years working for the CPR he knew very well how it operated. Of course the train left on time, but was almost delayed a few minutes loading all of the Gess/Rode items into the baggage car. Julianna was happy as the train pulled out. She did not feel the sharp pain of departure that she had leaving Volhynia. August, Pauline, Emily and Alvina were very excited about the move and anxious to get resettled. They were very happy that Charles and Emily were moving with them. Ludwig had traveled this line when he went out to investigate the area, but to the rest of them it was a great adventure, seeing more of Manitoba and traveling for many miles across southern Saskatchewan. They passed through many smaller towns and they enjoyed seeing the abundance of wildlife. Deer and antelope were plentiful, even some coyotes and a lot of badgers. Emil and Heinrich had great fun exploring the train. They were calmed down more than once by the conductor for exploring too aggressively. At each stop they wanted to get off and look over the town. Ludwig would let them off only if they waited till he got off first. That way he could have control of them so they would be on the train when it started to move. The train was scheduled to get into Cantaur at 9:00 that evening. Gustaf Libke was there to meet them with two teams and wagons. It was a happy family group that left the train and helped load the wagons with all their earthly possessions.

They settled in at the Libke home and it was a happy moment when they finally got to bed. For Ludwig and Julianna that wasn't until 3 the next morning. There was not much sleep that night. Everyone was up early and the mood seemed to be "is this really happening?" After a short trip they are starting another new life. Ludwig smiled—he had wanted to move to another country since he was a teenager. Now he was here and the real work was about to begin. Gustaf said he would take his team and a buggy to the land office in Swift Current 12 miles away. . They left an hour after daybreak. Julius was disappointed when Ludwig ordered him to stay behind in case his mother needed help. Gustaf was as excited as the homesteaders. Ludwig sat beside him and the conversation never lulled. August was with them, for he had written to the land office about filing a claim. He would be happy if they could find the correspondence. The trip was fast but would be much slower going back. When they arrived at the land office they waited in line. Eventually Ludwig laid out his identification and some ragged notes he had referencing the letters between them. Finally the agent was able to find the file. He turned to Ludwig and with a big smile said "Mr. Gess, you have a homestead located in the S.E. ¼ of Section 6-T17-R15." T stand for township, and R for range. They finished the signatures and Ludwig paid the filing fee and after an explanation of the costs to be paid later, he was a land owner with conditions. August asked the agent to look up his application. The agent finally found it and there was a lot of paper work to do, so he told August to come back next week and he would have his claim. He asked if there was any available land close to his for his brother Charles. There was an available quarter that bordered August's. He asked if it could be reserved for Charles. The agent said that was not allowed, but with a sly grin and a wink to August he said he thought it would still be available next week. The four left and Gustaf was as excited as they were.

They arrived home late that night. It did not matter, because they had accomplished more than they thought possible. A lot of the plans for the next day were discussed on the ride home. They would leave at daybreak with a team and wagon Julius and Charles joining them. They took along some shovels, picks, grub axes, hammer, nails and boards. The first job would be to carefully examine the property to see the best location for the farmyard. Gustaf would use his water witching talents to find the underwater channel.

The property was flat with only some rolling land on half of it. Ludwig stood on that slight knoll and took half an hour to turn around looking at the lay of his land. He had dreamed of this day for so many years. Finally he was here—from Volhynia to Success, the town three miles away. The three men agreed on the site for the farmyard, and Libke was finding abundant sources of water. They picked a place for the well, visualizing a barn built close by and fences. It was close to the house, yet distant enough. They were anxious to start digging. After four feet Gustaf opined they would find water within another 10 feet. They were happy and started back by late afternoon. Ludwig kept turning around to look at his land until it was out of sight. A big meal was waiting for them when they returned full of stories to tell the families. Julius was thrilled at being able to spend the first day with the men on his dad's new homestead.

Gustaf told the men that he knew of a team that Ludwig could buy. For Ludwig that solved a major problem. He would have to buy a wagon and start to build a house as soon as possible. The men noticed a lot of sod houses on both of the trips, and it looked like that was what they should be building. The plow would cut the sod and then it would be carefully laid out and built up until it was ready for the roof.

Gustaf told August that he had a pair of oxen broke enough to break land that he would sell. One was very big and one was smaller, a regular size. In later years the story was repeated many times about August started farming with a big ox and a little one. The price fit August's budget. Within a week the well was dug and Ludwig's homestead was busy with activity. Ludwig, August and Charles were more than aware that summer would not last too long with the huge amount of work that needed to be done. They were all concerned about adequate fencing to hold their teams and oxen. That concern was on top of having adequate housing and food for the long winter.

Gustaf was happy to take August and Charles to the land office in Swift Current to finalize their homestead applications. No better luck could two homesteading brothers have than to share a half mile property line. Each claim was 160 acres, a half mile square. They could share equipment and machinery and work the two pieces of property as if they were one. Charles, only about a month married, was now 450 miles away and already had a homestead.

The dream was taking shape. The hard work of plowing the virgin prairie, building a farmstead, and raising families was facing the three families. They proudly tackled it and knew that with the support of each other they would survive and prosper.

CHAPTER 11

−1907−
Fifth Move:
To Success, Saskatchewan

Within a month Ludwig's large sod house had been built with help from August and Charles. Julius's growing skills were a big help to his father getting the house finished. Out where their first prairie land would be broken for farming Ludwig and Julius used a one bottom plow set to cut a five inch deep furrow. They did their best, and the house when finished looked like professionals had built it. They made a wall that divided the house into a third and two thirds—the large side for bedrooms, the small side a kitchen/eating area. The house had four windows, and would be warm in the winter and cool in the summer. It would be adequate for the family of seven, but good crops could soon provide the family with a frame house.

They also built a small but adequate corral to hold the team. The temporary barn had vertical boards for the sides, and boards on the roof were covered with dirt. The south side was half enclosed, to provide shelter if the worst of the storms were to come. Charlie had traded work for a milk cow and his brother August already had two so he offered the cow to Ludwig. The barn would protect his farm animals so Ludwig could concentrate on gathering enough wood for the winter.

Julius had been there a week and was an immediate help to his dad as they moved forward. He was a strong growing young man who looked like he might reach six feet. He had finished confirmation and enjoyed the train ride to Cantaur. He told of meeting a family on the train who had arrived from Volhynia. He said they envied him getting off when he did. They had been traveling for weeks and still had a long way to go to British Columbia.

He was so happy to be with the family, who now considered him a grown man. He had finished school, was confirmed and now was ready to assume any responsibility that his father or uncles would give him.

The wet spring enabled Ludwig to break 10 acres of prairie. If the weather cooperated and he could buy or borrow the proper machinery to prepare the ground, Ludwig would plant those acres next spring. He would also need to get five bushels of oats and five bushels of wheat to seed on the new land. He would push to try to break more land if the rains came to keep the soil moist.

A neighbor Aaron, who lived two miles west of the homestead, stopped to visit while Ludwig and Julius were starting to build a small chicken house on one end of the barn. He had lived on his farm for several years and already was starting to build a new house. Aaron was there to hire Julius to work for him. He had been a carpenter by trade before he started farming and he needed help. He would pay Julius $15 a month plus room and board, with Sunday off, so he could walk home Saturday after work. Ludwig needed his two horses so they would not be available for Julius to use. Julius was excited to have the chance to do actual carpentry work. There would be weeks of sawing lumber, nailing, leveling and seeing that everything was square and true. Julius wanted the skills, plus he would be able to earn money for the family.

They agreed, and Aaron left knowing that the following Sunday night Julius would arrive at his place ready to start work the next morning. Ludwig and Julius finished the chicken house in time. It was small, with just enough room for a dozen chickens. Ludwig had helped a neighbor with a wagon mired in the mud. It took most of a day to get it out and clean up the mess. It was on the edge of another neighbor's property, so they wanted it left in proper condition. Ludwig did not want anything, but after a friendly argument he agreed to accept a dozen chickens.

In the central part of the homestead there was a small valley. It did not hold water and the soil was good, like the rest of the claim. There was about an acre in the lowest part of the valley that should be a wheat field, but it was covered with buffalo bones so thick that a plow would not be able to get through. Ludwig gave Emil, age ten, the job of picking up the buffalo bones. They marked out four places where he could stack the bones, placing the piles so the plow would be able to get by. Once the bones were hauled into Swift Current and sold, it would be easy to break those four little spots of sod. Even though he worked hard, it took Emil a few weeks to have the ground cleared of bones. Several times Ludwig, his brothers-in-law and neighbor speculated on how the bones happened to be concentrated in that patch. The only logical idea had to do with extended hard winters. It was thought that the buffalo would wander with the north cold wind and gather in the bit of shelter of this slight valley. As the crowd grew and the storm continued, eventually some of them froze to death. There were several full sets of bones, which gave credence to the buffalo dying in place.

Heinrich was becoming known as Hank. His mother was the last holdout, but eventually she too called him Hank. He and Emil started school in September. It was about a mile walk, and when the weather was cold and snowy their dad would harness up the team to make the run to school, though each year they missed many days because of extreme weather. The teacher, who lived on the school property, had to plan for unlikely weather. During school the fires had to be kept burning and ashes had to be hauled out. Teachers had their hands full when they accepted rural jobs. Some teachers kept a horse and buggy, others did not, depending on close neighbors instead.

Aaron observed the aggressive way Julius undertook his work—it was obvious after the stringers for the floor had been put in place and the sub flooring put down. The 2 x 4 framing was nailed in place for the first end wall. They had been checked and rechecked so they were in true square. The bottom of the wall was on top of the plate nailed to the floor. When all was ready to lift up the top of the wall, they walked toward the end of the house, continuing to lift up the wall that was resting on top of the plate. As soon as it was upright, Julius held the wall steady and Aaron used his level to be certain it was at 90 degrees. He nailed boards at a 45 degree angle to the edge of the floor to hold it in place. Aaron sighed in sigh of relief as they rested. Julius was happy—he had just experienced another step in building a structure.

They were rushing to get the house enclosed before heavy snow arrived. They worked faster to get the walls up and ready for the next step. Aaron had arranged for two extra men to be there in two days to help him cut the rafters and put them in place. The angle cuts of the rafters had to be exact and Aaron wanted help with it. That piqued the curiosity of Julius who was anxious to see the men mark the rafters so that were ready for the saw. He questioned the men about how they would know where to mark the rafters. The men said they would show him how it is done—the carpenter's square was marked to give the angle of the cut for the pitch of the roof. They saw his interest and let him mark some rafters under their careful eye. Little did Julius dream that in a few years he would be leading carpentry crews and teaching men how to cut rafters. Once the rafters were all up and properly spaced, sheeting was nailed onto them. Once the windows and door were installed snow could be kept out so Aaron could work on the interior. As the weather grew colder he installed the kitchen stove and kept a fire in it so he and Julius were comfortable as they finished off the bare walls. Julius at 14 and Aaron in his mid-forties had built up a good working relationship. At the end of three months Aaron said that he would have to continue alone after the end of this week. Julius went home Saturday afternoon and told his parents that his work for the time being was finished. He gave the money he earned over to his father who would use some of it to buy another milk cow.

The Gess home was comfortable and did hold heat well during the cold weather. Springtime would mean some more outside work for

Julius. When homesteaders dropped by to visit they mentioned that they heard Julius was a very good hired hand. But there was work to do at home, for more sod needed to be turned. This should be the year that they broke the most land. Ludwig wanted a better wagon and a better plow, but he was very careful with his money and bought only what was absolutely necessary. He decided to wait and see how the crop looked. He planted only 10 acres of crop, then he started to break land. He and Julius had drawn out a plan for their 160 acres. They reserved two acres for the farmyard out of the 40 acre pasture. That left 120 acres for crop land.

Late that spring Ludwig and Julius went to the land office in Swift Current. Julius applied for a Homestead Patent located about four miles east of Success, and about 2½ miles NE of Ludwig's homestead. It was the SW ¼ of Section 21 T17 R15 W3 Meridian. With that description it is easy to locate a piece of land. Julius gave his age as 22 on the application—in 1908 he was stretching a bit to qualify.

Julius was happy to have another sister, Lydia, born August 15, 1908. Her godfather was Otto Malchow, a close neighbor of the Gess family. As the oldest, his brothers and sisters all looked up to Julius. He would always be the tallest, thus always looked up to. They wanted his approval as well as their parents'. He enjoyed the role and most of the time lived up to it. Knowing that he would be gone from home before most of his siblings were teenagers left him sad—and he slowly learned that was the path his life would follow.

Julius read that in 1908 the province of Saskatchewan had begun the construction of a Capitol building. It would be a four year project and cost around $1.75 million. He thought constantly about it, feeling that he had to work on the construction of that building. More experience was what he needed, and he would work toward that. It was late fall, a hard time for finding work, especially carpentry, but he heard that a homesteader near the town of Success was building a large barn that was not yet enclosed. He told his parents he would go there to see if the owner needed more help. Ludwig let him take a horse and the buggy which Ludwig had bargained for. As he approached the farmyard he saw that the man could be in trouble if he did not get it closed soon, for he still did not have all the rafters up. He introduced himself and was surprised to hear that the farmer knew of him. There were two hired carpenters working, and Julius agreed to work for him with terms similar to his last job. This would be vital experience for him and he was anxious to start. Raising the rafters for a barn with a huge hay mow took all the strength of the four men plus an array of ropes and pulleys. His experience with Aaron gave Julius an edge that surprised the three men. He was gaining the experience which he sought to get a job on the Capitol building.

Julius worked there on and off through the winter. The farmer needed that large barn available for his eight horses, milk cows, and to start raising sheep. Julius was not interested in livestock. He liked using and fixing machinery when it was needed. He worked on those skills but always arranged his time so he would be available when his father needed him. They were very busy with two homesteads that needed work. This would be the second crop year for Ludwig, seeding all 60 acres that had been broken—40 acres in wheat, 15 acres in oats, and 5 acres in corn. There was a large garden with about two acres of potatoes in the hopes of extra potatoes to barter with for other food items. Ludwig was drawing on skills he learned in Poland and Volhynia now for his homestead.

Summer 1909 Julius was 16 and had 15 acres seeded on his own homestead. He and Ludwig had been very busy, for the future depended on the harvest. Julius could choose the work he wanted to do away from home, given his reputation. The work was getting easier as he learned more about carpentry. He would work all he could this summer at home and away from home. He set his sights on working on the Capitol in Regina the following summer. Emil at 13 would be able to pick up when Julius was not around.

Hank, now 10, was a very good hand and able to do a lot of the farm work very quickly, though he often needed to be tidied up. He was happiest when he was working around livestock. One day he went with his dad to the blacksmith in Cantaur. He was fascinated by what the blacksmith was able to do with a forge and some iron. They watched him repair a broken steel hook-shaped part from the plow and sharpen some plowshares. After that visit whenever there was a trip to the black-smith, Hank was to be found on the buggy. He often went alone for long walks in the neighborhood. Many times it was thought he had run away. Not the case, he just liked to explore—something he did as long as he lived at home.

As Julius worked on various jobs, he was comfortable knowing Emil and Hank would be getting the work done at home. The crops were looking good. They needed a good crop this year to bring in money to start building the large house they needed. The dream was there with the entire family. The conversation would drift toward a frame house whenever it rained, especially during a crucial growing period.

The harvest was good and there was grain to be sold. It was not a big crop, wheat averaging 20 bushels per acre at $.78 per bushel in 1909. Even so, the feeling in the neighborhood was one of satisfaction and most people were grateful. Many were new farmers harvesting their first crop. For the homesteaders with no farming background that first crop is a thrilling experience no matter the yield. It did not take long for reality to set in for a man new to farming. Many homesteaders left the big city to learn how to live off the land but soon learned that it would be a long, difficult life.

Ludwig knew the risk. Julius faced them and now was learning them first hand. He was quickly acquiring a good set of farming and carpen-try skills. Ludwig would survive, given a chance from mother nature. Julius would also survive given the abilities he was acquiring—and with youth on his side.

Two years after they left Winkler, Ludwig wanted to go back to visit his father Michael and brother Heinrich, and he wanted Julianna to go with him. She decided to stay at home—to take care of the children and prepare for another child arriving the fall.

Arriving in mid-August, he was warmly greeted by his father and Julia. Dinner that evening included his father-in-law Wilhelm, Caroline and their sons. Ludwig was surprised to find out that Heinrich was working in the States—he had left near the end of the previous year. A record was found of Heinrich Gess, machinist age 28, crossing the border into Canada March 8, 1910. He had traveled from Boston to St.

Allrad with $20 in his possession, having worked in the Boston area for a short time as a machinist. He heard of the demand for his skills in Pittsburgh, Pennsylvania, and near the end of 1910 he moved there and immediately got a job. It must have been a good job as he sent money home to his father.

Ludwig was able to visit their former neighbors and many of his fellow employees at the railroad yard. He enjoyed the time spent, but after two days he started worrying about his crops back home. It had rained a lot, which moved the harvest forward. The third day he boarded the train feeling refreshed. The trip was easy—no change of trains. Just get aboard, take a seat, and hours later be back home. He asked his father to visit them and they agreed on next spring. He had two new daughters since they had left Winkler whom he wanted to show off, along with his 480 acres and the two homesteads, counting Julius's claim.

In only three days the wheat crop had turned more golden, which meant harvest time was near. That evening there were ominous clouds gathering in the west, followed by a cold wind. During the night they were awakened by the sound of hail pounding on the roof. Heavy hearts would not allow any more sleep that night. Shortly after daylight Ludwig, Julius, Emil and Hank walked out to the fields to face the damage. About a third of the stand of wheat that had stood three feet high was laying on the ground, and some of the heads of the standing wheat were also damaged. It was a severe blow—one that they would have to accept as part of the risk of farming. Not only would they have to fear hail, they would have to deal with drought, grasshoppers, and heavy weeds growing in their crops. It was a part of their life. Whenever homesteaders met, the conversation within minutes always turned to weather conditions. Homesteaders had a hard life. The crop was still harvested, and for most who were in the line of that hail storm, yield was about 40% of what it would have been.

After the harvest Julius left for Regina to seek work on the Capitol building. His letter said that after waiting around for a week he was given a job working on a framing crew. Again his height and strong body was an advantage, and soon he was moved to work inside, out of the weather, with one carpenter, moving around the building doing cleanup carpentry. Where crews went through and did not finish every little detail, it was their job to complete the work. It was a good job and he respected the man with whom he worked with. The job was never ending and Julius was able to work through the winter. One job followed the crew putting up the wire netting and lath to support the plaster on the ten foot high wall. They left out a one foot section 60 feet long near the top. Their job was to nail 2x6 planks parallel to the plate at the top of the wall for anchoring hanging art work. The six inch gap was to be filled in with lath and wire netting for 60 feet. When that was finished they did the same thing on the other side of the hall. Julius liked the variety that added to his experience.

He rented a very small room with a bed, barely space to stand up, and only a couple shelves for his clothes. He ate meals in a common dining hall for the men working on the Capitol building. His room was cold so he welcomed morning when he got up and moved around to generate body heat. The room and dining hall were close to the Capitol. This convenience and the good meals overcame the tiny room and the cold nights he had to endure.

He regretted having to leave in April to help plant crops at both homesteads. His employer said he would like to have him again in the fall when the farm work was finished. Number one in his mind was helping to make the two homesteads successful. He and Emil planted most of the crop, which produced average for the area. There seemed to be adequate rain, but for some reason the production just wasn't there. The homesteading experiment was playing itself out. It would be many years before farming skills were able to produce crops with very little rain, but the homesteaders kept innovating against drought, grasshoppers, prairie fires, and inadequate prices for their meager harvests. The Gess and Rode families labored on. Hard times meant watching every dollar and constantly being on the alert for a way to bring in some extra income. Ludwig would try to keep two milk cows to provide for the family. Each spring they would hatch more chicks to supply the large family with eggs and meat, as well as trade for other food products. Ludwig was a seasoned trader when it came to swapping for items he needed. Those early years of learning in Volhynia kept them in food many times.

Julius went back to Regina late in September and began working again as a cleanup carpenter with the same boss. He found out later they transferred one man to another job so his boss could have him back. After a short time, his boss and he were moved to do rough framing for decorative work. Some of what they did was small and tedious work. The frames would hold finished decorative work of all types—from small designs on doors to large paintings covering huge spaces on walls. Julius knew that he would never again work on a building this size. He would someday have his own homestead and this job was a part of preparing for that time. Carpentry skills at that time were a real asset for anyone. It was hard work, and a carpenter who presented himself as such had to have the necessary skills. It took years to learn and Julius was investing that time.

Lillian joined the family October 30, 1910. Julianna and Ludwig now had three sons and four daughters. Mathilda at eight was a big help to her mother. The sisters especially enjoyed having a new baby girl in the family.

Julius would visit quite often with his uncle August. They both enjoyed talking about their life in Volhynia. August knew of Julius's carpentry skills and mentioned that he wanted him to help build a barn when he had enough money for lumber. Julius was excited to utilize his carpentry skills, which August did not have. As their visits continued they started drawing out plans and looking at locations.

It was a happy day when August was finally able to replace his oxen with a team of horses. Oxen were stubborn, hard to handle animals. His daughter Martha decades later wrote that he would take a load of wheat to Swift Current in the fall with the oxen, and bring home flour and staples for the winter. On one occasion the flies were so bad, the oxen took to a slough, toppling August and the supplies into the water. Farming those few years with oxen constantly tried his patience. Had the oxen both been the same size it would have helped some. August and Pauline now have three daughters: Emily, Alvina and Martha. He had built a single-ply frame house. It was very cold in the winter and the family was anxious for the day that they could build a house with siding and windows that could retain heat in the winter. The crops were not ample enough and the constant hard work to provide for basic necessities was never ending. Martha wrote, "Our father told us that in early days he and his brother-in-law drove a team of horses hitched to a wagon, with a rack to Moose Jaw to thresh grain. The wage was $1.50 a day for a man and $2.50 a day for team and rack. Such were the days of the pioneers!" Also mother told how the boys would hunt for and shoot badgers. They would skin them and remove all the fat. This she would use to make soap. She named this product Badger Soap. Mother said "it was an excellent soap."

Julius worked one more winter on the Capitol building in Regina until early 1912. His carpenter jobs after that were mostly helping neighbors build a barn or a house which left him busy most of the time. Another brother was born November 24, 1912. Reynold Ernest Gess was the first son given a middle name. He eventually took over the family farm and continued to farm it till he retired.

Ludwig was able to prove up his homestead late in the fall of 1912. The move west had provided a living, and now he owned the homestead. There were occasional sales and purchases of land in the area, and Ludwig stayed alert to any opportunity though he had very little money. He knew that sometimes a quarter section would trade hands for a few dollars, a promissory note, and a handshake. If a farmer was having a tough time and wanted to leave and try another occupation, he would be willing to negotiate. Early spring 1913 he happened upon an opportunity and he quickly moved on it, buying a half section of land which was the S ½ of section 7 T17 R15. He now had owned 480 acres. The land was located a quarter mile from where they lived. They would eventually move to that land where he built the large two story house which became their home.

August was ready to start building the barn after the harvest of 1913. He and Julius negotiated their terms and rushed to pour the foundation before frost started. Their plans had been drawn out for a long time and the location was easy. Brother Charles, who lived across the road, was there to help with the foundation, along with two neighbors, so the foundation work was done in one day. Julius, now 20, was directing the work, and with Charles helping the frame work rose rapidly. They were fighting weather and they needed to make every waking minute count. At sun up they were on the job, and soon they quickly finished the frame work. When they woke the next morning there was a foot of snow on the ground. This was a real shock, but they realized that at this early date the snow might disappear soon. It did, and they were back to work putting the shiplap boards on the walls. These boards were notched on both lengthwise edges to fit tight with the next board. It took several days to put it on the frame since Charles had to work at his place. The two story barn had a typical hay mow lower than similar barns. The shiplap covered the rafters as well.

With all the frame covered, August and Julius gave a big sigh of relief, though they still had a long way to go. The shiplap would be covered with siding that was six inches wide, with one inch over the board below it. On the corners, vertical finishing board was put up, same around the windows. They were constantly battling weather which was getting colder. Most days they had a fire going in a barrel that August had fashioned into a sort of fire pit. The roof still needed shingles.

The barrel fire pit had been made to use when a hog was butchered. 18 inches high, a large barrel was set on top of it and filled with water. When the water was heated, the hog was lifted up and into the hot water with block and tackle, a system of pulleys and rope that hung from a three legged derrick. When the bristles could be easily pulled from the hog, it was time to hoist it out and the butchering process continued.

That fire pit helped them warm up as they worked in freezing temperature. The windows were in and the shingles were starting to work their way up the roof. Nothing had been done inside—horse stalls, two stanchions for milk cows, pens for calves, and two bins for grain with walls from floor to ceiling. The front door—the last item to be built, sealed the inside against snow. The door would be eight feet wide and seven feet high, sliding on a rail on the top. The shingles were on and only a few boards of siding were nailed on before weather stopped them until next spring. But the snow would not get in the barn and some work inside could be done during the winter.

Julius was happy the way the barn turned out. He and Uncle August both enjoyed their time together and he saw the barn as an arrow in his quiver. He could always say, "I built August Rode's barn." Julius went home to spend the winter.

He was concerned about a possible conscription in Canada. He preferred not having to go away to the army, however he would gladly go if drafted. He also heard talk in Success that a large block of land might open for homesteading south of the border in Montana. He asked around and finally found out that it was in the Fort Peck Indian Reservation in northeast Montana. He saw the possibility of a new life opening up for him. At age 20 he felt he could handle a homestead. It was something that would not happen immediately, so he had time to think about it. First he had to decide if he wanted to homestead again, and in another country. He considered himself a veteran homesteader, plus he had carpentry skills that would be very useful if he did decide to homestead.

March 17, 1913 word was received that Julius's grandfather, Michael Gess, had died in Winkler. He and his father boarded the train for the funeral. The funeral was a sad gathering of many friends and family. The family that had lived close together in Volhynia was spread out. Wilhelm Rode and his family, who had left Winkler and moved to Verwood, Saskatchewan, reported that their homestead's wheat crops had been very good. (Wilhelm remained in the Verwood area until his death in May 1931.) Though sad, the time for gathering was appreciated. Michael's son Heinrich arrived home from Pittsburgh, Pennsylvania.

Julius helped his father with the spring seeding on all three parcels of land. There was more work available in Regina, working on a crew that was building homes. For three weeks he worked on the framing crew. But the workers all got together one day and decided to go on strike, to cut their 12 hour work day to 10 hours. They lost, but all of them went back to work. He worked there till harvest time and then went back home. After harvest he sought out more information about homesteads on the Fort Peck Indian Reservation. Seeing articles in Regina newspapers, he wrote to "The Homestead Office—Glasgow, Montana USA." About six months later he received a flyer about homesteads in northeast Montana.

After many discussions with his family and neighbors, he decided he would go to Montana after the harvest in 1915. With that decision made, his time was spent working, saving money and preparing for the move. He transferred his homestead to his father and he helped him prepare the foundation for the new house on the land that Ludwig bought. It would be a two story building adequate for Ludwig and Julianna's growing family, the land layout was better for a farmyard at this property than on the homestead. It would take a lot of time to complete the house, but they would move in when it was livable, and continue to work on it as time and money permitted. It was a big project for a homesteader, and Ludwig knew it would test his patience.

Julianna gave birth to Minnie the last child May 26, 1915.[11] Julius helped put the crops in that spring. After that he and his father decided on the layout for the house. There would be a root cellar under the kitchen. They had to dig that and shore up the walls to prevent it from caving in. After the root cellar was completed they laid out the perimeter of the house. It did not have the typical foundation, instead the house would rest on concrete blocks or large rocks dug into the ground. This was a precise job that called for the blocks to be perfectly level with each other.

Ludwig, Julius, Emil and Hank all worked to get the floor stringers in and lay the subflooring. In the kitchen area a door was cut in the floor for a stairway to access the root cellar. Julius had to leave to work for a neighbor who was building a barn and a chicken coop. This work lasted most of the summer. His help was crucial with the building projects because the neighbor's skills were minimal. He needed help with framing and especially the rafters. Ludwig and his sons had gone as far as their ability and time took them, then he hired carpenters to take over the job. Lydia's daughter Wendy related many years later that

---

11 Minnie stayed at home and took care of her mother in her final years. After Julianna's death Minnie worked as a nurse until her retirement. An automobile struck her in a crosswalk, and that changed her life. She had lingering effects from that accident and was not able to work anymore.

her mother said, "It was a wonderful house." There were many bed-rooms upstairs and the downstairs living room and the kitchen were the biggest in the neighborhood. She said that during construction the carpenters used to swear at Julianna and the children because they were always underfoot. Anyone who has worked around construction knows the danger and nuisance it is having little children around. Lydia also related that school in Success was a long way away, so her mother would take them halfway to Success and let them walk the rest of the way because she had to get back home to take of the many jobs she had. She said that after they got a little older the children took the horse and buggy and rode all the way to school. The parents of Lydia's best friend, Evelyn Forbes, owned a livery stable in town. Her dad would unhitch the horses and hitch them up again for the kids when it was time to go home. She spent a lot of time at the Forbes's, including sleeping over.

Ludwig and Julianna's farm house near Success, Saskatchewan.

They were all very proud of the house and many neighbors were invited to come over and see—and there were those who came to see it who had not been invited. They were warmly welcomed. Julianna also had a remarkable garden, including a big display of flowers (which she loved). Many people on the road from Success to Medicine Hat used to stop and admire it. But one of the kids would have to talk to the people because of Julianna's lack of English.

Julius started making plans to leave the middle of July. He had to concentrate on it, and that was not easy with the house being built and his father talking about harvest. His destination would be Wolf Point, Montana, a trip of 220 miles which he would make on a bicycle. In 1915 bicycles were very advanced, with inner tube tires and multi-sprocket gears, though his was a plain single sprocket. He carried extra tires, inner tubes and the tools necessary to fix any problems he might encounter. He would be riding over ground that had cactus, and gopher and badger holes, and creeks with sharp-edged stones. A loaded bike would make it easier to puncture a tire—and he knew he would have to push the bike a lot. The trip would be tiresome and would take at least a week, but he might pass some towns where he could spend the night, and there were farm homes that would take in travelers. If not he would sleep under the stars.

Julius wanted to stay for the harvest but he could not. He had to file papers when he got to the homestead office, and if it were too late in the fall the office might have shut down for the winter. He had to get there as soon as he could.

The family invited both the August and Charles Rode families over for Sunday dinner July 11, 1915. It was "blessings to you, Julius," as you leave for Montana. The families had grown. August and Pauline had five children, Emily 14, Alvina 10, Martha 7, Fred 4, Henry 1. Charles and Emily had three children Wilhelm 7, Bertha 5, and Alfred 1. Julius was leaving behind his eight siblings: Emil 18, Hank 15, Mathilda 13, Winnie 9, Lydia 7, Lillian 5, Reynold 3 and Minnie two months. It was a wonderful day, and sad as Julius's relatives had to leave to go back to their homesteads. Julius knew he would see them again soon, and his goodbye expressions reflected that.

At last the crop yields satisfied Ludwig. 90 acres of wheat, 20 acres of oats, and two acres of potatoes. It came at a perfect time and meant that with good prices he could continue building on the house. Out of his small herd of cows, after saving a steer for family use, he would have a few calves to sell or trade in the fall. Things were looking better for the homesteader that was born in Bielsko, Poland. In his 46 years there had been many stops along the way, but now he had found his home.

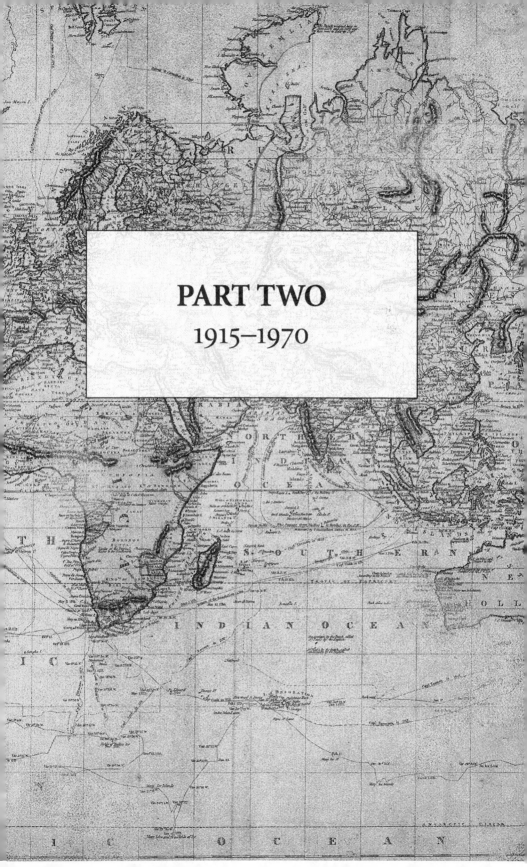

PART TWO

1915–1970

From Success, Saskatchewan, to Wolf Point, Montana, on This Bicycle—1915

The homesteader's son, Robert, and his wife, Merna, had sold the homestead. The remaining task was preparing for an auction on October 8, 2011. Preparation began in the spring. Machinery had to be moved and clustered for maximum exposure to potential buyers. Buckets, chains, compressors, and emery wheels were just a few of the many items that were separated into categories. A spot was made for antiques and just plain old "stuff." There was also a pile for iron and various unsaleable metal items, which were to be picked up after the auction for recycling. Having driven up from Townsend, Montana, their daughter, Sandi, would arrive for a week or two each month that summer to help during the preparation process. Her last visit was made a week before the sale was to be held. The heavy work was done, and tidying up was the order of the day.

Sandi walked through the huge farmyard, reliving the hard work done to get ready for sale day. Much of this trip would be a last for her, and she was feeling a flood of emotions. She approached the antique/old stuff collection, and her eyes quickly shifted to the iron pile a few yards away. She thought she saw handlebars sticking up from the other side of the pile. She ran over—and there it was: the bicycle her grandfather had ridden all the way from his father's farm near Success, Saskatchewan, to Wolf Point, Montana, in July 1915! She later learned it had been placed there by well-meaning friends who early on had stopped by to help. She carefully lifted it from the pile and wheeled it to her vehicle. Robert saw her and nodded, knowing what she was thinking. She later took it to her home, where it has remained. Then on May 18, 2017, the rest of our family heard the startling news that the homesteader's bicycle is still with us.

CHAPTER 12

— 1915 —

Julius Leaves by Bicycle

Julius left Friday morning July 16, 1915. He followed the road that took him to Cantaur, where they had arrived from Winkler in 1907. He recognized people he knew, and they were surprised by the traveling gear on his bicycle. His brief stop was a refreshing break before he continued on his way.

Julius carried a compass and a map, but relied mostly on local knowledge for direction. He bypassed Swift Current to save miles, but he would be returning to visit, so this was not a final goodbye for him. His goal was to reach Wymark before dark. He stayed at a travelers rest home that evening, and after a hearty breakfast he was ready to start pedaling. He was advised by locals to stay in Ponteix[12] that night,

---

12 In 1908 Father Albert-Marie Royer from the Auvergne region in France established a parish and hamlet called Notre-Dame d'Auvergne north of Notukeu Creek, Saskatchewan. Five years later, the townsite was moved south of the creek when the Canadian Pacific Railway laid track there. After the move, the community was renamed Ponteix after Father Royer's former parish in France (Le Ponteix, commune of Aydat). Notre Dame D'Auvergne Catholic Church, a brick and concrete structure in Ponteix built in 1929, features twin steeples and houses a large wood carving of the Pieta, which statue came to Canada in 1909 and was saved when the 1916 Church was destroyed by fire in 1923. Abbot Jerome Webber of St. Peter's Abbey in 1954 said the oak statue, once covered in pure gold, was made in France over four hundred years ago and was saved by peasants during the French Revolution.

about 30 miles away. It proved to be unique, with friendly people who were French-speaking, though some spoke English. The small Catholic Church in town, he heard, was planning to build a large twin-tower Church plus a convent nearby. He stored that information.

On Sunday the 18th the weather was cool and Julius was riding on his bike early, looking forward to getting to Mankota, a distance of about 24 miles. Out on the prairie it could have been any day of the week. Traveling over mostly rolling hills and crossing two creeks was still work, yet easier than he thought it would be. Julius needed rest from the sun and wind, and constant travel exhausted him. He got to Mankota late afternoon, but there was no place to stay. He was prepared for that and asked a local person how far he was from the Montana border—30 miles if he went due south. He reviewed his maps, and calculated that he was about 55 miles from the border town of Opheim in Montana, about where he wanted to cross. As he was leaving Mankota to ride a few more miles before bedding down, a person along the road called out inviting him to stay in his house. Julius took him up on the offer and gladly slept on the floor.

Julius was on the road early, riding in a southeasterly direction with storm clouds gathering behind him. It was humid, muggy weather. About noon, the temperatures dropped dramatically, promising a storm and possibly hail. He had been following a creek with no trees around. Ahead he saw what looked like a homestead shack, so he pedaled as fast as he could for it. The place, with a small barn beside it, had been abandoned. He chose shelter in the barn. He stayed to let the ground dry out some before he started traveling again. It was Monday and he had traveled a long way already, so he would stay here overnight and leave for the area north and east of the Opheim border crossing. A lot of wildlife—deer, partridges, prairie chickens and some antelope—were seen near the road, which always made him feel good. He had passed the halfway mark many miles back, so he felt relaxed, at the same time knowing that the big job was ahead of him. He was thrilled at the prospect of applying for a homestead. His mind was whirling as he traveled. He reached the border about three miles west of the official border crossing. He could calculate the distance from the border after he reached Opheim. By 1915 border crossings had become more formal, and registering at the border was expected. But exhaustive record searches of Julius's border crossing produced no results.

He stayed that night in a boarding house and headed southeast again in the morning through lush grass and rolling terrain along the Poplar River Valley, ideal cattle country. In the days of cattle drives, cattle were driven to this area to graze and fatten up for the eastern markets.

This part of the trip fed Julius's dream of homesteading. He soon felt that he must have reached reservation land, and he saw that the soil was good. He prayed that his homestead would have the same good soil.

He had been pushing his bicycle most of the time since he left Opheim. The grass was very thick and the hills steeper. He realized that he would be sleeping under the stars that night. After looking for a couple hours he found a suitable place to put his bed roll. His food supply of smoked beef had him longing for a change of menu.

In the morning he was able to ride his bike on level terrain. Near noon, he came upon a valley that he estimated was up to seven miles across, with pockets of water in the valley floor. He assumed the creek would flow only during spring runoff and heavy rains. With his sense of dead reckoning, he felt right going southeast. He picked a coulee that he could climb out of on the other side to declining ground where he could ride for a mile before pushing the bike again. He coasted down the easy slope, but his joy came to a quick end, soon as the front wheel went over a rock and the crank sprocket broke. He could still push it to the bottom of the valley.

After resting he made the long slow climb out of the valley, stopping many times to view what he would discover later was Cottonwood Valley. Pushing the load was strenuous, but he came out on flat ground.[13] He reached the crest of the hill and marveled at the complete change in terrain. In a quarter of a mile he looked to the east and saw what could be homestead buildings. He left his bike in the trees and cautiously approached the house. Henry greeted him and said he and

---

13 Thirty years later as we were looking at some of the valleys near the Rauch home, he commented to me that he thought it was the valley he came up with his bicycle. I recall a very rare puzzled look on his face. What an opening to ask questions of course. I regretfully did not.

Lydia ran a sort of way station for travelers such as Julius. At times the floor was so full that if someone wanted to turn they would all have to turn at once—a story that survived for many years. They chatted for hours and Julius was fed. Henry offered to let Julius borrow a saddle horse so he could go to Glasgow for a new sprocket.

The next morning was Sunday July 22nd. It had taken Julius seven days to get here to the Fort Peck Indian Reservation. He did not want to leave for Glasgow, but there was no other choice. He had talked many hours with Henry, who suggested that the first thing Julius should do was to apply for citizenship. There was still a lot of land in the immediate area that was not spoken for, and he urged him to put in an application for a homestead here.

The trip to Glasgow, 45 miles as the crow flies, was long and tiresome. He thought he could make it in three days without pushing the horse too much. It gave him a chance to view the land and explore homesteading activity. He liked the countryside that he rode over. Wildlife was abundant which always warmed his heart. After another night under the stars he rode into Glasgow and found the needed sprocket. He passed the busy land office. He wanted to go in and get acquainted with some of the process, but the mass of homesteaders precluded that and it was time to get started back to the Ferdina place. About 30 miles out of Glasgow Julius came upon a sheep herder's wagon and a large number of sheep. Julius talked to the man who said there was a "band," over a thousand sheep. No homestead shacks were visible and this was free grazing area. With the Homestead Act having been approved, that type of available land would not last long. They visited for a couple hours and Julius realized he needed to get back on his trail. Raising sheep was new to Julius, and he enjoyed learning about it and the shepherd's life, alone with his sheep and only his two dogs for companionship. Julius's preference was raising grain, and he could not wait to plow the first furrow on his own homestead. That night he slept again under the stars and rose before daybreak to return the horse. He saw many deer and some antelope—the first time he had seen this many since leaving home. Many times partridges and pheasants flew up as he rode by. He was learning a lot about the area where he hoped to spend his life. He arrived back at the Ferdinas' place in time for the evening meal. He had much to talk about, and Henry was very interested in his impression of the countryside and how it compared to where he came from in Canada. They fixed the bicycle before it got dark and he was ready to continue his journey in the morning. Henry thought that with an early start and a little luck he could get to Wolf Point before dark. Julius was ready.

The morning of Tuesday July 27th he headed straight south as Henry had suggested, toward some hills. To go around them would take much longer than to stay on course, he rode hard, getting off to push his bike only a few times. He saw Wolf Point when he was about a mile from it, an hour before sundown. He rode up to within a hundred yards of the Great Northern Railroad tracks, got off and slowly pushed his bike up to the tracks. The town was south of the tracks and his eyes were taking in everything in front of him. This was going to be his town: The place to sell his grain, to sell his cattle, to buy groceries, and a place to get on the train to travel east and west. It was a bustling town with a lot of activity on the main street. There were shops for anything he might want or need. His interest settled to a manageable level, and after making a couple of inquiries, he was guided to a boarding house. He had arrived on the Fort Peck Indian Reservation and in Wolf Point after a long bicycle ride and a horseback trip to Glasgow.

Julius was tired, more like exhausted—even at age twenty-two. He realized he needed to rest. The bed was a welcome sight. With his bicycle and possessions secure, he blew out the candle and went to sleep.

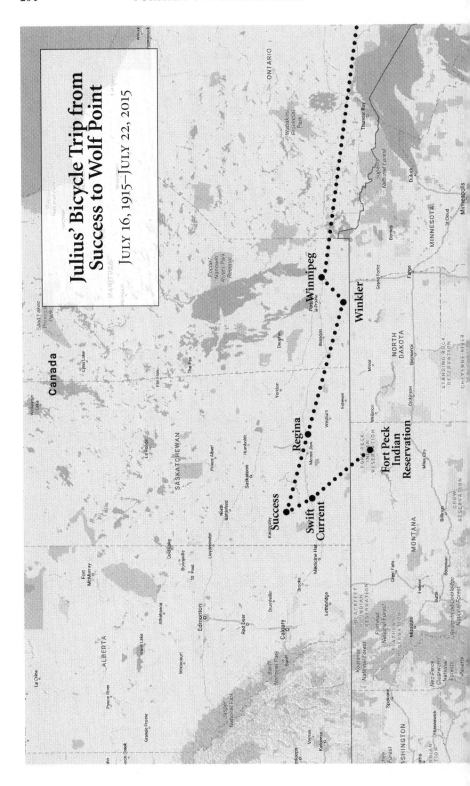

CHAPTER 13

– 1915 –
New Life Begins—Army Service

Julius woke feeling much better, even though he needed more sleep. He realized the importance of returning to Glasgow and getting his citizenship application started. There was a lot of building activity in town. Two two-story buildings were in the early stage of construction—the first floor was for a storefront, with offices on the second. The foundation was already in. Julius did not waste any time finding the man in charge and asking him for a job. Saturday July 29th, 1915 Julius began his first job in Montana. The boss was soon very impressed, and the job was good and just what Julius needed. He decided he would stay on till the buildings were done or until the winter weather shut them down.

He filed his "Declaration papers" August 7th, stating his intention to become a citizen. This was an important step toward his filing for a homestead.

He took the train a couple times to go to Wolf Point to talk with folks about good areas for a homestead. When he mentioned the area straight north, before the Cottonwood, he always got a favorable reaction. On the second trip to Wolf Point he ran into Henry and Lydia Ferdina who had come to town with a team and wagon to buy food staples for their way station. Traffic would soon be stopped by winter, but they were buying for next spring's guests. It was like two long lost cousins meeting, when they got together. He told them he had filed for citizenship and would soon file for a homestead. They suggested he consider some of the land south of where they lived if any was left.

On October 19th, 1915 Julius filed his application for Homestead No. 036465, W½ SE¼ Sec. 13 & NE¼ and W½ SE¼ Sec. 24. T31N R46E, 320 acres @ $3.00 per acre (total of $960). He paid $1.00. On November 17th the balance due of $191.00 was paid. Along with the application were "Corroborating Affidavits" including "Affidavit of Witnesses as to character and reputation of Applicant." He filed an Application for Amendment.

The locator dropped him off at the rooming house where he would get some rest and catch the train for Glasgow. The 50 mile trip was made with quick stops in Oswego, Fraser and Nashua. He got off the train and went to the land office. He expressed his desire to amend the application and swap the 240 acres in Section 13 for the 240 acres in the east half of Section 24. He said that after seeing the land he wanted to have it all in one rectangle, rather than have part of it separated by a half mile which made fencing difficult, and he preferred one block a mile long and a half mile wide. Indeed the requested land to fill out the half section was available.

He continued doing carpentry in Glasgow, except in the hard winter months. His ability was in demand and he gladly accepted all work offered.

The Homestead record states that Julius built his house (homestead shack) April 16, 1916. With a little help, the tar paper shack could have been enclosed in a couple days.

Julius kept a record starting April 14, 1916, the day he established residence on the W ½ SE ¼ Section 24. He stayed until June 30th, his record stating that he had 50 acres broken when he left. He does not state what he did when he left, but he probably returned to Glasgow to work. He arrived back on the homestead August 18 and stayed for one week. October 18 he resumed residence and stayed two weeks, returned again December 1st.

Finally on November 17, 1916 the land exchange was granted. Julius's homestead became E ½ Section 24, Township 31 N, Range 46 E as he had hoped.

His farmyard was placed about halfway between the outside borders on a slight knoll with a gentle slope on the west side. The land on the east side continued level, but dropped off as it approached his eastern border of the half section. On the north side of the farmyard the land sloped into a coulee. The shack was about two hundred yards from the southern border of the section line. He had dug a well and built a shack 12 x 16 covered with shiplap and tar paper nailed down with lath.

When he received correspondence from the Interior Department requesting the second of five payments for $153.40, he asked for an extension till next year saying "so late in the spring of 1916 when he established his residence that he was not able to secure anyone to do the breaking and get his land under cultivation in time to justify him in putting in a crop." He would have no income to make the necessary payment. His extension was granted.

Julius had also built a shelter from the cold Montana winter for his horse—three-sided, with as much of a roof on it as the lumber left over allowed.

Julius was drafted into the US Army October 2, 1917. He was sworn in at Plentywood, Montana, the county seat of Sheridan County where his homestead was. Roosevelt County was later formed out of Sheridan County by the Montana Legislature in 1919. The story in the family is that one day he went to Wolf Point and was advised that he was being drafted into the Army and he had to leave immediately. There is no evidence to confirm or deny that bit of oral history.

Julius wrote a letter dated October 16, 1917 to the US Land Office in Glasgow, Montana. (two weeks after being inducted):

Gentlemen,

I wish to notify you that I am in the Service of the US National Army, and wish that you hold my homestead, and allow no

one to interfere with it. The description of my land is, E ½ of
sec. 24 T. 31 R 46 Montana Mer. Fort Peck Indian Reservation.

Yours truly, Julius Gess

(Old address) Volt, Montana

Present address

10th Battalion
166 Depot Brigade 40th Co.
Camp Lewis, Washington

The letter was immediately forwarded to Montana Senator Henry
L. Myers who was the Chairman of the Committee on Public Lands.
He sent a letter to the Commissioner of the General Land Office at the
Department of the Interior:

> *Dear Sir,*
>
> *I desire to call your attention to the inclosed letter from Julius*
> *Gess a Montana homesteader on the Fort Peck Indian Reser-*
> *vation, but now drafted into the Army and located at Camp*
> *Lewis, Washington.*
>
> *He desires certain information relative to his homestead status*
> *and if you will kindly advise me I shall be obliged.*
>
> *Yours respectfully,*
>
> *H L Myers*

The record shows some correspondence about legislation pending
for people in the service with homestead payment responsibilities.

Julius served with French forces March 6, 1918 to January 1, 1919.
Family correspondence indicates he was serving in the Lorraine, France
area. He served his time as a Military Policeman. No doubt his 6'1½"
height helped him receive that appointment. He was a Pvt 1/c Co-1st
Air Service Mech Regiment.

*Julius and soldier buddy reading War
news in the International Newspaper.*

He was discharged July 5, 1919 in Cheyenne, Wyoming with papers saying his character was excellent, his services honest and faithful, no A.W.O.L. He is entitled to travel pay to Wolf Point, Montana and paid in full $143.25.

Julius got back to his homestead as soon as he could. He was very anxious to get back on his land. When he got there his enthusiasm was quickly dampened. He had been robbed of what machinery he had and everything that was not nailed down. His homestead shack had not been bothered on the inside. Most of the boards had been taken off the horse shelter. He was disappointed but not broken, though it was too late to plant crops. He would do what he could with the land to prepare to plant in the spring and pray the rains would come.

The fall of 1919 Ludwig, August, and Gustav Libke traveled to Volt to bring him a team of horses, a much needed gift from his parents. The secondary purpose was to look over the countryside—Ludwig was considering moving to the area. They made that trip in a "Democrat," a light buggy with tall wheels and a springy ride, pulled by a team. The team for Julius trailed behind the wagon. After resting up a bit they left the homestead in the morning and rode many miles looking at land over that several days. But Ludwig did not see what he thought was good land. After resting up the three men started back to their home near Success.

October 11, 1920 Julius wrote the following letter:

Mr. Clay Tallman:

Dear Sir, I am writing you in regards to my homestead on the Fort Peck Indian Reservation. Serial No. 036465. Must I pay the interest on this land Nov 1st. If so where will I get the money from. I was in the Army 2 years and got out so late last summer that I did not have a chance to prepare my land for this years crop and consequently I have raised practically nothing and will not have enough to pull me thru another year. I must borrow money somewhere, but do not know where just yet.

Tell me will the Government insist that we pay up. Will they treat faithful soldiers in such a way. This land should be given free to us considering that loss we have had in depreciation and stolen property while away in the Army. There is one fact certain I cannot pay up the interest, unless I wish to take chances on starving myself to do it and that I do not propose to do.

Hoping to have a satisfactory answer from you immediately.

Yours Truly

Julius Gess

Volt, Mont.

Julius received a response dated October 29 that his interest payments would not be due until two years from the date of discharge from the Army, July 5, 1921.

July 14, 1920 Julius, a subject of Great Britain, renounced his alliance and fidelity to any foreign prince and particularly to George V, King of Great Britain and Ireland. His document states he emigrated from "Swift Current, Canada" arriving by "private conveyance" (bicycle). He had lived in the US for five years and had lived continuously for the last year in the State of Montana. He had been discharged July 5, 1919 so he met that qualification.

October 30, 1920 the Final Affidavit of Homestead Claimant was filed. Two neighbors had to attest to the fact that he had lived on the property and that he had cultivated the ground he said he did. Those neighbors were Richard Jacobson age 33 and John C. McLachland age 31. Mr. Jacobson left the area in the 1940s, but Mr. McLachland stayed in the area and was friends of Julius and his family till their deaths. He farmed until his sons were old enough to take over the farming.

He stated on his Final Affidavit application that the following ground had been broken and the acres planted:

1916 Broke 50 acres of ground.

1917 Planted those 50 acres to wheat. Yield 9 bushel per acre.

1918 Same ground planted to wheat. Yield 5 bushel per acre.

One of the neighbors planted and harvested his 50 acres while he was in the Army.

1919 Same ground summerfallowed.

1920 Broke 50 acre and seeded to flax. No crop. Old ground 37 acres in wheat,

13 acres in Oats.

Total land in Cultivation 100 acres.

Improvements to the homestead.

House 14 x 30 feet   Barn 34 x 36 feet

Granary 10 x 13

The well he dug was listed.

2½ miles part 2 strand and part 3 strand wire fence.

Total value of improvements was listed as $1,000.

April 1921 Julius's oldest sister Mathilda arrived to help him on the homestead. She cooked and kept house for him until she left to go back home December 21, 1922. It was a huge help to him as he tried to manage farming, his cattle and the horses.

The following news item appeared in the weekly *Wolf Point Herald News* in 1922 under the Volt News section. "Miss Matilda Gess was the honor guest of a surprise birthday party at Liberty School." The party was Saturday November 25th, the day before her birthday. Liberty School was about ten miles from the homestead. She had been invited to attend by a young couple in the neighborhood. Mathilda had been with the family when they arrived from Volhynia, having traveled in her mother's womb. She was born five months after they settled in Winkler.

January 2, 1922 the Department of the Interior advised Julius that although he had "proven up," the final certificate was being withheld because the final payment for the land was still outstanding. They further stated that when all payments were made, if the records showed no objections, a final certificate would be issued.

His crop was totally destroyed by hail July 21, 1923 yet the interest due was $65.28. The Department of the Interior was threatening to foreclose. Julius wrote letters to ask for extensions and describing the crop destruction. The extension was granted.

Julius's sister Winnie arrived to help him November 1923. She was listed on Border crossing record as 16 years and 7 months of age. She liked to work on his homestead and talked about it in later years as being a good experience. She related how one of the bachelor neighbors gave her the eye every time he came around to "borrow" something from Julius.

Julius was very creative when it came to dealing with homestead payments, lack of rain, and hail storms. He wrote to the Department of the Interior and asked that his land be reappraised. "He wrote that portions of the land was traversed by deep ravines and coolies" and was not suitable for any purpose other than grazing. He also stated that "there was a great amount of gravel mixed in the soil, actually, in all the land." The Department lost his first letter for a reappraisal and they acknowledged the second letter. October 17, 1925 the Department of the Interior denied his request for re-appraisal. The Superintendent recommended that no change be made to the original price of three dollars an acre. Julius had tried and he would continue to do his best job at farming, hoping for rain and no hail.

He improved the farmstead as he could with very little income. He had a two story house that was impressive, given the era and the farming conditions. The barn had been built so his precious horses had protection from the cold windy winters. He had managed to buy a Model T coupe. Although it was not known for sure, photos indicate it may have been quite new. The struggle continued and the terrible disappointments seemed to not let up. Bad crops, drought, hail, strong winds, and unfavorable prices for what was harvested were just a few of the obstacles that the homesteaders of that time endured. Many left the land and went to find work wherever they could. Julius told Victor about homesteaders who had been foreclosed on by the bank, which auctioned off all of the farmer's equipment, livestock and household goods. The farmers would get together and bid pennies on the items and then give whatever they bought back to the farmer—the homesteading spirit was one of helping each other. Even though they lived miles apart, they acted as neighbors. (Author's note: I saw this referenced several times. I recall watching Julius meet someone whom he hadn't seen in a long time. A meeting like that prompted a handshake and often a reference to being neighbors. Recalling one trip when we went to the Cottonwood Valley to get a truck load of gravel, we stopped at a farmhouse to ask directions. The lady recognized Julius and greeted him with "long time neighbor." She made reference to old time dances that everyone used to attend as they bantered a bit before he asked for directions. This event happened in the late '40s.

There were many community gatherings where people could visit and catch up on the latest. Dances were held during the warmer months, and people would travel from miles around to attend. One such dance was held in the Nels & Nettie Lund's barn. The location was close to the Ferdina wayside station, three miles from Julius's homestead. Another location was a large community hall called Silver Star. It was north northeast of Ferdina's place and south southwest of the town of Scobey. Huge dances were held there and many from the Volt community traveled the distance to attend. In those days the road from Wolf Point went straight north on the Powder River Trail, crossing the Cottonwood and continuing to Scobey. The road went right by the Silver Star community hall. Children also attended the dances. If people were lucky there would be a room where the children and some mothers could spend time. If the room cut out some of the sound, the children might be able to sleep. Most of the time there was no room and children fell asleep on piles of jackets. More important than the dance was a chance to catch up.

The following news item appeared in the *Wolf Point Herald News* in 1926, day and month unknown: "The Powder River Trail from Wolf Point to Scobey is now so well marked it can be traveled at night. The road is in good shape. The trip is now less than 60 miles, more than half of it is graded."

Julius was one of the first in the community to have a radio—from a radio kit that he put together. It was his way of tapping into the outside world, amazed that with the radio he could get instant news. His political interests grew as he listened to what was happening around the country. He no longer had to read in the paper what might be days old. This interest grew into a politically active life.

Melvin Ferdina related that he and his father Henry would drive to Julius's place many evenings to listen to station CFCN in Regina. Melvin said that the earphones were clamped on his head and he had to push against them to hear, causing small blisters on his ears. Those three men would eventually own television sets and spend hours watching whatever was most interesting.

This was the time period when most homesteaders bought a Model T, which gave them mobility and greater travel opportunities. It was a new world for the homesteader when he got his first car, most likely a Model T. Mechanical travel meant one could drive many miles to visit someone on a Sunday, or drive to a special spot to picnic. It was a wonderful experience to crank up the Model T, get in the car, and then leave—in contrast to harnessing the team and hooking them up to the buggy and then travel at a slow pace. Horses, while providing the ability to move about, were limiting, and getting the horses harnessed and hitched up took a lot of time and effort. Teams needed year around attention—hay, water, grazing and shelter. Some homesteaders lovingly referred to their horses as "hay burners." At ten cents a gallon, a dollar's worth of gas would take them a long way. It was a treat for the homesteading family to go to town to see a movie. Church was rarely attended because of the distance to town, so on occasion the Lutheran families attended a service or special event at the Mennonite Church closer by. The Model T was there and, with proper maintenance, waiting to travel. The mechanically inclined homesteader quickly learned how to take care of his precious automobile. They had to be cranked with care, and many a greenhorn broke his thumb if the engine quickly backfired as they were trying to start it. The proper way to grasp the crank was to keep the thumb on the same side as the fingers. The newfangled machine gave Americans out in the country the ability to move around, hastening the development of the countryside. It helped to fill a social void as travel to neighbors and events was more possible.

In 1926 the following news item appeared in the Volt section of the *Wolf Point Herald News.* "Eight Volt farmers—Ben Thompson, Julius Gess, Frans Borgeson, Henry Ferdina, Alfred Johnson, Art Schwan, Nels Lund and Russell Hanson—graded a stretch of road four miles long running past their farms. They were unassisted by county or town and did the work because of benefits to their community." Those men would tackle jobs with whatever equipment they had. They did it because they knew they were gradually improving the quality of their lives.

Working together like that hastened the development of their community.

CHAPTER 14

— 1920S —
Model Ts and Romance

Newspaper clippings of the Volt community in the early 1920s indicate that Julius Gess was a well-known and respected farmer with an interest in community affairs. He caught up on the local happenings at the Volt store and Post Office.

Henry Jantz delivering mail to the Volt Post Office
to be picked up by the homesteaders.

217

Because Volt had a Post Office it was on the map. Mail was picked up in Wolf Point by Henry Jantz and delivered to Volt as well as to the Waska Post Office in the Cottonwood Valley and to Lustre, several miles west and a bit north of Volt. Henry Jantz's mail wagon, pulled by a team of horses, was light-weight with tall wheels, the taller rear wheels about four feet high. The seat had springs, and the long box, a foot high, was big enough to hold the many sacks of mail. The Volt store carried staples, shoes, pants and items that the homesteaders needed between trips to Wolf Point. Just as important was the time catching up on what was happening in the neighborhood.

Julius made the eight mile round trip to get his mail a couple of times a week. On a particular trip in April 1926 he heard there was going to be a dance that Saturday night in Nels Lund's barn. The rest of the week the dance was on his mind. Finally Saturday night came and he cranked up his Model T for the three mile trip to Lund's place. The whole neighborhood was there, for the dance was in the hay mow.

Julius kept a record of his meeting Alma, as well as their subsequent meetings.

Saturday evening April 24, 1926

There was a dance at Lunds Barn. There I seen a girl who I thought to be a married woman I asked Mark [Mark Blankenship] her name and found her to be Alma Applegren. I danced with her a few times. I thought she was just the girl for me, but, I held back not wanting to spoil a good thing by too rapid action.

May 1, at the normal training dance she was again present and we danced oftener then the first time, and she told me that she would not be present at the dance on May 8. I did not feel so very badly about it, but thought I'd like to see her again. May 12 was Field day at Volt. I knew she would be there as her sister Agnes was one of the teachers taking part, it was a very chilly day and I went there more to see her then anything else. We were together quite a bit that day and we kind of agreed to meet at the old time dance the next Monday nite. I went to the Legion meeting that nite and I thought the meeting would never come to a close finally one of the boys had to go to work and I jumped up with him so then they made us stay and have ice cream & cake. When this was devoured I lost no time getting to the dance hall there she was and we danced a lot together and talked quite a lot. By this time I felt myself sinking very rapidly. We had the home sweet home dance and she agreed to come to the dance in her own car on May 22. I was there but she failed to show up. I felt pretty badly about it and was quite disappointed and really did not enjoy myself as much as usual.

May 23 was Sunday and I lost no time getting to town and I met her in front of the Lutheran Church, she invited me up to dinner which was just what I wanted her to do. After dinner we took a little car ride of some 20 miles and had some refreshments when back in town. After that we went to her house, there we had a little lunch, the cake & coffee was delicious after this I left and mad a date for Wed nite May 26th. We went to the show that nite and after the show had some Ice cream then I took her home, we stayed in the car when we got home and had a great visit—after a while I got a hold of her fingers and hands a little later I got my arms around her I felt that if I wasn't in love with her, there I could not say what it was I knew very well that there was no keeping back I had fallen indeed, and since there was no resistance the first Kiss was placed on her wonderful lips then I knew that every thing was as I wished it to be and presumably as she wished it to be.

May 29, we started to a dance, but we never got there stopping on the road several times I found it very difficult to drive the car and do what I should so finally we found an very good parking place near her home on this nite I asked her a certain question to which she did not give an answer, it having come so soon I did not care as I had not planned on asking her for about 2 weeks and I felt certain that the answer would be what I wanted anyhow.

June 2 we had another very pleasant and loving visit. At this time we talked of various things and wedding plans I was so delighted to think that I could be so lucky to find such a good loving and Christian girl in the Wolf Point vicinity, something that I had waited for such a long time, and I pray may God bless her and keep her for me. Now I feel more at ease and she does not seem to be a phantom anymore, something that may slip away at anytime, she seems very real to me now. I will be very disappointed if I don't see her at the dance on June 5- June 6 we both had the best time so far of our lives. We took a drive out to my farm we had wished to keep this a secret but it was observed by 2 neighbors, however we did not mind as our behavior was strictly what it should be. On June the 8th I seen her again for a little while, she was not feeling well. The dance of Sat nite & the long ride on Sunday tired her out very much and I hope that she will get well speedily. During the week from June 6 to 12 we met and were together 4 times she is a real Pal and the more I see her the more I love her. We are very happy when together. On June 13th we met again and had a grand time talking of various things at this time we found that we were not engaged yet, so when I asked her to be my wife, she said "I will". It made me so happy! Besides I liked the answer a lot better then if she had said yes. I am indeed a happy man, and I will spare nothing to make her a happy woman. I am writing this on the 17th of June, and I haven't seen my Alma since Sunday four long days and it will be tomorrow night before I will see her. I don't know how I will stand it I should be happy since we have had 1 3/4 inches of rain since Sunday and I am glad of it too as it will put the wheat in such shape so we can go thru with our plans nicely. But I have a queer feeling since this after noon and it bids fair to keep on until I see her again. I do hope that she will decide to remain at her present home this summer and not go east. As it would certainly make me very lonesome. June 18 was the dance at Benrud. My Alma came out and met me at my house and we went to the dance in my car. We had a great time. On June 22, I came in to see her we went to a show called Uncle

Toms Cabin. The show was great, but the time we had after the show was greater by a long ways. At this time she got her diamond, and the poor child was completely put out she was so surprised. She certainly is the dearest girl and I know that she will be just the nicest pal & Wife to me. On June 24 we had another very pleasant visit. We of course talked of a good many things as usual, she went to a convention at Plentywood so I will not see her again until June 28. We were together quite a few times from the last date and July 11, on July 6 we took in the Stampede, and dance in the evening also the following nite. On the eleventh we went to Church to hear M. Gram give a play called the Fool it was great. After this we took a drive and had some refreshments and I did not get away from her home until early on the 12th. (The record ended with this last entry.)

During a celebration for Alma's 95th birthday, long-time Wolf Point resident Norman Nedrud had a story to tell. He said that Alma chaperoned the Wolf Point Luther League group as they traveled to Plentywood for the convention June 25–27, 1926. He said that the Luther League teased her about marrying a guy named Gess. He said she got a lot of teasing and took it in good stride. I told Norman that wasn't the first time I heard comments about the name Gess.

Alma talked many times about her meeting Julius at Lund's place in April and how they were married five months (so soon) later on October 1, 1926. She enjoyed telling about the wonderful feeling the evening he slipped a ring on her finger. The romance grew more intense and Julius put lots of miles on that Model T traveling back and forth to visit Alma.

He was doing a financial two-step that fall. The Department of Interior demanded that he make a payment of $481.85. He gave a sworn statement that his crop yield was very light and he could only make a partial payment. They agreed to accept a $200.00 payment and put off the final payment for one year. The receipt shows he purchased a beautiful 3/8 of a carat diamond ring from Sears Roebuck for $106.25. The expense of an extended honeymoon in the Model T further strained the budget. Victor thinks the Department of the Interior would have allowed for Love expenses.

The wedding invitations were sent out for a Candlelight Wedding at the First Lutheran Church in Wolf Point at 5:00 in the evening. This was a newly formed congregation and they were the first couple married in the Church. The Church at the time was in the basement, as that was as far as construction had gone.

Two weeks before the wedding a Bridal Shower was held with 50 ladies in attendance. Games were played and wedding photos of those married were shared with the ladies.

The planning continued and soon the wedding day arrived.

The following is the *Wolf Point Herald* newspaper account of the wedding:

> *Gess-Applegren: Last Friday evening in the Lutheran Church the Rev. A. O. Johnson united in marriage Miss Alma Amanda Applegren and Julius Gess. A large crowd of friends and relatives attended the wedding and the reception which followed it.*
>
> *The bride entered the Church on the arm of her father, G.S. Applegren, who gave her in marriage. The wedding march from "Lohengrin" was played by Miss Lucille Zimmerman. The bride was preceded by her bridesmaids who were her sisters, the Misses Ellen and Agnes Applegren. Dainty little Miss Jean Bjorgen was flower girl. August Applegren was best man.[14]*
>
> *The bride was lovely in an exquisite gown of white beaded georgette and a long veil of white tulle, arranged in cap shape. The bridesmaids wore dainty frocks of a delicate blue shade trimmed in silk lace to match. The flower girl wore a pink dress of the same pattern as those worn by the bridesmaids. During the reception which followed the ceremony Roland Thom gave two violin solos and Miss Helen Listerud sang. Both were accompanied by Miss Lucille Zimmerman.*

---

14 Julius's brother Emil was going to be the best man. Something unforeseen happened and he was unable to make it so August was called upon to serve.

The Church parlors were attractively decorated with a number of floor lamps arranged about to give a cozy air and cedar boughs banked around the altar. Mrs H. A. Schoening and Mrs. William Zimmerman had charge of arranging the decorations.

Mrs. Ole Erickson and Mrs. Anna Sethre had charge of the refreshments. The young ladies who served were Elizabeth Strand, Harriet Strand, Blanche Pipal, Beulah Thom, Edna Kjensrud, Anna Olson, Florence Olson, Hulda Nyland and Ruth Nedrud.

Mr and Mrs Gess left the morning after the ceremony by car for an extensive wedding trip. They will go to Glasgow, Great Falls and afterwards to Canada. After their return they will be at home on the groom's ranch north of town.

The bride is the daughter of Mr. and Mrs. G. S. Applegren and is a well known and popular member of the younger set. She is a graduate of the schools of Winthrop, Minnesota.

The groom has resided in the north country for many years, coming here from Canada. He has a new modern ranch home there and is among the most well known and successful of the north country residents.

Back row: August Applegen, Julius.
Front row: Agnes (Alma's sister), Alma, Zimmerman girl,
Ellen (Alma's sister).

The next morning everyone in the wedding party got dressed up again for a session with the photographer. It was 1926 and photos in Wolf Point could only be taken in natural light. After the photos were taken, and best wishes for a safe trip were said, the newlyweds got in the Model T and headed west.

The following is a record Alma kept of their travels. It was an ambitious trip including some health care, beautiful scenery at Banff, Calgary a big city and a visit to his parent's home near Success, Saskatchewan.

The following agenda was written by Alma (with the exception of a small amount by Julius) in a small 2.2 x 5.2 inch 1925 Plymouth Binder Twine Memo Book. It was discovered by Victor Gess April 14, 1998 while going through pictures and papers found while cleaning out Alma's house March 31, 1996. It was copied exactly as written. Much of what she wrote was in short phrases apparently to accommodate the small memo book. While the account does not go into much detail about the trip, it does tell the exact route that was taken:

Left Wolf Point Oct 2, 4:30 arrived in Glasgow 7:20. Stayed in Shannon Hotel room 12. Speed registered 11,934 in Wolf Point Speed reg. 11,987 in Glasgow, left Glasgow 8:45 Oct 3. Saco 10:40 ice cream, roads fairly good from Glasgow. Boudin 12:05 roads fairly good onto Malta had chicken dinner at City café, arrived 12:50 Left Malta at 1:25 bad road thru Wagner and Dodson graveled road from Dodson on. Stopped at Harlem for ice cream arrived at 3:25. S.R. 12112 Arrived at Havre 5:10 Speed reg. 12157. Left 5:20 Arr. in Big Sandy 6:40 roomed at Montana Hotel room no 27. Oct, 4th beautiful morning had breakfast at Big Sandy Café. Predictions for road to Great Falls, bad Arrived in the beautiful Great Falls at 12 o'clock had dinner at cafeteria next door was Columbia Hotel where we had a real nice room no. 77 on the 2nd floor. Then we got 1 dozen Asters and a 2 doz. Roses for Mrs A.O. Johnson sent them to Dr. Keenans office also to Dr. Edmonson had teeth finished on Oct. 5. Done a little shopping. Oct 6 we drove out to the Great Falls on Missouri and left G.F. at 10:30 reg. 12310. Then on thru Power and stopped at Dutton for dinner at 12:30 Speed reg. 12351 left Dutton 1:05 Arrived 4:20 in Shelby speed reg. 12412. Seen Joe Djersdof. Had one blow out and one flat tire North of Conrad, arrived in Sunburst 10 Min to 6. Roomed at Northern Hotel room No 39. Oct. 7 Left Sunburst at 8:40 Speed reg. 12443 Arrived at Sweet grass at 9. Custom place then on to Coutts only a few roads 2nd Customs Canada. Speed reg. 12452 one oil well here. On our way to Lethbridge we went thru sugar beet country. One picture taken, Arrived in Lethbridge at 12:10 some good graveled roads. Street cars almost as large as Great Falls but not near as busy. Roomed at Hotel Dallas room no. 17. Had supper and breakfast at Halsom Bakery. Left Lethbridge at 9:30. Speed reg. 12537. This was Oct 8 Arrived in Carmangay stopped for dinner at Grange Hotel. Speed reg 12578. Left here at 1:15 Stopped at Nanton for pie & coffee (at Liberty) 22 miles out of town got stuck in mud was assisted by farmer Arrived in Calgary at 8:30 Speed reg. 12681. Oct 9. (following written by Julius) By J.G. This morning we went out and had breakfast then we went out shopping and just before noon the male part of our party went and fixed up the car for tomorrows trip and the female part wrote a letter to our sister. After dinner we went to a show saw the Dempsy Tunney fight pictures after we went to see the C.F.C.N. broadcasting studio and the City park in the evening following this the old lady took a bath and the old man washed his feet that's all. By J.G. Oct. 10. On Sunday morning we left Calgary at 8:30 Speed registered 12682 at 11:20 we arrived in Gleichen at 11:20 WheatBelt. At Bassaro at 12:30 we stopped for dinner here it snowed had more or less all day. At 7:40 we arrived in Empress snowing hard. 225 miles from Calgary. On Monday Oct 11. We started out for Success had dinner at Cabri Made Success at 3 o'clock. The End (Oct 9–11 written by Julius) (the photo on the next page was taken of the honeymoon couple on the steps of the Success farm house was taken on October 17, 1926) Homeward bound After 10 well spent days at home with our folks on the 21st day being a clear and beautiful A.M. we were again ready to start. Our speed reg. 13180 left (thurs.) Oct. 21, at 8:05 o'clock for Moose

Sunday October 17, 1926—Julianna front white dress, Ludwig white shirt, Julius looking over Ludwig's left shoulder, Alma to Ludwig's left.

Jaw arrived at Moose Jaw at 10:40 stopped at Canadian Café for pie and coffee. Speed. Re. 13242 started again at 10:50. About 2:30 finally found Emil after 3 left for Regina arrived there 5:15 Speed reg. 13___. Roomed at Metropole room no 38 Oct 22, We arose 7:45 breakfast at Savoy Café it was rather a dark morning as it was snowing a trifle. This being our 3rd week anniversary. Oct 23 we left Regina 8:15 Speed reg. 13376 at 11:30 we reached Ogema had dinner. Speed reg 13451. 90 miles to Scobey 11:50 off again. (The record ended here. Nothing about the remainder of the trip.)

They arrived at the house Julius had built early evening October 23rd, after a three week honeymoon trip. It was a dream trip that covered about 1600 miles. Now it was time to settle down, and this newlywed couple was ready to do it. It was 12 years since Julius had put in his homestead application. He had survived all the hazards that had driven many of the homesteaders away. He had the basics all set up for a lifetime of farming—a good two story house and a big barn. Now he had an automobile. His goal was to make the final payment of $321.84 to the Department of the Interior next October and receive the Title for his 320 acre homestead.

Alma's parents and siblings had moved from Winthrop, Minnesota to Wolf Point in March 1915. Her father had homesteaded 320 acres a mile north of the railroad tracks that ran through Wolf Point. Her brother John had homesteaded 320 acres that was 8 miles north of Wolf Point. John worked his homestead, married, raised a family and lived on his homestead for many years. Her sister Anna had also filed for a homestead that was near John's. Her premature death in 1917 cut short her homestead dreams. They made the move filling three immigrant railroad cars used to transport farm machinery, household goods and some livestock. They moved in March and Alma had to remain in Minnesota because she had not finished Confirmation class in the Lutheran Church at Bernadotte, Minnesota. It was very important to the family that she complete her studies and be confirmed, which happened June 13th. The next day she took a train from Winthrop to Minneapolis where she changed trains for the trip to Wolf Point. When she arrived in Wolf Point, her mother met her with a one horse buggy and took her home. When she arrived it was raining heavily, so the station agent offered to take the luggage into the depot where they could pick it up in the morning. When they went down in the morning, her trunk was still sitting by the railroad tracks. Her clothes were ruined.

Alma worked for Sherman Cogswell's general store and Indian trading post in old town Wolf Point by the Missouri River. Eventually the town moved a mile north, next to the Great Northern Railroad tracks.

After a few years Alma's father decided to start a dairy, as there was none in the area. The family all became expert at milking cows. They sold milk in town, delivering to businesses and residents. Little did she know that her milking skills would help them survive the depression of the thirties.

Within a few months a milk cow was purchased. This was needed because children would require milk. The idea was to sell the cream when they were producing enough, which was profitable. Julius did not have milking cows in the plan when he built the barn so he had to build stanchions and cement gutters. Eventually there was enough room for eight milk cows. Later on, every Saturday there was a trip to town to deliver either a five or eight gallon cream can to the train depot, where it was put on the next train east, to the creamery in Williston, North Dakota, a distance of one hundred miles.

Chickens were raised and eventually enough eggs were produced to take to town to sell. This was what helped them get through the depression. Many homesteaders did similar things. Their practice of milking cows ended sooner than it did on Julius's homestead. Good things are hard to stop. Eventually hogs and cattle were produced in numbers that helped the farming budget.

Julius was a man who preferred the land and wanted to earn most of his living from the seeds he put in the ground. He did not like raising cattle and having to farm with horses. It was a happy day when he could buy a tractor. He dreamed of the day when you put gas in the tractor, hook it up to that particular piece of machinery, and go out to the field. This was a big difference from catching the horses, harnessing as many as six of them, and lining them all up in front of a piece of machinery. He couldn't wait till that opportunity arrived.

In the spring of 1927 Julius seeded his crop with a six horse team pulling the drill. (Seems like a lot of horse power to pull the drill.) The discs on the drill came together in the front and were about three inches apart in the back. The spread would allow the seed room to drop. The big wheels would come along and pack the seed covered by dirt that had fallen back over the seed. The discs were lowered into the ground 4–6 inches, and the work of moving them through the dirt began. Note on the picture that there is only one line going to each of the outside horses, enough to control the six horses. The four in the center were squeezed into doing what the outside two were directed to do by Julius.

The all-purpose Model T also grinds grain.

Julius was able to make the final payment of interest and principal before the deadline in October 1927. The Department of the Interior approved the issuance of a Patent for his homestead February 1, 1928. At last the homestead was his. It had been 13 years since his application had been submitted. He had struggled most of those years. This was home for him and his family, and he would continue to work it to the best of his ability. He thought with more land and hard work he could provide a good living for his family. Now that the homestead was his, he was free to add land to his farm. Because of a technicality he had been unable to buy more land until he received the Patent. With homesteaders leaving, the possibility of being able to buy land near his place was good.

The Model Ts of the day were a versatile piece of machinery. They were not thought of as just a car for transportation. Some even used their "car" in the field to pull light machinery, though maybe there were a few snapped drive shafts. Julius used his Model T to grind grain for the cattle and hogs. Imagine a single bachelor on his homestead able to buy a Model T. A supply of gas would be necessary to get it home. That involved five gallon gas cans, and several of them. The buyers of the Model T soon became very proficient at fixing the car whenever it broke down. Of course there were times when the breakdown meant that it needed to be taken to someone with more mechanical ability, so the sight of a team of horses pulling a Model T was not unusual.

CHAPTER 15

— 1928 —
Struggles and a Growing Family

For the arrival of their first child, Julius built a crib and Alma made blankets. They had planned for Alma to go to her parent's home to await the arrival. February 1st when the time was close, they would take her to the midwife birthing center less than a mile away. Julius prepared the team and sled for the trip. He had built a light frame to cover their legs and mid-section, enclosed it with a tarp and put a small stove on the floor. Alma reported that when they left they just headed south, not following any road, though there were some roads in the community—but Julius knew the quickest way was to head out across the prairie. With a fire in the stove, the tarps and blankets covering them, she said the trip was comfortable, and that it did not seem to take very long. No matter what her later thoughts were, it most likely took a full day. Julius returned home the next day, and on February 5th he wrote a letter to Alma saying the calves were looking good, he was watering the plants, and it is a nice day with the thermometer reaching 40. His letter sounded as if he did not like being a bachelor again. He rode his mail over to the Volt Post Office.

He also got news of his daughter's birth by mail. Helen Lorinda Gess was born February 13, 1928, healthy and with good lungs.

Being the middle of winter Alma and her baby stayed at her parents' place. Julius was getting a little anxious as time moved on and his family still was not home. He wrote the following letter:

Feb 24, 1928

Dearest Alma,

How are you these cold & stormy days & how is the baby. I hope you are both felling fine and strong. I wonder where you are now. I will address this letter to 402 as I think you are home by this time. Will I have been plastering & painting everything is painted with new paint.

The big room looks real pretty with the light colored walls. The ceiling in the Kitchen has given me oodles of trouble and just yesterday I went over a few spots it looks pretty good now and I hope it will stay so a while. Well I think you won't hardly know this place when you come here again to live.

The plants & fish are still alive also the yellow dog but I may shoot him if he don't get better soon now he eats twice a day and lays under the porch the rest of the time. I had intended to have feed today but it's a little too windy & cold. I may go to the store this afternoon and see how the car runs in the new snow. There don't seem to be so much so now but then the ruts are all full, if it only lets up. Then it won't be long before we will be going to town again. I don't know just when I can come now as I don't want to be the first one over the road, but I thought if you would be ready to come out next week. I would come in then if not before. I am getting very lonesome for you. If you don't come out soon I will be an old hibernating bachelor again as I am already sleeping in my underwear see? Well I churned this morning but have done nothing with the butter.

The radio works real good. I heard Senator Jim Reed Lambasting Coolidge last nite from Denver. He certainly had the dope on them.

Well honey if you don't see me before Sunday then write again. So I know just how you are making it.

Your loving husband says so long with lots of kisses. Julius

Finally on Saturday March 3rd, a clear day, Julius was able to drive to town to get Alma and the baby. It had not snowed for a couple of days and the road had been traveled so he did not have to break a trail. Such a difference—taking an hour to get to Alma's parent's place rather than the full day it took in the sled. It was a great homecoming. He had been a bachelor for over a month and Alma did not say a word about the condition of the kitchen as she walked into it. They were a happy family, Helen was doing well, and the joy of that new baby was exciting for them.

A new routine was working its way into the Gess family. Taking care of the baby, milking cows, feeding hogs, and planning for 100 chicks to arrive in a month. They both knew that routine would be with them a long time. By the end of April if not before, crops would be planted. Before then he would prepare seed and make sure the harnesses were all in good shape.

A field of crested wheatgrass—a hearty perennial that thrives in arid climates like the Fort Peck Indian Reservation—had been planted for his winter hay supply. It is usually cut and stacked for feed, and not grazed, and hauled into the barn by the team pulling a four wheel hay rack. While Julius would be inside the hay mow stacking it, whoever was helping was on the hay wagon pitching hay into the barn—a hot and sweaty job—but he did not mind as the alternative would have been no hay crop to put away for winter use.

In a good year the granary was full, with hay to get through the winter and have some left over. The garden was growing in size and requiring more work to process what it produced. Butchering a hog or a beef required several days to prepare the meat. Chickens were butchered and canned in quart jars in the pressure cooker. These went into the basement for storage until used.

The family was concerned about the health of Alma's mother, Amanda, a beautiful name passed on as Alma's middle name. She had not been feeling well for months, though she still went through the daily routine. She rested during the day which was something she had never done. Alma and her siblings were vigilant, stopping by more often to check on her. Sister Agnes had married in December 1927 and was living with her husband Martin on a homestead he had acquired from Casper Grondahl about 30 miles NNE of Wolf Point. Sister Ellen left home in October 1928 to go to college in Valley City, North Dakota. Brother John called her home to be with their mother whose health was rapidly deteriorating. She had RN care for about a month, then Ellen accompanied her to a hospital in Minot, North Dakota. She was very weak, but on the trip home she and Ellen were able to have some conversations. She died December 19, 1928 and was buried December 23rd in the King Cemetery, next to her daughter Anna who died in 1919. The cemetery was named after an early Presbyterian missionary couple, Rev. Richard and Cynthia King who had moved to Wolf Point in 1893. They had a son, Kenneth, in 1894. Two months later Rev. King died, and Cynthia chose to stay in Wolf Point. There are also several headstones marking the burial of Indian scouts and prominent Wolf Point families. That cemetery was eventually referred to as the Indian Cemetery, after Lyman Clayton Sr. bought some land and started the Greenwood Cemetery. Greenwood was the maiden name of Mrs. Clayton. Most future burials took place there.

The death of Alma's mother was a shock to the family, and especially to Alma who had just become a mother. Ellen stayed home with her father that winter, but left again in the fall of 1929 to return to college.

While mourning the death of her mother, Alma and Julius were preparing to become parents again in the middle of the summer. Several things would be different. The trip to Wolf Point would be in a Model A instead of a sled. Summertime weather would not be a problem, unless a heavy downpour got in the way of travel plans. Alma's mother would not be there to help in those first few days after the baby arrived, but no doubt Julius would be able to go to Wolf Point to get them when they were ready to go home. Arrangements had been made for Helen to stay with Ellen at their dad's homestead a mile north of Wolf Point. The summer was hot and there were some sandstorms caused by fields being plowed in the spring for seeding, leaving bare soil still waiting for roots to take hold. When hot weather came too quickly, it drew the moisture out of the ground, which strong winds blew high in the air.

Saturday July 20th the family loaded up the Model A and left for Alma's father's place. It was a comforting drive with a little bit of going home and a lot of sorrow for missing her mother, though Ellen would be there to care for Helen.

Lorraine Charlotte was born Friday, July 26, 1929. She was a healthy baby and it was a happy day sometime later when she let out with a big laugh. A week later the family of four headed back to the homestead. Alma said, "I never get caught up with what I have to do." The garden always had something ripe at this time of the year. There were tomatoes ready to be picked and canned. The tall golden reddish wheat waved in the breeze and seemed to say they were getting closer to harvest time. Alma had the help of a girl from town for August and September who was paid 50 cents a day, which help made life a bit easier.

With cold weather in the air there was a rush to prepare for a winter of freezing temperature and snow. The garden had provided food for the winter and chickens had been butchered and canned. Quart jars lined the shelves in the basement.

Then came the fateful day that would gain the attention of every American and countries around the world. The stock market had been slowing down most days as the end of October neared. On October 29, 1929 the stock market crashed, a day that would forever be called Black Tuesday. Over 16 million shares traded and billions of dollars were lost, wiping out thousands of investors. Stocks were so low that there was nowhere to go but up. The market did rally for a few weeks, but then it slowly dropped and the country slumped into the Great Depression. By 1932 the stocks were worth about 20% of what they had been in 1929. The stock market crash was not the sole reason for the depression, though it accelerated the global economic collapse. By 1933 half the banks had failed and the unemployment rate was 30%.

Julius would listen to the radio hoping to hear some words of hope. He and Alma wondered if they would be able to survive and hold onto their farm. They did not realize how well positioned they were for the years ahead. As they talked to neighbors, they realized they had been doing just what was needed to get through the tough years. They would try to milk more cows and raise more chickens so they could sell more cream and eggs. Julius's main interest in the news was what was happening politically. He appreciated living in a free country and was very curious about its inner workings. He quickly became more familiar with the politics of how things got done and was frustrated with inaction by Congress. He could not understand how seemingly fine pieces of legislation would languish in Congress and never be turned into law.

There were many things that came together to create his political interest. First and foremost was his farming interest. He felt that the farmer, be he a new farmer or a homesteader like himself, should be presented with a fair market price for his product, which was grain and livestock. During the twenties and thirties when it was unusual to harvest a high yield, he should be able to get a price for his crop that would at least cover the cost of production. This issue he carried with him and worked on till he turned the farm over to his youngest son. He traveled to county, state and national conventions in pursuit of that goal. Did he ever think about where he was born and the way farming was done in those days? What about the years in Saskatchewan working on his own homestead and his father's and his neighbors'? Did he think about those formative years that had honed his skills at farming? Those great years gave him the ability to farm his homestead and hold onto it during the roughest years of the depression. Most people that knew him would probably answer no—he did not think of those days. He was always thinking ahead and laying out plans in his head, preparing for the worst possible day that might confront him and Alma.

Even if he did not think about those days, he was drawing on them all the time. But it must be mentioned that the Germans who emigrated from Volhynia and the Volga region of Russia did not talk about their lives back home. Some of that can be traced back to leaving because of undesirable political situations. They felt that families and friends left behind might be feeling the sting of their having left, though the situation at the time the Gess/Rode family left Volhynia was not subject to beatings by soldiers. They were only looking for an opportunity and a better place to live. Julius inherited that typical German blood of the time, looking for a better place to live.

The decade of the 1920s was about to close, and Julius was not looking back. He was determined to keep a positive view and pray that the depression would soon be over. Little did he or most people know that they were about to experience or observe tremendous suffering, with millions of people out of work with the last ounce of hope drained out. Julius wrote his congressman and senators suggesting things that he felt could be done to improve conditions. He was always doing things to improve his lot, the family's, or the community's.

He never gave up, and when Saturday came it was the day to go to town to sell the eggs and cream. Those two checks helped buy groceries, and the basement was always well stocked.

Yes, the Gess family was more than ready to enter the next decade. Julius and Alma did most of their work themselves as a couple. They would do the butchering themselves even though there were willing neighbors who would trade work with them. The tall German felt that he could accomplish more by himself than trading work with someone. Apparently he did not value the social time spent with neighbors as they were doing the job at hand. He was a no-nonsense man.

CHAPTER 16

— 1930s —
The Dirty Thirties

Trepidation was the mood of everyone as they entered the fourth decade. Unemployment had thrown many out into the streets. Innovative unemployed men sold fruit on street corners. Money, counted in pennies, was hard to collect. Dejected grown men of all ages were seen everywhere. Suicide rates climbed. People started moving—moving to what they thought was an opportunity. But many found their move did not improve their lot. Some moved to be near relatives, but reports came back describing unhappy situations.

Though established May 26, 1926, the depression made Route 66 famous. The highway began in Chicago, then it went through Missouri, Kansas, Oklahoma, Texas, New Mexico and Arizona to end in Santa Monica, California. It served as the major road for those migrating west, especially during the Dust Bowl of the 1930s. People who established businesses along Route 66 did well as the road's popularity increased. Loaded Model Ts traveled the road to California hoping for a better life. The 1939 movie "The Grapes of wrath" had travel scenes on Route 66. Because they had been living it, Julius took the family to see that movie. Five year old Victor remembered the scene where a huge Caterpillar tractor destroyed a home. He imagined his own house being crushed—an image imprinted on his mind that never left. When he viewed that movie in later life he became very agitated when the Caterpillar destruction scene appeared.

When people left the Volt community they headed in different directions. Rain, a much milder climate, and job prospects attracted many homesteaders to the Seattle area. The Volt homesteaders had come from all walks of life. Some had no background in farming, having come from the middle of a big city. After years of backbreaking work, drought, grasshoppers and low prices the thought of returning to the kind of place they came from was very inviting.

Julius owned his land and all the improvements on it. If absolutely necessary he could pledge his land at the bank for a loan, but he would do that only if his back was against the wall. Like many of that era, he did not believe in borrowing money unless all other options had failed. He kept thinking about what he could do to bring in more income. He considered raising hogs, since he could produce the feed for them and he had some experience in the early '30s, but there was already too much livestock on the market and prices had dropped disastrously.

Officials with the New Deal believed prices were down because farmers were still producing too much livestock and small grains. The solution proposed in the Agricultural Adjustment Act of 1933 was to reduce the supply. So in the late spring of 1933, the federal government carried out "emergency livestock reductions," buying six million hogs from desperate farmers nationwide. Cattle were purchased by the hundreds of thousands and shot and buried in large pits. The farmers could hear the dying squeals of their animals. They felt that the animals should have been used to help feed the hungry nation. These actions were quickly changed as the AAA was amended to set up the Federal Surplus Relief Corporation (FSRC) which distributed agricultural products such as canned beef, apples, beans and pork products to relief organizations. The government continued to buy farm products and pass them on to people who needed food. Every cent at the Gess household was watched and accounted for. Eggs retailed at 5 cents a dozen, bread cost 9 cents a loaf. A gallon of gas was 10 cents and stayed at that price during the thirties. A pair of single vision glasses cost $3.75. Alma many times repeated that during the depression she had toothpicks on her grocery list three times before she felt she could spend the money to buy them. Clothes were mended and if the patches got holes in them, the patches were mended. Socks were mended by weaving thread back and forth and then changing directions to create a checkerboard design across the hole, a money saving craft called "darning socks." Clothes were handed down, or if not needed in the family they were exchanged or given to neighbors. Flour sacks and feed sacks were saved and made into clothing for the children. It was common for a girl to not have a store bought dress until she was a teenager. Shirts were made for boys and they wore them to school as did their schoolmates. If it were absolutely necessary to see a doctor the homesteader would go to town and wait in the doctor's office until it was his turn. Doctors saw whoever showed up—and many visits were not paid for. Everyone was affected during the worst years of the depression.

1930 Julius and first child Helen, next to Model A.

The small Lutheran community was east of the Volt road, and the homesteaders west of the Volt road were mostly Mennonites. These two communities began approximately 15 miles north of Wolf Point and continued north for about 20 miles. The Mennonite Community extended many miles west. The Mennonites were fine neighbors. They did not wear differentiating clothes or eschew certain items of comfort like many Mennonite Communities did. They were God-fearing, and as evidence of a community became obvious, building a Church quickly became a priority.[15]

It had been over 15 years since Julius filed papers for his homestead. Julius never talked about the past, only discussing the present or the future. Now the family can only wonder what his thoughts were those days that he quietly walked around the homestead thinking and planning. The plans he made in his head were rarely transferred to paper. He was seen one time drawing out a rough plan for a granary on the back of a big envelope. He would make a list of the lumber needed when he went to town for that purchase. Deciding where to plant crops would take time and he would write down which fields would be planted to each crop, but most of his management was in his head.

He walked tall as he surveyed his homestead, which always had six to ten horses and a small herd of cattle. Eventually he would gladly sell all of the horses. When it was decided that they needed another milk cow one was selected from the range herd. After the birth of her calf the idea was to train the cow to go into a stanchion in the barn. It was rare that the cow liked that idea. Usually a rope went around the cow's neck and the rope was thrown around the stanchion for one person to pull. The other person or two would push and coerce in any way that might get the cow to move forward. After much tugging and pushing, the cow would step forward and her neck would go in the stanchion. She was fed some oats to encourage her to like staying there while she was relieved of her dairy product. The next step usually involved putting "kickers" on the cow. This was a store-bought device with hook shaped flat irons on a chain placed over the cow's back legs above the knee joint. The chain could be drawn up tight. Without any danger to

---

15 Several decades later two of these Churches disappeared as farms were sold as the rampant consolidation of land continued. It did not take long for a vibrant community to disappear with only a family or two left. Driving through the farming countryside one can usually see weathered buildings of a homestead. Letting the imagination take over, the community comes to life with schools, Churches, many men in the fields working the land—a temporary picture which can only live again in the mind of the person driving through.

the new milk cow, it would reduce her ability to kick the brave person doing the milking. The first few times the cow was milked, this process was repeated. Soon the cow did not need the restraint, and it wasn't long before she would walk into her place and wait to be milked. It wasn't until the 1950s that Julius bought a Jersey milk cow bred to be milked. She produced much more than the range cows. All those years milk cows had been "converted" from Herford range cows, as the homesteader could become more productive by using his range cattle.

The homesteader had to watch his herd of cattle closely for any sign of illness. It was a tough day to look out at the pasture and see that a calf had died during the night. Black leg sickness was deadly when it struck. Vaccinations later became available to lessen the possible attack. Losses like this were very painful, as it was usually the six month to one year old calf that was attacked. So much was the small cattle herd depended on that the loss of a single animal was deeply felt.

Julius's grandfather Wilhelm Herman Rode died May 6, 1931. He was about 90 and had lived with his wife Caroline and his son Dick in Verwood, Saskatchewan. He is buried in the Verwood cemetery about a mile northwest of the town. Alma told Victor later in life that whenever they went to Canada to visit Julius's family they would stop in Verwood to visit with Dick Rode.

When Helen was four years old February 1932 and sister Lorraine was several months shy of three, Julius and Alma began to think of school attendance for Helen in a couple years. That would need some planning and it would change their daily routine. Maybe he thought of his first day at school so far away in Volhynia. We can only speculate on that.

Julius wanted another building. The farmyard had a large house, a big barn and a chicken coop. His building would garage his Model A sedan, and there would be room for a shop, for all of his tools, anvil, and much needed forge. There would be two granaries for different types of grain, and room to clean the grain in preparation for seeding. Above the ceiling he would have room to store items that needed protection from the weather. This would be a major building project with the footprint about the size of the barn. He needed the granary space so he could hold over crops if he felt he could get a better price later on. Like the house and the barn, he built it bigger, with an eye to the future. He carefully lined up the forms using his compass pointing to true north, adjusting for the magnetic variation. His building would be square to the other building in the yard and to the section line, which was the road going by the farmyard.

The land had all been claimed years ago, so there were no new people moving into the neighborhood. The neighbors' half section homesteads dotted the landscape—so close and yet so far away. There were many neighbors one could see, but it was not as if they were next door. Bordering Julius's homestead on the north was Albert Eggum, his brothers Martin and Carl, and a sister Ida. They were a reclusive Swedish family who came from Minnesota. They stayed in their modest two story house. Bordering the homestead on the west was the homestead of Ben Thompson. Mr. Thompson was a bachelor for many years who late in life married a delightful lady who had been a school teacher. To the north was the Ferdina family whom Julius met when he was traveling down from Canada in 1915. On the north side of the Eggum family was the homestead of Alfred Johnson and his wife Signe. To the east of Julius's homestead was the homestead of John McClaughlin, a small man with a big heart who eventually moved to Wolf Point, though he spent time on the farm when it was seeding or harvest time. During some harvests when the yield warranted it, large harvesting crews would quickly get his crop in. August Nelson's homestead was south of the McClaughlin's land. Mr. Nelson was a bachelor and never changed that way of living. He would take the train back to his home in Minnesota soon after the harvesting was finished. As the spring thaw was well underway he would return from Minnesota to plant his crop when the weather allowed. South of his land was the homestead of Red Sutter, one third of which was fine farmland, though the balance was creek–bottom, boggy land that with an abundance of grass, was capable of carrying many head of livestock. A mile south of Julius's homestead was the homestead of Jim Johnson. He had a small house with a full basement, on the top of a hill where it was fully exposed to wind and snow. It may have been one of the reasons he left in the thirties for opportunities elsewhere. West and a half mile south was the homestead of Abe Weins. His land was very sandy, and during the dry thirties, his dirt would join other dirt in the sky during a high wind.

Julius's first tractor. Wagon used to haul grain put in sacks to Wolf Point.

Julius bought his first tractor at an auction sale in 1930. The John Deere was far from new, as the $70 price reflected. It would be a start for him, and he anxiously began fiddling with it. If the tractor ran well, it would simplify his farming—no more catching horses, harnessing and hooking them up to machinery. What a concept. And he was a part of that revolution in farming! Maybe in the near future he could get a bigger, newer tractor. He would need more land to be worth buying a new tractor. It was possible to buy land even though their income was very little because homesteaders who wanted to leave would arrange to have the purchaser takeover the homestead obligation. If the land had been proven up, they might sell on contract. All they needed was some money to leave and travel to their destination. During the depression some farmers just packed up and left, leaving land fallow for years till someone paid the back taxes to own it. Julius wanted more land but was not quite ready to take the step. He would wait and watch to hopefully be ready for an opportunity.

The times were still very tough. New hope was shared by many on their homesteads as Franklin Roosevelt was elected President in November 1932, for he had been a reform governor of New York from 1929 to 1932. He had promoted the enactment of programs to combat the Great Depression during his governorship. He was inaugurated March 4, 1933 when the depression was at the lowest point. A fourth of the workforce was unemployed. Two million people were homeless. 32 of the 48 states had closed their banks. People were panicked and looking for any word of encouragement. He came into the Oval Office with that valuable experience, and promptly put it to use. People across the nation were gathered around radios as they listened to their new president offer encouragement, and they responded. He quickly took the reins and laid out an agenda, promising to keep them informed. He finally began to tackle the agriculture and Dust Bowl issue.

Though the tough life in the thirties continued, Julius and Alma's family continued to grow. Victor Ralph Gess was born the afternoon of May 10, 1934 at 422 Fallon Street in Wolf Point, a birthing center on the north side of town. A proud father had his first son and he went downtown and bought a five pound box of chocolates for the nurses. The story was told many times about being at a picnic near the big Missouri River bridge. Victor suffering from eczema was still in a basket, so he must have still been a very small fellow. Rhoda Gross, a family friend and prominent Wolf Point citizen, was standing there and looking down in the basket. Julius saw what she doing and asked the childless Mrs. Gross if she would like to have one. She looked down in the basket again, turned to him and said "Who'd want it?"

On the day of Victor's birth dust blew from the northern part of Montana as far as Detroit and Cleveland. Dust from various parts of the Country at times reached the Atlantic Ocean. Being able to write his name in the dust on his White House desk had a huge impact on President Roosevelt. He imagined what it was like out on the plains. This simple demonstration was a force behind his desire to find solutions to the problem.

On August 6, 1934 President Roosevelt addressed a large audience at Fort Peck and signed a bill to construct the Fort Peck Dam—the largest earth filled dam in the world—that gave jobs to 11,000 people. It helped the towns in the area. Businesses were now busy, motels were quickly built, many restaurants and bars opened and prospered, though they all knew that the great economic benefit in the immediate Fort Peck area would last only a few years. When the work was done the many towns built up quickly disappeared, though small crews were still needed for maintenance and to oversee the spillway gates and the generators producing all that precious energy.

In 1936 Dust Bowl farmers saw their first ray of hope. Hand-picked by President Roosevelt, Hugh Bennett accepted the herculean task of presenting topsoil saving techniques to the farmers. He introduced contour farming and led efforts to plant millions of trees as wind breaks. He persuaded Congress to approve a federal program that would pay farmers to use new farming techniques. By 1937 the soil conservation campaign was in full swing.

Robert William Gess arrived August 2, 1936. On that same day American athlete Jesse Owens won four gold medals and broke two world records at the Olympic Games in Berlin. The depression was dragging on, however signs of improvement were being noticed. That day butter toasted pecan ice cream was 27 cents a quart, shoes for men and women with a "mystic arch" sold for $4.95, sterilized pillows 70 cents, a three piece bedroom set cost $69.50—as advertised in the *Chicago Tribune*.

Julius had been farming solely with the tractor for several years, though the horses were still used for hauling hay. At times the big sorrel named Bill was used to move dirt around the yard, pulling a scoop-like device called a slip which had two wooden handles to guide the loading and dumping. Victor recalls watching this from a distance, worrying that the long one-piece reins that Julius had over his shoulders would drag his father if the horse suddenly spooked. All turned out well on what was to be the last time the horse was used to move dirt. Using the horses became more infrequent—and that did not upset Julius.

Unemployment continued to drop and reached 14.3% in 1937, almost 7% lower than the year before. The economy was gaining steam. The construction of the Golden Gate Bridge was completed. A domestic air flight record was set: Los Angeles to New York in 7 hours. More people were employed, more people owned a home and a car. People were feeling better. Americans took pride in these accomplishments. The average cost of a new house was $4,100, average wages $1,700, a gallon of gas was still 10 cents, hamburger meat 12 cents a pound, average price for a new car was $760.

Julius listened to the news and felt more optimistic. The Roosevelt fireside chats informed those who wanted to feel connected, and that included most of the citizenry. There was still much work to be done, which the President always mentioned as he was signing off. A little more rain fell that summer. Julius was optimistic that maybe the drought was ending.

Feeling that the depression was nearing its end, he bought a half section whose northeast corner touched the southwest corner of his homestead. 640 acres would mean more planning and more seed preparation. Next spring he was ready to seed, and the land had all been farmed so it was easy to plant. No sod to break—just drive the tractor with the implements to the land and farm.

As 1938 was unfolding Julius spent extra time listening to the news on the radio. He was interested in what Hitler was doing and threatening to do. He understood that Hitler could become a force to be reckoned with, which deserved a very close watch. Intently listening to the President whenever he spoke provided him some relief. In spite of it all, Julius and the family decided it was time to buy a car. They went to the Dodge dealer in Wolf Point to see the inventory. The story told many times by Alma was that Victor wanted a blue Dosh, Dodge! Julius ended up buying a 1936 Lafayette four door which was driven several years into the early '40s. Even though storm clouds were hanging heavy over Europe, the manufacturers were producing cars, trucks, tractors and farm implements. With the agriculture outlook improving, the farm equipment manufacturers closely watched the crop predictions so they could provide whatever farmers needed to grow their crops. Julius would improve on his machinery whenever he saw an opportunity that he could afford.

One early morning at the end of summer the family saw the farmhouse of Red Sutter burning. Victor stood on the bread box and looked out the window toward the southeast and watched the flames shoot high. That sight was burned into his mind and the image never left him. As the crow flies it was about three-fourths of a mile away. The Sutters and their daughter left soon after that disaster, never to be heard from.

Eventually Julius bought that half section as well. It added 50 acres of crop land, and the balance was good grazing with a wide boggy area with several pools of water. A small partially sub-irrigated alfalfa field near the swampy area provided several welcome cuttings during the season. This gave him summer grazing for his cattle with no concern for water. An adequate fence was his only concern. Julius now owned three half sections, 960 acres.

As he added more land—which required a lot of extra work—the cost of production per acre or bushel was lowered, for that cost was spread over more acres. He had provided the base for his operation by building up his farmstead. He carefully maintained his machinery so breakdowns would not hold up seeding or harvesting. New machinery and farming techniques always caught his attention, and he quickly figured out whether or not the idea would benefit his operation.

Things were looking up and the optimism was felt by most people, though there were still the dreadful Montana winters to prepare for. Coal was mined at a location about six miles from the homestead. Each fall farmers would go to the mine with their tractors to scrape dirt from the coal. Some digging was necessary, and danger was always lurking. In the late thirties a tragedy at that mine happened on a day when all the men in the neighborhood were at the Volt school for a meeting (the purpose not remembered): the Fachner boys were digging coal when a large overhang of coal collapsed. Arlie was able to get Ernest out. They both worked feverishly to free Julius. When he was finally released from a heavy load of coal, efforts to revive him failed. Julius Fachner was 14. They rushed back to the school and broke the tragic news.

Funeral services were held at the Mennonite Church. That death had a profound effect on Helen, who was about 10 and his classmate. At gatherings when the "old days" were discussed, she would often bring it up, talking about how small he seemed in the casket.

Farm accidents ending in death happened too often. Machinery was new to the farmers and safety first was not impressed as it should have been. Farming with horses was of concern, especially if there was a frisky one in the group. But whether farming was done with horses or machinery, the danger was always there.

As the fourth decade was coming to a close, Americans became more optimistic. Improvements that President Roosevelt had made years earlier were taking effect. His continued conversation with the American people continued to give them hope. There were agricultural measures put into place and more rains were leaving the Dust Bowl days in the memories of those who had survived them. Maybe, just maybe there would be a hint of prosperity for the homesteader who held on through all the difficult years. The dream of new machinery, a bigger house, moving out of a homestead shack might just happen. There were more smiles on faces when they met in the store or came over for a visit. Conversations had definitely changed, noticed by journalists and radio commentators. Perhaps the dream of applying for a homestead had been a good idea after all.

CHAPTER 17

— 1940s —
The Landscape Changes

Homesteaders were smiling as the forties began. Average wheat yields started to climb because of farming techniques and there was more much-needed moisture, a trend that would continue for several decades. Size of farms was also increasing as many of the homesteaders on the Fort Peck Indian Reservation realized that they were in a competitive business with constantly increasing costs. Some were content to stay with their homestead and not expand. Others kept an eye open for any opportunity. Julius proudly worked his 960 acres. Did he take time to think about life in Volhynia with small parcels of land? Probably not, he only thought about the present and looked ahead to plan so there would be no surprises.

In the new decade Julius and Alma had three children in school. Winter weather took planning, but there were enough children on farms close by that efforts were joined to get children to school. Julius and Alma realized the importance of school, so missing school or being late was not an option unless sickness required being in bed. They wanted their four children to graduate from high school—and hopefully more education beyond that.

Unsettling rumbles kept coming out of Europe as Hitler continued to build up his war machine. Many of his supporters in this country were becoming suspicious of his authoritarian actions. Julius listened to his radio. He had served in France during World War I and he understood the unpredictable nature of Adolph Hitler. He felt that barring a catastrophe life on the homestead, life for his family was going to continue to improve.

The golden wheat fields of 1941 proudly waved in the wind. A large yield was being looked forward to. Julius was getting his 12 foot John Deere combine ready as harvest was nearing. Help would be needed to get the crop in, and seasonal workers were usually available. It was a matter of connecting with them and agreeing on payment. Victor remembered such a bargaining discussion taking place on a Saturday in the front yard. A young man drove into the yard wearing cowboy boots with aluminum heels and said he had been working several miles east in the Benrud Community. He wanted $30 a month, a good bed and lots to eat. Only problem was that he could not start for a several days. Julius was only willing to pay $25 a month. As the bargaining continued Julius said he would pay $30 if he would start Monday. The man could not do that and they parted ways on a friendly basis. Julius did get the crop in and it filled his granaries. There was much to be thankful for.

It had been 26 years since Julius filed his application for a homestead. He had been married 15 years, had four children, and fortunately he had good health. He was 48 years old and in the prime of his life. Neighbors were wonderful caring people who could be counted on if a need arose. Willingness to help was strong in the Volt Lutheran and Mennonite communities. The dust storms of the thirties were almost a thing of the past. Mobility was increasing as more and more cars and trucks found their way onto the farms. After all those tough years of struggling to survive, there seemed to be not much to worry about.

Then the other shoe dropped. December 7, 1941 just before 8:00 a.m. Hawaii time the Japanese attacked the naval base at Pearl Harbor. In two hours they destroyed 20 ships, including eight enormous battleships, and more than 300 airplanes. More than 2000 soldiers and sailors died and another 1000 were wounded. The day after the assault President Franklin D. Roosevelt asked Congress to declare war on Japan. Congress approved his declaration with just one dissenting vote—from Montana's Senator Jeannette Rankin. She said, "As a woman, I can't go to war, and I refuse to send anyone else." Shortly after the attack Japanese Admiral Isoroku Yamamoto said, "I fear all we have done is to awaken a sleeping giant and fill him with a terrible resolve." A memorable phrase by President Roosevelt was "a date which will live in infamy."

Three days later, Japan's allies Germany and Italy also declared war on the United States, and again Congress reciprocated. More than two years into the conflict, America had finally joined World War II.

Life in the Volt community and the country changed forever. The "war effort"—just two words—were repeated millions of times in the next few years. Roosevelt had resisted getting involved in the European war, but his attitude had been changed for him. All thoughts were about converting to a wartime economy. Automobile factories were dedicated to building airplanes, trucks, tanks and all the thousands of items that accompanied them. Shortages and rationing were the order of the day. Rationing stamps were treasured. Tires were rationed. Many arguments happened at the window of the rationing office at the Roosevelt County Courthouse in Wolf Point. As Julius was approaching Wolf Point one day, a tire on his one-ton truck blew out beyond repair. He went to the rationing board to get a coupon for a tire. It was mounted and he was ready to head home. A few miles out of town another tire blew out—no other choice but to head back to the ration office and plead for another coupon. More than once the family said they would have loved to have heard that request from Julius.

People were encouraged to start a Victory Garden if they didn't already have one. Alma responded with a huff when a neighbor announced that she was going home to work in her Victory Garden, for Alma and Julius always had a large garden probably unequaled in the neighborhood. It was during this time that Julius started experimenting with an orchard—several varieties of apples, cherries, sand cherries and choke cherries, and planted a long row of raspberries which he would show off with great pride. He carefully tended his orchard and each year would proudly pick the first ripe apples. The orchard yielded apple sauce, raspberry jam and cherry jelly.

Crop yields were good during the war years, and some farmers were able to put some money in the bank. The rains came and the dreadfully long winters piled up snow pack that melted adding always-needed moisture.

Homes were being modernized and Julius would not be left behind. He obtained some generators that he reworked to produce electricity. One winter the family watched him rewind those generators in the house where it was warm. Julius cut the right length 2 x 6 and used his plane and pull chisel to carve out a propeller to exact specification. Victor watched as he worked on it, carefully planing off some wood on alternating sides till it balanced perfectly. When all was ready he fastened the completed wind charger to a small tower on the top of the barn. When the wind blew the generated electricity traveled by wire to charge three rows of batteries in the basement of the house. Red, yellow and green markers contained in a tube would move to the top when they were full. They were monitored closely, and when all three markers dropped, the family knew that the wind must blow soon or there would be no electricity for light—time for the kerosene lamps again. Julius soon built a larger generator, and an 18 foot tower out of 2 x 4s to accommodate it. The tower was about 20 feet from the house

Even though Julius had electricity for his home, he had been reading about The Rural Electrification Act of 1936 which provided federal loans for the installation of electrical distribution systems to serve isolated rural areas of the United States. He wasted no time writing to his congressman and senators. He explained the need for electricity on the farms and asked for their help to push for legislation that would hasten the process. He talked with people locally who might be able to start the wheels turning. He would not hesitate to contact the Montana congressional delegation on any item he felt was of value to the farmer and the community.

Alma's father Gustaf Applegren died after a short illness on September 3, 1943. He had been born in Sweden in 1862, but his family left for New York March 8, 1869. They spent several weeks in steerage while the wind-propelled ship made its way to their new country. They settled in the Winthrop, Minnesota area. Gustaf married Amanda Setterman in 1889, a year after she arrived from Sweden.

The national news was all about the wars being fought and the war effort. The government promoted the sale of War Bonds in increments of $25, $50 and $100 to finance the war effort. It was a big investment for most people to buy a $25 bond, even when sold at a discount to be cashed out at face value in ten years. There were scrap metal drives, aluminum drives—anything that could be construed as aiding the war effort became a drive. Victor and Robert collected the silver paper inside cigarette packs and gum wrappers from a hired man that was a heavy smoker, though they received no medals for their contribution to the war effort.

Julius noticed land for sale in an ad in the Wolf Point Herald—the homestead of Jim Johnson, who had left his homestead years before. The half section was located a mile south of his farmstead and would fit into his farm very well, though only a few acres on the east side had been broken. He estimated that 270 acres would be suitable farm land. He bought it for taxes, and a couple years later, with the help of a hired man named Glen McWilliams, he began breaking it with an old tractor that had iron lugs. It was a big job to keep it steered in an approximate straight line, but after working the soil several times the land produced well. It was flat to slightly rolling, making it ideal for seeding and harvesting.

Julius added land that adjoined his holding as it became available. The expansion was slow, and with better equipment he was able to keep up on the work. He had been heard a couple times by people opining about how his boys would be a big help when they were a little older. The family continued to milk cows and they kept a lot of chickens to sell eggs. The rains continued to come and there were wonderful crops during most of the '40s.

The war had a direct effect on many families. Homesteaders' sons were being drafted into the service. Many servicemen did not return home for three, four or five years. Many did not return at all, as they had made the ultimate sacrifice. And servicemen and women's lives had been changed forever—carrying wounds and psychological scars. However they did not talk or complain about their time in the service. The attitude was that the country needed them and they had gladly gone and served. They were part of what was ultimately called "The Greatest Generation." After fighting in the war they came home and seemed to integrate easily back into civilian life.

Victor recalls being with Julius when he met a neighbor and the topic turned to the war. The neighbor was complaining that his sons were about to be drafted into service. The discussion went on, and finally Julius said it is our duty to answer the call if it comes, saying "I was drafted into the first World War and I gladly served—though when I came home my machinery had been stolen." He then added, "If my boys are drafted they will have to go." That is how the conversation ended. The sons of both men were drafted, served and all returned home.

The war was controversial and many animated conversations were held about it. The Mennonites basic belief was against war and serving in the military. A very few of the neighboring Mennonite young men were conscientious objectors, but served in various camps that provided help to the war effort. Because of the ferocity of the war, some of the conscientious objectors were not welcomed home as the servicemen were. It can be said that the whole country was behind the war effort, even if they disagreed with it.

Victor recalled talking with an older boy in school about the war. The older boy said that "Hitler said when they win the war they are going to put a soldier on every farm in America." That was enough to scare nine year old Victor. It was several years before he realized the quotation was probably not authentic. Everyone thought about the war. Just about every family had a close friend, neighbor or family member in the service. Victor remembered attending a memorial service in Wolf Point for the son of a Church member killed in Luzon, Philippines. The weight of that service death was felt by the whole town and the sadness of that event had a profound effect on him at his young age.

For a couple of years in the early forties the Gess children all attended Volt school at the same time. Helen entered High School in 1942, Lorraine followed two years later. Soon after that Victor began driving a green 1928 GMC truck to school. It was a faithful vehicle that got himself and Robert to school on time for many years. Because it did not have a heater it made for anxious moments getting to school or home where a fire was burning. When arriving at school the engine was covered with a heavy blanket for protection against the below zero weather. During the morning, noon and afternoon recesses the engine was started and kept running long enough to heat it up to last till the next time it was started. Some very young school children were given grown up responsibilities—and they handled them well. Other school children also drove to school though heavy snow and low temperatures brought out parents to drive the children both ways.

In the spring several country schools in the district would get together for a field day. It was a great way to get acquainted with other young people in friendly competition at various games. A softball game among the schools closed out the day.

The teachers typically lived in the basement of the school, decorating it to their liking for the nine month stay. One teacher, Francis Romo, signed a one year contract to teach at Volt school. He and his wife arrived with a small chicken coop and a milk cow. It worked out well for him, and the animals had an ideal place to stay for the school year. There was always discussion about country schools getting the best-qualified teachers. One argument was that a lot of teachers wanted to teach in country schools where they could be divorced from the politics of town school systems.

The President appeared very tired in photos taken at the Yalta conference February 4th to 11th. President Roosevelt, Prime Minister Winston Churchill and Premier Joseph Stalin met mainly to discuss the re-establishment of the nations of war-torn Europe. On April 12, 1945, while sitting for a portrait in Warm Springs, Georgia, President Franklin D. Roosevelt said what may have been his last words—"I have a terrific headache"—and fainted. He died two hours later of a cerebral hemorrhage. The nation was in mourning as they followed the news waiting for their president to be laid to rest. Vice President Harry Truman became President and asked for the nation's help as he grew into his new job. He became famous for the bronze saying on his desk: "The Buck Stops Here."

The war had been raging in Europe and rumors of Hitler's death had been on the news, but turned out to be untrue. The Western Allies and the Soviet Union captured Berlin with the help of Polish troops. Finally the Germans unconditionally surrendered May 8, 1945. Alma told Victor to get on the bicycle and go out in the field and advise his father that Hitler was dead for sure. Even with the war still on, Julius had been able to purchase a used bicycle for the children. The $5.00 purchase was worth many times that, as the children had years of riding enjoyment.

On the other side of the globe the once mighty Japanese fighting forces had been dramatically weakened. Hiroshima was destroyed by an atomic bomb August 6, 1945. It was followed by a plutonium implosion bomb on Nagasaki August 9. Surrender papers were signed by the Japanese on the USS Missouri September 2, bringing an end to World War II.

An exciting different life was the topic at the supper table. Would the factories manufacturing war machinery quickly convert to farm machinery, automobiles and trucks? New tires that could be bought anytime would be so appreciated. Travel restriction to Canada had precluded visiting during the war. Julius was anxious to visit his mother and siblings—how long before restrictions would be lifted? Rationing and coupons, would they soon go away? Dramatic changes with peace was the order of the day.

Julius reflected and talked with neighbors and relatives about the new day. In 1945 at age 53, he felt the dream he had 30 years ago had been fulfilled. He had a healthy family, a mortgage-free farm, and thankful for his father's dream of leaving Volhynia in 1902. There were very few Germans left in Volhynia during World War II. The few that were there were threatened by the Russians from the east, and the Germans from the west were suspicious of them. Julius never said much about his lot in life. He did say several times that he felt the citizens of Canada had not have the opportunity in life that he had. His appreciation for his country was shown by his willingness to do whatever he could to better the community. Not having to concentrate on aiding the war effort would mean time to explore improving life. Julius dreamed of a new tractor, maybe someday a new car.

With all the good news and optimism after the war, the family knew it would soon be facing sad times. Alma's sister Agnes died September 9, 1946. She had been ill the past year, but the family was always hopeful she would fully recover. Alma, her brother John, and sister Ellen were the remaining members of the family. So sad to lose a well-loved sister that did not see her 39th birthday. Her grieving husband Martin and son Glenn were left to carry on. Glenn at 15 helped his father with the many tasks that needed to be done. Their grief was shared by the family and their community.

Julius was frustrated that machinery and parts were not becoming available as quickly as needed. Because it was a 28 mile trip to Wolf Point each way when a quick trip was needed to get parts for machinery that had broken down, he decided that he needed a welder. With the war having just ended, there were none available. He decided to build his own and ordered an instruction book. He used a Model T engine from a truck that was no longer used. There was a lot of electrical rewinding that had to be done, but soon the day arrived when he could try it out. He had built it on four steel wheels and parked it outside of the shop. There it stayed for many years until a 110 volt welder replaced it.

Victor watched him agonize over a broken combine sprocket soon after the war. He went to town for a replacement, but none were available. So he went home and began to build up a sprocket by adding beads of weld on the sprocket housing that fit over the shaft. More welding, more grinding the sprocket into shape. In effect he had built almost all of the sprocket with his homemade welder, grinder and talent. That welder saved him many 60 mile trips to get repairs. He also made a cement mixer using an old barrel, shaping the top of the barrel so it curved in to hold water. Without the welder he could not have made the mixer. He wanted a garden tractor, but again none available so he made one with a 1.5 horse Briggs & Stratton engine. He welded lugs on the steel wheels so it would pull without slipping when he wanted to go deeper.

Helen went off to Concordia College in Moorhead, Minnesota and graduated in 1950. Lorraine graduated from High School in 1948. She worked several years at Stephens Mercantile in Wolf Point till she married in 1954. Robert was showing interest in tools as his father had at that age and he became an excellent fixer, admired by friends and family.

Julius continued to work on getting electricity into the community, to be free of depending on wind. Unlimited electricity meant the community could have electric drills, welders, compressors or any electrical tool that would make farming better. A yard light would be a welcome addition to every farm. It would take a few more years, but the reward would be worth the wait.

Electricity started running through installed lines and wired homes and outbuildings April 29, 1948. Julius was ready. The house had wiring updated, the shop and the barn were wired. A yard light was ready high up on the windmill. Finally the switch was thrown and Julius's homestead was lit up. That welder that Julius built was now pushed aside for a store-bought welder that plugged into the wall.

Volhynia to Volt! Fifty-six years of age and look at his life: a loving wife, four children in their teens, a large farm, money in the bank, a new car, good machinery and now electricity on the homestead out in the country, 28 miles from town. No wonder his brother Emil commented on a visit, "Julius is not as serious as he used to be. He is more relaxed now."

The mailbox was 1¾ miles from the homestead. As Lorraine drove up to get the mail one day, she noticed a man standing by the mailbox. As he approached the car she asked, "You're dad's brother, aren't you?" He said "Yes, and I hope he'll be glad to see me." She drove into the farmyard and Hank and Julius saw each other for the first time since 1915. Catching up was the order of the day. He told about his four children—his oldest son was attending the University of North Dakota. He had graduated with an engineering degree. Alma commented when the men were outside, "He must have a lot of money, if his son goes to the University."

All three of Hank's sons were in the service during World War II. Oldest son Harvey was a paratrooper. As the war was winding down, Harvey and three other soldiers were sent out on patrol. They came upon Hitler's castle and cautiously waited to be approached by German soldiers. Nothing happened, so they moved closer. A door was open, so they stepped in. Tension was very high, but finally they realized there was no one around. They looked it all over and Harvey collected several souvenirs including Hitler's razor. He was released from the Army in April 1946 and that fall entered the University.

Ludwig and his son Hank never got along. One afternoon in September 1916 they had an unpleasant argument. The next morning Hank left home. He went to see his friend Hiram Benzinger, a neighbor who lived nearby. The two of them left to make their way to Verwood, Saskatchewan, a distance of about 140 miles. There they visited with Hank's cousin, Dick Rode, son of Wilhelm, who suggested they change their names so they could not be traced. Hank took the name Harry Rhodes, added an "h" to his mother's maiden name. But to the rest of the family he was always Hank.

The two traveled on to Regina where they worked for a few months before Hank joined the Canadian Army February 15, 1917 at Winnipeg, altering his age to meet the requirements. He served in Canada, Britain, and France and was discharged March 28, 1919 at Winnipeg. He worked various jobs for several years and ended up in Estevan, Saskatchewan working in a mine. He met Fannie McKibben, and after a brief romance they were married October 9, 1923. They eventually moved from Estevan 18 miles south to Noonan, North Dakota. There he worked in the coal mine and also continued perfecting his blacksmithing skills. Three sons and a daughter were born in the next nine years.

Hank's siblings and parents always speculated about where he was or if he was still alive. After the family moved to their new farm near Yellow Grass, Saskatchewan, only 90 miles separated them.

On a train ride in Saskatchewan in 1948 Hank began a conversation with a brakeman who he discovered was his sister Tillie's husband. He suddenly felt homesick and asked about the family. His father had died, but his mother was alive, living with her youngest daughter Minnie in a comfortable house in Yellow Grass. When Hank arrived at their door, his mother did not believe it was him and asked for some proof. He took his left shirt sleeve off and showed her the scar from the hot water that had scalded him when they lived in Winkler. He had been gone 30-plus years. His family had no idea that he had any siblings and were overwhelmed with all the relatives. Hank had eight living siblings, their spouses, plus 14 children among them. That fall most of the family gathered at Hank and Fannie's farm in Noonan to celebrate their 25th wedding anniversary. It was a wonderful opportunity for his family to put names and faces to their new relatives. Hank was in Alaska at the time, where he worked for six months to a year since 1939, then he would return to the farm. The pay was very good and he loved the adventure. He would ride the rails to Seattle and then continue to Alaska on a commercial vessel.

Julius was happy to have his brother home again. Many times phone books in various towns had been checked to see if his name was there. The topic about where Hank may be always came up when members of the family gathered.

A very proud homesteader with a new 1947 Hudson.

The late '40s was a time of optimism, good crops, and enjoyment of the peace time economy. Julius was participating and enjoying every minute of it. He was a happy homesteader when he arrived home with a new four door Hudson automobile. He had survived all these years of drought, grasshoppers, hail, and dust storms, and now he and the family were enjoying success. Gatherings at Church, picnics or with another person inevitably brought up the purchase of a new car, tractor or other equipment. The nation was still basking in the glory of winning WW II and the quick economic recovery. Occasionally hail would hit small areas, and the damage ranged from insignificant to 100%—especially difficult if it hit the same area two years in a row. Insurance would cover much of the loss, however it did not take the place of a crop completing its cycle.

In 1949 car manufacturers were busy promoting their latest designs. One day in science class at Wolf Point High, Victor's teacher Mr. Zeller said that the new classy 1949 Chevrolet was on display in the dealership. After school Victor and several of the class members went to look at the latest. They wondered around the car, sat in it and looked under the hood. They were happy to have seen the amazing latest. Automobiles were the topic of conversation for high school boys in that era. They prided themselves on being able to identify a car a half mile away.

Julius the Homesteader was happy to close out the forties. His memory of those early days and especially the thirties moved further behind him. He only thought of the present day and the future. We don't know and can only speculate that he may have referenced those early days as a lesson learned. He was growing in his ability to get up and speak at meetings. If he had something to contribute, he would be on his feet expressing it at a Church meeting or a farm meeting. The family many times speculated about what he would have been if he had more education. He upset some people, but the person was probably better off having had an encounter with the Homesteader. There was much to be learned from him, and part of that lesson included visiting his homestead where he proudly showed off his orchard and what he was doing in the shop. What he did and who he was started developing back at the village of Shinufka in Volhynia. That and his life experiences made him who he was.

With all that behind him Julius was anxious to take his family into the fifties.

CHAPTER 18

— 1950s —
The Exciting Fifties

The Homesteader's children were continuing their education, working on the farm, serving in the military, and getting married. Grandchildren started appearing during the '50s. There were rumblings among farmers and farm reporters asking when the price for grain would go up. Farm machinery technology was improving and the price for it was climbing, as was the desire for more land to help offset this disparity.

It was about this time that word circulated in the neighborhood that a second generation farmer, Dennis Nelson had bought a new combine. It was a "self-propelled" Massey Harris combine that cost $5,000. The price was unbelievable to many people—but they soon found out that prices would go up for farm machinery and it would become a struggle again to buy what was needed. What an invention, but what a price! How could a farm pay for such an expensive machine? Yet with this combine a man could do what took two to accomplish with the pull combine. This was another welcome revolution for grain growers. Two people could now easily harvest a crop of several hundred acres. Augers

265

started showing up on farms to unload grain and to load it on trucks for delivery to the grain elevators. Before, grain had been shoveled from the granary into the truck box to get to market. All the new items showing up on the farm would be constantly improved—and with that the price would increase.

Julius had a front row seat living the great homestead experiment. It seemed a good way to settle the land and create homes and develop towns. There may not have been another way to do it even, if they had wanted one. There was emotional expense since many who homesteaded had to leave for various reasons. Most were not prepared for the life, and when the tough times came, they left. Consolidation of the half section homestead was inevitable.

Julius purchased a Dodge truck with a large box capable of hauling 200 bushels of grain. Big change from 30 years earlier when he put wheat in sacks and loaded them on a wagon pulled by two teams to Wolf Point. It was a three day trip—one day to get there, one to purchase what was on his list, and the third to travel home. Now it could take less than an hour to get a load of grain to town. No wonder he was beginning to talk about retirement—he was tired. But retirement was still be a long way off.

Wheat is sacked, loaded, ready for three day trip to Wolf Point.

In this arid region strip farming was standard practice. The strips that lay fallow had to be cultivated to kill the weeds. But cultivated strips were subject to blowing in a dry year. Julius heard about a machine that would skim under the ground, cut the roots of the weeds and leave the stubble covering the soil. It was called a Noble blade, this machine kept soil from blowing and it retained moisture with the cut foliage protecting against the blazing sun. Julius was first in the community to own one. He knew the value of saving soil, having seen it blowing away during the thirties. The Noble blade became a common sight in fields. When the new crop was planted, any remaining foliage was tilled into the soil with the seed, to help raise crops with very little annual rainfall.

Television was arriving and Julius was interested. He said many times he would only watch it during conventions and speeches. Other than that he said he wouldn't waste his time. It took a while before acceptable reception was available and Julius soon discovered that he enjoyed watching whenever they were broadcasting. In the early days the test pattern would show till a program began, sometimes running for hours. Julius used his radio and generator experience skills to put up his own antenna and connect it with the television set. Eventually good signals were received from the Williston, North Dakota station. Television was a source of entertainment for Julius the rest of his days.

The Homesteader was wanting a new combine—the old John Deere pulled by a tractor was prone to multiple seasonal breakdowns. He had enough money in the bank and he decided it was time to own a self-propelled combine. He also bought a Massy Harris, but as Julius was prone to do, he changed many things on it before its first trip to the wheat field. He changed the location of the tool box, moved the switch to raise or lower the cutter bar, and mounted an umbrella. He also increased the size of the hopper that held the grain by putting a six inch extension sideboard around the top. Finally he was ready and the golden fields of wheat were ready to be harvested. What was he thinking as he drove that new combine to cut that first 10 acre field just steps from the southwest corner of his half section homestead? Did he think about that day in 1915 with the locator when they found that section marker? Probably not, for Julius was always thinking about the next step. He now had to steer the combine and keep the cutter bar at the correct height. He would soon learn the rhythmic sound of the machine and be able to detect a foreign sound that needed attention.

The fifties were filled with family activity. Victor graduated from high school and was inducted into the army December 10, 1953. Helen married Fred Amestoy March 29, 1953. Lorraine married Richard Keller April 4, 1954. At both weddings Julius showed up with an 8 mm movie camera—he was always checking out items new to him. He even developed films. He bought a violin. He was always going to learn how to play it, but other things held more interest for him.

When it came to automobiles he usually chose the road less traveled. He went from a Lafayette automobile to a four door Hudson and then to a Desoto. Finally in 1953 he bought a four door Pontiac. That car was turned over to Victor when he got out of the Army September 9, 1955. Ten days after being discharged he was enrolled at Montana State University in Bozeman. For the next six years he would go to school during the fall and winter quarter. After the final quarter tests were finished, he would pack up and go back to the homestead to help farm.

Julius had done what he could to encourage neighbors to sign up for telephone service. The neighborhood had gotten together years before and put up a telephone line going to about a dozen farms. This was done by nailing a 2 x 2 on a fence post and stringing the telephone wire to an insulator on each post. It worked well, and each farm had a designated ring. The homestead's was two longs and a short. It was best to not discuss anything confidential with the person you had called because most of what was covered in a phone discussion was usually heard a second time in the neighborhood in the following days. If too many people picked up the phone to rubber-neck a call, it could weaken the signal to the point of being difficult to be heard. A caller would shout, "Some of you get off the line so I can hear," followed by a few clicks. Northeastern Montana Telephone Cooperative Association was organized in 1950 by people in rural areas wanting telephone service. The first members purchased several farmer-owned systems in the area (most of these ran along a fence line, similar to the Volt community telephone system) and began building a new system.

Telephone service reached the Volt community in 1954. At first each line was a six party system. Soon that system was converted to private lines for everyone. No more listening in on someone's conversation.

Full telephone service was a huge tool for the farmer living many miles from towns they needed to access. A phone call might save having to drive long distances to get information or order parts.

Julius witnessed another convenience and wondered what would come next. He knew what it was and just hoped that it would happen. He wrote many letters and had many conversations with neighbors regarding getting a paved road from Wolf Point north past Volt school, continuing till it reached Wall Street. The road heading west was named Wall Street because many families surnamed Wall lived on the road. The gravel Volt road was heavily traveled and lacked proper maintenance, which caused many tire repairs and blowouts. Gas tank repairs from rocks pounding them causing gas leaks were a constant frustration. Most farmers' gas tanks did not have a smooth place on the bottom because of the rock assaults.

After much lobbying, letter writing, and meetings the Volt road was approved for paving. The paved road meant much to the communities that lived near it or accessed it—no more gas tanks pounded out of shape by rocks. A pleasant smooth ride to Wolf Point was a dream come true. The road was well made with wide ditches and an easy slope off the road in case someone headed for the ditch. Julius had ridden a bicycle to this country and now he could ride on a paved to Wolf Point.

His next project was to get six day delivery of mail. He wrote letters to his congressman and to Senator Mike Mansfield urging them to support six day mail service for the North Star Route. It was eventually approved and widely appreciated.[16]

Grandchildren began arriving in the mid-fifties and continued for the next 20 years. No families would rival in size the families that Julius

---

16 Senator Mansfield served in the senate from January 1953 to January 1977. Julius and the senator knew each other well. In March 1955 Julius and Helen, with a group of Montana farmers, visited Washington D.C. Victor was in the Army stationed at Fort Devons in Massachusetts. He took time off and met them when they arrived in Washington D.C. He toured the sites with their group and was with them when they met with the Montana Congressional Delegation. Senator Mansfield spoke to the group and Julius asked him several questions about agriculture. Senator Mansfield was considered a friend of agriculture. Senator Mansfield returned to Montana after serving 24 years in the senate, 16 of them as the majority leader which was a record. In April 1977 President Jimmy Carter appointed him ambassador to Japan which he served for 11 years, also a record.

and Alma came from. Julius had ten siblings and Alma had five. Alma's brother Victor died in May 1901 and she died 101 years later.

Robert entered the service October 9, 1959 and served two years in Korea. He returned to the homestead and farmed as though he had never left. He married Merna Marie Smith October 1, 1967. In the next eight years daughters Sandi, Shannon and Deanna joined the family. Their grade and high school education was in Wolf Point, which required a daily round trip bus ride. Excelling in their scholastic abilities was another proud reason for Julius's happiness.

CHAPTER 19

– 1960s –

The Settling Sixties

The fifties had been generous to the Homesteader. He longed for the day when demanding chores didn't beckon and someone else would care for the soil he tilled. To that end he and Alma bought a house in Wolf Point January 27, 1961. It was rented out until they moved in the summer of 1963.

Victor married Hollie Carlson June 10, 1960. Her daughters Cynthia and Catherine brought the number of grandchildren to five. In the next year Victor was graduated from Montana State University.

Tragedy struck the family when Lorraine's husband Dick was killed April 10, 1961. A speeding vehicle coming out of a curve careened across the country road and hit Dick's car as he turned to avoid the oncoming car. Dick died within minutes after the accident. This shock to the family left Lorraine alone with Jule, a month short of her 6th birthday. The tragic mood turned to happiness as six months later Pamela Sue was born October 3rd. Jule proudly helped her mother take care of her baby sister.

Julius contented himself knowing that he would soon be living in town. The move was made during the summer of his 72nd year. He enjoyed his new life and easily transitioned into that role. Alma said that whenever he wanted to go fishing she dropped what she was doing to join him. He would go his favorite fishing spots on the Missouri River, but he was not a patient fisherman. If he didn't get any action he would go try another spot. Usually they would have to buy fish on the way home if that was what they wanted for dinner. It gave him some relaxing moments after a lifetime of rushing to do the necessary chores at the homestead.

Julius could linger around town without feeling that he had to rush out to the homestead. For a man that had always been on the move, he slowed down and smelled the roses. The house did not have a garage, so he built one attached to the house. True to his farmer nature he soon had a workbench set up with an emery wheel to assure that Alma always had sharp knives in her kitchen. He could fix things and make smaller items that he needed around the property. He was a happy man and seemed content leading the new life.

The Church was across the street—a quick walk and they were at the front door. Alma became involved in the ladies' activities at the Church. One of her favorites was helping a group make quilts to send to service personnel and to the Church synod headquarters. Quilting was done with ladies working on various spots around the frame. It was a production line process without the line moving. One of the quilt ladies told Victor, "That corner over there was Alma's, and she was always there doing her job."

When they began spending winters in Arizona it was an easy adjustment for Julius. He so appreciated the mild winter that he had dreamed of for years. The heavy snowstorms of the '40s never left him. He loved being where there was no reminder of them, though Alma would've been happy staying in their home in Wolf Point. She was always comfortable in her own place and was not as affected by the cold weather.

They bought a comfortable mobile home in Apache Junction, a suburb of Phoenix. The mobile home park was a perfect match for them. They quickly made friends in this middle class park with a variety of people. Every fall they looked forward to returning to the warm climate and the friendships they had made. Julius had always been a very political person and was always ready for a rousing discussion. Sometimes those discussions would get very animated with raised voices. Victor discussed this with his mother. Surprisingly, she said as soon as they got to the mobile park there was no mention of politics. Julius knew that he was in a tight-knit community that may not have any interest in his views. To get along and thrive in that community, he knew it was best to leave politics alone.

Alma quickly made friends at the Park and enjoyed participating in crafts, the coffee hour or whatever might be going on. Julius would join other men and take long walks in the desert behind the Park. Typical of Julius, he had put up a little shed behind the mobile home where he had a workbench with a vise and several tools so he could fix things.

They explored the area around Phoenix and watched new construction. He marveled at how an area could keep growing and never seemed to stop.

They soon learned that a short trip would take them across the border into Mexico where he could get his dental work done for a much lower price. One winter Victor and family spent Christmas with them and one of the outings was a much appreciated trip to Nogales, 180 miles through Arizona desert with expanded views and many large cactuses. The trip passed through Tucson, a rare town on the way to the Mexican border.

Christmas with the homesteader and Alma, Apache
Junction, Arizona. The author Victor, James, Cynthia,
Catherine and Hollie

Back home in Apache Junction, Julius proudly took them to the zoo and drove by the University. He showed them where a Mafia boss lived on the top of a hill. He was very curious as to why he chose to live on top of a hill where everyone could see him. They decided that he lived up there so he could see anyone who might be coming to visit him. Julius was intrigued with that idea, and tried to understand why that well-known man might have so many enemies.

Soon after arriving in the Phoenix area for the first time, they made plans to visit Hank's three sons. Harvey, Harold, Allan and their families were always happy to visit with any of Hank's extended family. There were many happy visits during the years that Julius and Alma spent winters in Arizona.

November 22, 1963 Julius was watching television and thinking about the upcoming trip to Arizona. The news bulletin came over that President Kennedy had been shot. It was followed shortly by another bulletin that the president was dead. Julius commented on the wonder of television that made it possible for him and hundreds of millions to see the proceedings that led up to the funeral November 25th. Julius felt the same grief as millions that took away his young president. He talked about the twisted mind that could commit that horrible crime.

There were very few people in the United States that did not feel affected by the assassination. Many times the television showed men crying as they heard the news. It was as if everyone in the county had voted for him, though the reality was that the voting was very close. He had the sparkle, the grin and that great sense of humor that endeared him to friend and foe alike. His press conferences were always looked forward to. He had a way of turning a reporter's hard question into an answer and a happy event. The country was in mourning for a long time. Even at the time of this writing, whenever the assassination is mentioned tears can often be seen welling up in people's eyes. The country changed and it happened as Lyndon Johnson transitioned into the presidency. The new president's personality was not as engaging, and some of the population were slow to accept the sudden change. Young people clung to President Kennedy and did not relate to President Johnson, who was one of the most accomplished politicians in the century. He understood how government worked and how to get legislation through congress. Even with those talents and abilities, it was hard for some people to feel connected to him.

The technology that provided television during this sad event may have been a defining moment for Julius. Imagine hearing about an automobile sometime after arriving in Canada in 1902. Eventually seeing an automobile, and the joy of his first ride. Then he chose technology in the form of a bicycle to make his trip to Wolf Point. No one knows why he rode a bicycle and not a horse—may have been that he was saving money for work horses and would buy them after being assured he would get a homestead. His life had been absorbed with technology and how he could improve it. Sitting in front of the television set which high technology created, how could he not help but marvel about the creation? He appreciated fine technology because he had lived it on a lower level.

Julius and Alma welcomed four grandchildren during the '60s. Lorraine named her daughter Pamela and her son Michael. Julius dubbed Victor's son James, the Crown Prince.

Family gatherings were getting bigger. Although Julius did not display much affection, he would break out in a big smile whenever his grandchildren arrived, and when they wanted something they soon learned how easy it would be to get it from Gramma.

The family was scattered. Helen, Fred and family were living in Missoula. Helen was finishing her teaching credential and would soon move to Nashua, 35 miles west of Wolf Point. Lorraine, Harold and family lived in Hardin. Victor, Hollie and family had moved to California in 1964. Robert was operating the farm and would until it was sold in October 2011.

CHAPTER 20

− 1970S −

The Easy Seventies

Julius and Alma had been traveling to Arizona for several winters. They looked forward to going there and were always anxious to return in the spring. Julius knew the route, worked out shortcuts, and detoured around long-range road construction. One fall they planned to leave later than usual. During that time Julius was hospitalized for a short stay and many times mentioned how cold it was at night in the Wolf Point Hospital. Those sub-zero windy Northers are hard to keep out of any building.

Harvey, Julius's oldest nephew, had expressed an interest in meeting, for he was curious about his father Hank during his early years. Julius related that at age 14 he himself was working every day that he could get a job, so with Hank seven years his junior, he did not spend much time with his brother. He did relate that Hank was full of energy and burning off that excess energy sometimes got him into trouble. He recalled Hank having been disciplined at school by having to stay home a couple days. Nothing serious, and Julius could not recall anything else out of the ordinary.

Those nephews continued to marvel about the huge family they had suddenly acquired. When any members of that family got together they would talk about Hank's family living so close and yet so far away. His three sons and daughter were loved and admired by all the relatives.

While in Wolf Point, Julius received a call from his brother Emil. He said he was not feeling well and he wished they would drive up to Weyburn, Saskatchewan to visit. Julius and Alma drove up to Emil and his wife Mary. Alma said that after visiting for a few hours, Emil was back to normal. He simply missed his brother and needed a visit. Julius was beloved by his siblings and their families. They saw him as the big brother who left home too soon. The youngest, Minnie, was two months old when Julius left on his bicycle on July 19, 1915.

Once he left home for Montana and filed for his homestead, there was no doubt in his mind that was his home. He often expressed the advantages of living in the US as he saw it. He would refer to the Canadian's loyalty to the Queen. That did not fit in with Julius's character. Tough, independent, hardworking, God-fearing and love of family is what made up his character. Victor recalled a visit to the Canadian cousins in the late forties. He said they saw Model As and Model Ts still in use. After the war Canada began to prosper, so it did not take long for Canada to be on par with the United States.

In 1970 daughter Helen and her daughter Heather moved from Missoula to Nashua where she had an elementary school teaching contract. Lyndon stayed in Missoula to finish High School. The move was a planned event, as she wanted to be closer to her parents and relatives. She was happy with the move as she quickly assimilated into the school system and Church. She married Robert Robbins, a Nashua resident, April 9, 1971. Nashua was their home, and with their deeply implanted roots they never considered leaving.

The seventies decade would bring several grandchildren's marriages. Clinton John Amestoy was the first and only great-grandchild born in the seventies. The future would bring many cousins to their generation who carried on the tradition of getting to know each other.

The homesteader and Alma
celebrate their 50th anniversary.

The summer of 1976 a 50th year anniversary celebration was held for the Homesteader and his bride. Though their wedding day was October 1st, it was decided a summer event would allow more people to attend. Brothers Emil and family and Reynold and family from Canada attended. Many from Alma's family attended. All of the Homesteader's children were there with their families. The event was held at the homestead, and the yard was full of automobiles. Imagine an event like this 60 years earlier in 1916—the yard would have been full of teams and wagons. The following Sunday the Church in Wolf Point recognized the anniversary, and it was celebrated during the coffee hour.

What else was there for Julius to look forward to? He wished for better health as he had not been feeling well. They left for Arizona at the usual time. The trip was uneventful and they were glad when they reached their winter home. It usually took a couple days to get settled in. Groceries and some housekeeping supplies needed to be purchased. Soon they felt very much at home and quickly fell into their usual routine. At about 9:30 people started coming out of their mobile homes and headed for the recreation room. Coffee was ready, prepared by residents taking turns. When the coffee was drunk and conversations finished, they headed back to what they had been doing.

Julius still enjoyed taking a morning walk, but he did it moving slower. The doctor in Wolf Point thought that cancer may be return-

ing. Tests were not taken, a discussion he and Alma had many times.
They struggled about what to do regarding his health care. He did see
a doctor in Phoenix late winter 1977 who suggested he have tests taken
when he got back home.

The results showed some cancer, but should not be of much concern. He felt good that summer and traveled again to Canada to visit
his brother. He enjoyed his time there and opined that they were only
a few miles from each other—only 180 miles apart, which now was
a three hour trip. While there he saw Emil's son Elvin and daughter
Doreen. Emil's other children—Douglas, Clifford and Beverly—lived
away from Weyburn.

It was an emotional departure with assurances that they would see
each other soon. Since 1915 Julius had traveled to Canada often, and his
family returned the visits. The family always felt the Canadian relatives
lived so much further away than they actually did. The border helped
create that impression, for during WW II the families could not cross
the border in either direction. Julius watched the newspaper closely
after the War for news that travel restrictions were lifted. Finally the
borders were opened and visitors were welcome.

Late summer Julius had bouts of feeling weak, but then he would
gain his strength back and feel good for a few weeks. The family was
gathered at the house in town. Sunday everyone headed back to their
respective homes to prepare for school and be ready for work Monday
morning. Julius was resting on the couch when Helen went in to say
goodbye. Helen repeated many times his response: "The Lord be with
you."

Julius and Alma left home for Arizona before Thanksgiving. They
stopped in Billings and visited Lorraine and family. All went well until
they reached Provo, Utah. Julius was not feeling well and the doctor
they found suggested he check into the local hospital. After a comfortable night in the hospital and armed with some new medication, they
continued down the road, but with Alma driving while Julius rested.
They spent one more night on the road. The next afternoon Alma drove
into the Apache Junction Mobile Home Park. Several people saw them
arrive and they knew something was wrong because Alma was driving.

They settled in and started enjoying the warm weather and their friends in the Park. Julius was doing better and Christmas was celebrated as usual. Julius and Alma attended Lutheran Church services in Phoenix when they were there for the winter, along with a huge influx of "snow birds." Alma told of hearing that council meetings got very animated as people with differing views discussed options for handling the large influx.

The last few days of December 1977 Julius was moving slower. His face reflected pain and concern. Alma knew his condition was deteriorating. She chatted frequently about it with her close friend Lilly in the Park. They both knew that Julius would have to be hospitalized soon. He had been hospitalized many times the last few months for similar symptoms. This time she knew it was worse.

January 1st Alma and Julius agreed he should go to the hospital for a "checkup." She drove him to the emergency room and he was promptly admitted. Consultation with the doctor several hours later told her that he was seriously ill.

New Year's Day 1978, being on Sunday, was celebrated on the January 2nd. Julius's nephew Allen and his wife Billie were celebrating the day at Victor's place in California. Early afternoon Victor answered a call from his mother. She said that Julius was in the hospital and the doctor told her that he would not leave alive. Victor said he would leave as soon as possible to be with her. Lorraine said she would leave the next day.

Victor said goodbye to Hollie and son Jim at the Oakland airport. The short walk into the airport was one of the longest he had ever taken. Many memories flooded his mind as the plane climbed high out of the Bay Area. He thought about driving to school at a young age. He pondered how his dad gave him and his brother adult responsibilities during their pre-teen ages. Did he consciously do that to teach them how to handle life? Maybe it was a bit of that, having a job that he knew the boys could do. After all, Julius did those things under more trying conditions when he was that age. Victor never questioned what was his father's best intent. Julius loved his children and his action constantly demonstrated that. The airplane ride to Phoenix seemed to take only a few minutes. The memories and questions about the next few days never left his mind. He was greeted at the airport by his mother and sister.

Julius was glad to see them, and when he heard Victor's voice he said, "Oh Vic, I didn't know you were here." The three visited Julius every day, and that Sunday they went to Church. Victor and Lorraine got to see the Church crowded by the "snow birds." Finally they were able to work their way to the Pastor who had visited Julius the day before. They expressed their thanks for his visit and the Pastor consoled them as he knew Julius was very weak.

The extra time was taken up with planning for the move back home for Alma. The mobile home would be sold to someone in the Park who had shown interest. It was decided that Victor would drive their car home, towing a trailer with their possessions. That would be a three or four day trip dealing with some heavy snowstorms.

They visited Julius on Sunday the 8th and it was obvious to them that he was very weak.

That evening Alma wanted to eat out. In her later years she enjoyed eating at different places, motivated by not having to cook.

They watched the evening news and went to bed wondering what the next day would bring.

At 2:30 AM January 9th Victor answered the phone. The caller confirmed his thought. The Homesteader had breathed his last. He would be buried in the Wolf Point Cemetery January 14th—his 85th birthday.

Appendix

Volhynia

Volhynia is the province in western Ukraine that lies against the Polish border. At one time most of northern Volhynia was covered with forest, but the spread of agriculture over the past 150 years leaves less than a third today.

For centuries Volhynia had belonged to the Lithuanian Commonwealth. It was later acquired by Poland through a marriage of royalty. In the first partition of Poland in 1772, the region was annexed by Russia. With the Treaty of Versailles after World War I, Volhynia was split in half. The east remained part of Russia while the west was returned to Poland. After World War II the entire region of Volhynia was made part of Ukraine, which in turn was part of the Union of Soviet Socialist Republics.

There were Germans scattered throughout Volhynia. Mennonites attempted an early farming settlement but most did not stay long. The first major and more permanent migration of Germans into Volhynia did not occur until the mid 1830s. These were primarily of the Lutheran faith. By 1860 the German population was still only estimated to be 4-6000, but after the 1863 Polish rebellion, Germans began to flood into Volhynia. Most of them came from Congress Poland, the central and eastern portion of modern day Poland, established after the defeat of Napoleon at the Congress of Vienna in 1815 and governed by Russia until 1918. Most of the Germans settled in a broad band extending from Wladimir Wolhynsk in the west to half way between Zhitomir and Kiev in the east. 1900 census figures indicate there were approximately

200,000 Germans living there. In addition to Lutherans, there were Baptist, Catholic, Mennonite, Moravian, and Reformed.

Daniel Mendelsohn in *The Lost—A Search of Six Million*, there is a joke that people from that part of Eastern Europe like to tell suggesting why the pronunciations and the spellings kept shifting. A man who is born in Austria, went to school in Poland, got married in Germany, had children in the Soviet Union, and died in Ukraine without ever leaving his village.

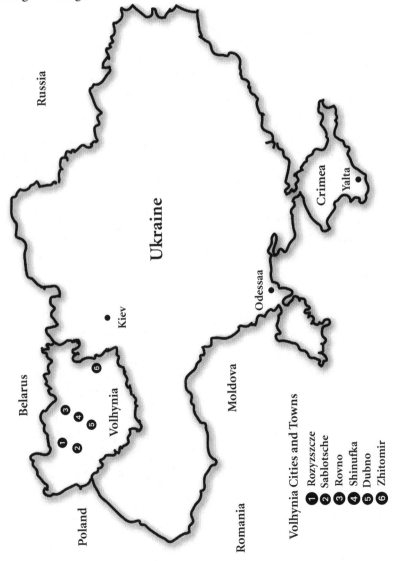

Fort Peck Indian Reservation

Around the start of the 20th century, as European non-Indian settlers proceeded to inhabit the boundary areas of the Reservation, the prime grazing and farmland areas situated within the Reservation drew their attention. As more and more homesteaders moved into the surrounding area, pressure was placed on Congress to open the Fort Peck Reservation to homesteading. The events leading to that end follow.

The Reservation is 100 miles long and 40 miles wide, bordered on the south by the Missouri River, the West by the Porcupine Creek, the East by the Big Muddy Creek, and the northern border line 40 miles distant from the center of the Missouri river. It encompasses 2,093,318 acres. The total of Indian owned lands is about 926,000 acres. There are an estimated 10,000 enrolled tribal members, of whom approximately 6,000 reside on or near the Reservation. The population density is greatest along the southern border of the Reservation near the Missouri River and the major transportation routes, US Highway 2 and Amtrak on the tracks of the Burlington Northern Railroad.

The Assiniboine and Sioux were both gradually pushed westward onto the plains from the woodlands of Minnesota by the Ojibwe, who had acquired firearms from their French allies. The Assiniboine eventually developed into a large and powerful people with a horse culture that hunted the vast herds of bison that lived within and outside their territory. They dominated territory from the North Saskatchewan River

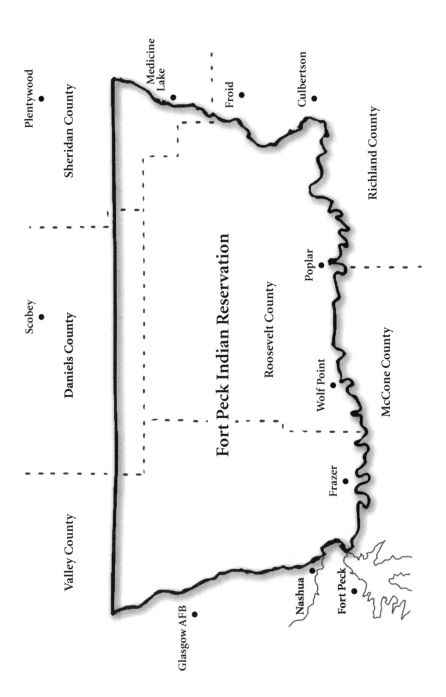

in the north to the Missouri River in the south including portions of modern day Canadian Provinces. The hunting of bison by American and Canadian hunters destroyed their nations' food source and led to the breaking up of the confederacy.[17]

In 1886, at the Fort Peck Agency in Poplar and Wolf Point, the Sioux and the Assiniboine Tribes exercised their sovereign powers and agreed with the United States government to the creation of the Fort Peck Indian Reservation. In 1888 Congress ratified the agreement, concluding three years of negotiations. Comprised of parts of four counties it is the ninth-largest Indian reservation in the United States. For Montana it was the last step in the opening of the west with the Great Northern railroad to coming through in 1889, and their statehood. The resident population in the 2010 census was 6,714. The largest community on the reservation is the city of Wolf Point.

Congress passed the Fort Peck Allotment Act May 30, 1908 which called for the survey and allotment of lands, and the sale and dispersal of all the surplus lands after allotment. Each eligible Indian was to receive 320 acres of grazing land in addition to some timber and irrigable land. Parcels of land were also withheld for Agency, school and, church use, as well as for use by the Great Northern (Burlington Northern) Railroad.

On July 25, 1913 President Woodrow Wilson proclaimed the Fort Peck surplus lands of 1,225,849 acres available to the applicant willing to pay from $2.50 to $7.00 per acre.

The railroad and affected towns were busy as homesteaders arrived. Mainly of German and Scandinavian descent, they soon occupied their dream half section of land. Little did they know of the hardships they were to endure. Those who had determination and experience would persevere to become successful homesteaders.

The great homesteading experiment continued on the Reservation. In retrospect, in spite of the hardships, it was probably the best way to develop the area. It took many years to play out, yet the desire to have family farms occupy the landscape slowly slipped away. Small towns lost many of their businesses and residents. Contributing to this was

---

17 Wikipedia

the box store phenomenon that enticed customers from more than a hundred miles. Changes continue as fewer and fewer homesteads remain in families.

Disagreements did occur between Indians and homesteaders, some perceived, some real. The Indian felt the intrusion of the white man on his ground where he had hunted and fished for millennia. The homesteader felt that he helped develop the Reservation which provided education and health care for the Indian family. While true, the services were not always well received. There was the occasional white man who took advantage of the Indian. At various times the Indian tried his hand at farming or raising cattle, sometimes at the behest of a white man who was friends of an Indian or who married an Indian.

The Indian connection would open the door to acquiring land. However, there were Indians who started farming or ranching on their own and were very successful at it. Their knowledge of the area since birth was an asset that the homesteader did not have. In such a case the admiration of the homesteader was a feeling of pride in the Indian. Many Indian people went on to make a name for themselves. One was oil painting artist William Standing who was born in 1904 and grew up near Oswego, located between Wolf Point and Frasier. Mr. Standing died in an automobile accident near Zortman, Montana in 1951. Many young Indian men competed in the local rodeos. The more talented followed the circuit. Floyd T. DeWitt, a white man, also made a name for himself as a sculptor. His interest changed from painting to sculpture when he entered the Rijksakademie in Amsterdam, Holland.

At various times a farmer noticed that his fence had been cut when Indian hunters wanted access to hunting grounds. Had the hunters asked permission for access, most would have been surprised if it were not granted. However, the instinct was there because thousands of years instilled the feeling of ownership. What their ancestors and the US Government decided years before did not come into play. Opinions about the Indians and the white man getting along are as numerous as the trees along the Missouri.

Gess Family Photographs

Julius Gess with son Victor, on horseback.

Winter 1934–35. l-r: Lorraine Gess, Reynold, Julianna (Julius' mother), homesteader Julius, sister Lydia, sister Minnie, Mary wife of brother Emil holding son Elvin.

Volt School 1942: The store is upper left, open until the late 1930s.
Back row: Marbie Hanson, Helen Gess, Sibley Hanson, Helen Hanson, Lorraine Gess
Front row: Larry Funk, Gladys Funk, Dorence Hanson, Vern Hanson, Victor Gess,
Dale Funk.

1937. Lorraine, Helen, Robert, Victor

Victor sitting on the fender of a 1936 Lafayette automobile. Missouri river bridge in the background.

1937. Great Depression comic relief.

More Great Depression comic relief.

The Gess Homestead, 2010

No. _____
1809

036

UNITED STATES OF AMERICA

DECLARATION OF INTENTION

Invalid for all purposes seven years after the date hereof

State of Montana } ss:

County of Valley

In the District Court

of Valley County, Montana

I, Julius Coan, aged 23 years

occupation Farming, do declare on oath that my personal

description is: Color White, complexion Fair, height 6 feet 1 inches

weight 172 pounds, color of hair Brown, color of eyes Blue

other visible distinctive marks None

I was born in Valenia, Russia

on the 14 day of January, anno Domini 1 893; I now reside

at Glasgow, Montana

(Give number, street, city, or town, and State.)

I emigrated to the United States of America from Swift Current, Canada

on the vessel private conveyance (bicycle) (If the alien arrived otherwise than by vessel, the character of conveyance or name of transportation company should be given.); my last

foreign residence was Swift Current, Canada

It is my bona fide intention to renounce forever all allegiance and fidelity to any foreign

prince, potentate, state, or sovereignty, and particularly to George V., King of Great

Britain and Ireland, of whom I am now a subject;

arrived at the port of no port of entry in US or, in the

State of Montana on or about the 20 day

of July, anno Domini 1915; I am not an anarchist; I am not a

polygamist nor a believer in the practice of polygamy; and it is my intention in good faith

to become a citizen of the United States of America and to permanently reside therein:

SO HELP ME GOD.

(Signed:) Julius Coan

Subscribed and sworn to before me this _____

[SEAL.]

day of _____, anno Domini 19

August 5

(Signed:) Peter Bradley

Clerk of the District Court

By O. E. Settins Clerk

Deputy

About the Author

Studying his family's movement for decades compelled his writing this story after finding his late father's christening record. Victor began an intense ancestral search. Records slowly became accessible after the Berlin wall came down in 1989. In the mid-nineties, his family genealogy research quickly grew to eventually include over three thousand family names. Lacking an organization for Congress Poland, Volhynian research, Victor started a discussion which resulted in the formation of The Society for German Genealogy in Easter Europe, SGGEE. The formation started at the July 1998 Conference. He visited Volhynia and found the birth village of his father and several related ancestral villages. Studying his family's genealogy for decades compelled him to write this story.

Made in the USA
Columbia, SC
14 July 2017